Eliseo,
Happy reading!
John Klopfer

A Quest for Immortality

JOHN KLOPFER

authorHOUSE®

AuthorHouse™
1663 Liberty Drive
Bloomington, IN 47403
www.authorhouse.com
Phone: 1-800-839-8640

First published by AuthorHouse 7/27/2009

ISBN: 978-1-4389-6492-8 (sc)
ISBN: 978-1-4389-6491-1 (hc)

Printed in the United States of America
Bloomington, Indiana

This book is printed on acid-free paper.

Dear Readers,

In conjunction with Butterfly Hope, I am donating twenty percent of my proceeds, from this book, to cancer research. Ten percent will be donated to general cancer research, or a one-time donation for research on a specific cancer. The other ten percent will be donated to colon cancer research. It is my belief that if we all work together, we can find a cure for cancer.

Butterfly Hope was founded on three principles. The first is to provide hope to all people diagnosed with a terminal illness, their families, and their loved ones. Hope through education and awareness of all alternatives for treatment of the body, mind, and spirit. The second is to create awareness of the need for early detection. By doing this, Butterfly Hope is hopeful that legislation will be created to mandate that insurance companies cover tests for early screening. Early detection can save hundred of thousands people the pain of battling a terminal illness. Third, Butterfly Hope is dedicated to raising money for cancer research.

For more information visit: *www.Butterflyhope.com.*

Happy reading,

John Klopfer

This book is dedicated to Lori Bari, a true friend and companion. Lori is my beloved paramour. Without Lori's encouragement and belief, this manuscript would have never been completed.

Acknowledgment

I would like to acknowledge Diane Childs for the valuable assistance she provided me in editing this book.

Chapter I

Tuesday

*Like as the waves make towards the pebbled shore, so
do our minutes hasten to their end.*
—William Shakespeare

The mist was swiftly sweeping off the raucous sea, enveloping the poorly maintained shack known as Caribbean Charkey's. C.C.'s, as called by the locals, had been a mainstay of North Daytona for many generations. For those seeking fresh deviled crab, grouper, lobster, or almost any type of seafood, this was the place. The prevailing thought was that you could get acceptable food in a fancy chain diner, but for a real treat to the palate, a trip to C.C.'s was a must. Unless referred by the locals, it was a place that visitors feared to tread.

The pale gray rented Toyota Avalon pulled into the driveway of Charkey's a little past 8:30 PM as most of the regular crowd was thinning. Dr. Carollyn Morris-Bower slowly stepped from the car onto the graveled parking lot and peered at the dilapidated restaurant. Taking a deep breath, she noticed the sting of the salty air in her nostrils. Being from Chicago, this was an unusual sensation. Keeping her eyes focused on the restaurant, she motioned for her two sons, Jason, fourteen, and Nathaniel, eight, to join her.

Carollyn casually looked around the surrounding area. With the exception of a few houses, the entire area was deserted and dark. She imagined what it would look like on a clear evening with the Milky Way lighting up the black abyss.

The trio walked up the creaky wooden steps to the deck, peering at the sand below. Though the porch was almost totally engulfed with fog, Carollyn could see it was in obvious need of much repair. The splintered railing that surrounded it was rotting; the wooden floor was riddled with holes and cracks. Rusted nails that had once secured the screen were still in place. A worn American flag proudly stood at attention on the outer porch. Two gas sea lanterns hung from the ceiling, illuminating the unfinished picnic tables used for dining alfresco. Three giant banana ceiling fans swirled gently to keep the air from stagnating.

"Welcome to Caribbean Charkey's," came a shrill greeting from the far side of the porch, which startled the three visitors. Again, the greeting sounded, "Welcome to Caribbean Charkey's." Peering through the haze, they discovered their host was a beautiful macaw.

Carollyn and the boys slowly approached the cage. Unlike the porch, the cage was in pristine condition. Its sterling silver rods extended to the roof. The cage continued past the width of the porch and into the restaurant. A luscious tree sprouted from the center of the confine with fresh vegetation covering the ground. The parrot was a majestic red with wings trimmed in gold and blue. Faded yellow feathers traced the black eyes that were cloudy and dimming. Even though he had seen better days, the old bird held his proud head high.

"Welcome to Caribbean Charkey's," a gruff voice resonated from a corner table.

The once again startled patrons turned to an old bearded man smoking a stogie. The man was clad in a seaman's hat and was resting his weary body on a cane. A white polo shirt with thick navy blue horizontal stripes draped over an oversized stomach and was tucked neatly into khaki shorts. His right stationary eye was sparking blue while the left eye was hazy displaying the cataract that was robbing his vision.

"That your bird, mister?" Nathaniel shouted as his mother tapped his shoulder in an attempt to lower his voice.

"Well," the man laughed, "I think it is more like I'm his man." The old man, hopeful the vivacious young boy would have more questions, graciously invited the family to join him.

As predicted, the boy had more questions. "What's his name?"

"Charkey," the old man replied. Then he took a puff of his cigar.

"How'd he get a silly name like that?" Nathaniel asked.

The old man chuckled. "My grandpappy named him after an army buddy who saved his life on three or four occasions."

"Really?" the boy stammered with excitement.

"Yes, sir," the old man continued. "Sergeant Milford Charkey." The man hacked as he emitted smoke from his lungs. Pointing toward the cigar he moaned apologetically, "Only vice I have left."

"Sergeant Charkey," Carollyn sighed knowingly.

"You heard of him?" the old man asked with surprise.

"The legend of Sergeant Charkey was taught to me in a history lesson," Carollyn nodded. She was prepared to say more; however, she chose to remain silent.

"Well then." The man prepared for a story. "You are aware of the Battle of Chickamauga, where General Braxton Bragg led the Confederate Army to one of its greatest victories. They were under heavy fire, with no regard for his safety, Sergeant Charkey pulled eight or nine severely wounded Confederate soldiers from the line of fire. One of those soldiers was my grandpappy. If it were not for Sergeant Charkey, I wouldn't be here talking to you."

"River of death," the parrot interrupted.

"That's right, Charkey. In the local Indian dialect, 'Chickamauga' means river of death. That defines what this town was. The terrible battle took place on September 18 through September 20, 1863. Sergeant Charkey was shot in the chest, close to the heart, as he was pulling the last man to safety on the eighteenth. The trail to the confederate field hospital was blocked, so Grandpappy and another soldier switched uniforms with three dead Yankee soldiers and proceeded to take Sergeant Charkey to the Union hospital."

"Johnny Reb was always deceitful," fourteen-year-old Jason mumbled inaudibly.

"Grandpappy, with a badly wounded shoulder, and the other enlisted man carried him to the Gordon Plantation. The estate had been transformed into a makeshift hospital by the Union." The man paused to gather his thoughts. "The journey to the plantation was a six-mile hike through treacherous terrain; they found themselves hiding behind giant oaks to dodge fire from fellow Confederates. When they reached the mansion, Grandpappy said he marveled at its majestic presence. The lane leading to the house was outlined with rows of chestnut trees. He recalled how surreal it was; on the right side of the lane all the trees were covered in green. Those on the left were overflowing with red and brown leaves, symbolizing the carnage raging around it. As the two men tugged Charkey up the seventeen steps to the porch, the other man collapsed, dying of his own wounds. This was a testimony of his great bravery in saving his compatriot. Legend has it that at the height of the battle, two inches of blood bathed the parlor floor of the mansion. Grandpappy insisted that the doctor, who was really reduced to being a butcher, tend to the sergeant first. The sergeant held Grandpappy's hand tightly as they attempted to dig the bullet out of his artery, then his hand went limp. He was dead. Charkey was one of thirty-five thousand men who died in that battle."

"The doctor removed the bullet from Grandpappy's shoulder without the assistance of anesthesia. He said it was the most excruciating pain he had ever experienced. To assist in controlling the pain he bit on a bullet, chipping a tooth, while the doctor performed the procedure. At daybreak, as his wounded shoulder continued oozing blood, he slipped out the back door, rejoining his troop in battle. Some say that Sergeant Charkey and other soldiers, many of them masquerading as Yankees, still haunt the house today." The man paused to ensure he had a captive audience. "Reliable legend has it that he pulled many more men to safety during the final two days of battle. Of course, with him being dead, that doesn't seem likely."

"Where's Chickamauga?" an impressed eight-year-old asked.

"North Georgia, almost in Chattanooga," the old man chirped. "It was an important battle to prevent the North from progressing to Atlanta." The man coughed. "It was really an extension of the battle of Chattanooga. Chattanooga was a vital rail port that served as a channel keeping supplies running to all the southern troops."

"Shame that they won," a sullen Jason mumbled under his breath as his mother gave him a warning stare to be polite. She did, however, share his anguish of an unjust era in history.

"That it is," the man said to the young African-American boy, with sincerity in his voice.

"What happened to your grandfather after the war?" Carollyn asked.

"Grandpappy grew up on a cotton farm near Savannah." Looking directly at Jason, he continued, "Yes, his parents owned slaves. But you must understand that their church said it was all right. The book of Proverbs commands 'treat your slaves well.' At least, that was Grandpappy's reasoning, not that it's right. According to family history, their slaves were well treated. My ancestors were zealous followers of the Christian faith. They were so charmed with the doctrine of Charles Wesley, they followed him to Savannah. I believe it was in the 1700s. Eventually, due to some of his less-than-charitable doctrines, he was ceremoniously invited to leave town. My family having settled in, elected to stay. Not wanting to go back to farming, Grandpappy and his brother drifted south to Florida. Grandpappy, always the adventure seeker, became a fisherman, and my Uncle Luther created a seafood restaurant that is now known as Charkey's."

"How can slaves be well treated?" Jason protested angrily.

A heavyset blonde waitress, dressed like the old man minus the hat, emerged on the veranda with menus. As she handed them the menus she asked for their drink orders.

Jason wanted to throw the menus on the ground and leave; however, he caught a glance from his mother through the corner of his eyes and knew they were staying.

"Bring the lady a bottle of Charkey's, on the house," the old man blurted out presumptuously, and then nodded to her for approval. "And give these lads some of our freshly squeezed lemonade."

"That would be fine," Carollyn whispered.

"As Benjamin Franklin so poetically proclaimed, 'Beer is proof that God loves us and wants us to be happy,'" the old man quipped.

Carollyn smiled.

"Captain," the waitress inquired of the old man, "may I bring you lemonade, too?"

The old man nodded as he bent to pick a penny off the ground, ignoring Jason's question. He did not want to get in an argument on the morality of his ancestors. Even if they erred in owning slaves, he felt the importance of holding his heritage with pride. The fact that several of the slaves followed them to Florida, and several others stayed on at the family plantation, was a testament to their treatment. The man chose not to mention he believed that due to their uneducated status the slaves would have perished if left to their own devices.

"Hey," Jason pondered, "if this Charkey character died in Chickamauga, how could he save your grandfather's life three or four times?"

The captain chuckled. "Excellent point, and a worthy explanation you shall have."

"Poor Abe," the parrot squawked, interrupting the man's chain of thought. "Good Friday; good-bye, Abe."

The old man shook his head. "For reasons obvious, Grandpappy was not a big supporter of our sixteenth president. According to my daddy, the two days that stuck out in Grandpappy's memory were January 1, 1863, the day the Emancipation Proclamation was signed; and the day Lincoln was assassinated. He said that the president had no right to make a proclamation affecting a country he was no longer governing. According to him, the only person that could render slavery illegal in the Confederate States was Jefferson Davis."

"On April fourteenth, 1865, Good Friday, John Wilkes Booth assassinated President Lincoln. Coincidentally, that was the fourth anniversary of the Confederate's victory at Fort Sumter. That was a day my grandpappy and many other southerners celebrated for years. They felt that Booth made an ordinary Good Friday into a great Friday." The captain coughed, harshly.

"That is a shame," Carollyn interjected sadly. "The action of a misguided individual changed the course of history."

"Misguided? Or inspired?" the old man offered. "It all depends on which side of the fence you are on. Booth and his co-conspirators were viewed as heroes by many in the South. Most in the North, but not all, would label them treacherous villains."

"I would choose the latter," Carollyn was quick to interject.

"I am not disagreeing with you," the captain added. "It doesn't really matter; the deed was done."

"It is sad that his life had to end when the nation needed him most," Carollyn continued. "President Lincoln was a great man. Not only for ending the brutality of human bondage, but also for preserving our great nation. If not for Lincoln, our country as we know it would not exist. If he had allowed the southern states to secede, what would have prevented other states from doing the same? The United States would have become a splintered nation. 'A house divided can not stand.'"

"As stated in the book of Matthew," the captain acknowledged, "though many attribute the quote directly to Lincoln. However, I believe the death of the president allowed the citizens of the South to put their hostilities behind them and move on."

"There are historians who would strongly disagree," Carollyn said in an intellectually superior tone. "Some people claim the plan for reconciliation was delayed due to President Johnson's lack of Lincoln's vision of forgiveness and unity. The assassination occurred at a crucial time in our history. If the president had lived, there would have been less carpetbaggers pillaging the South and taking advantage of its politically weakened condition. The hostilities from the North would have evaporated more quickly. Those hostilities affected both white southerners and the blacks. By most accounts it affected the newly ordained black citizens more." She paused for a few seconds, debating whether to continue. "Remember, Andrew Johnson was a southern, from Tennessee. Undoubtedly, he had many friends that were former slave owners."

The man peered in her eyes. "It was Andrew Johnson who declared, 'The better class will go to work and sustain themselves, and they ought to be allowed to vote, on the ground that a loyal negro is more worthy than a disloyal white man.'"

"I believe," Carollyn continued the debate, "that he also stated that the negroes were second-class citizens. Johnson was definitely no Mr. Lincoln."

"Perhaps," the old man agreed, grudgingly. Though he had a remarkably different viewpoint of the president's vision he knew it was futile to debate it. Gazing at the penny, he continued, "When the U.S. mint introduced the Lincoln penny in 1909, in commemoration of the president's one hundredth birthday, Grandpappy called it blasphemy. He vowed never to use it; would only use the Indian head penny. Said the Indian penny had been around since 1859, and there was no use replacing it. He felt having a president on a coin, especially Lincoln, was reminiscent of the monarchies of Europe. It had no place in a democracy, even if Lincoln thought he was king."

"Must have had something against repressed races," Jason mumbled under his breath. "Wants to own one and have another one to stuff in his pocket."

A seagull landed on the porch to eat a leftover french fry that was lying on the ground.

"He must have been real upset," Jason mocked, "in 1959 when the mint placed the Lincoln Memorial on the back."

The man looked at Jason, "Are you a member of the Numismatics Society?"

"Excuse me?" Jason asked.

"The society of coin collectors," the old man coughed. "Numismatics."

"What makes you ask that?" the teenager asked, mildly curious.

"Not many people, especially of your age, know the Lincoln Memorial replaced the wheat leaves in 1959." There was a pause for a second. "Of course the penny received another face lift in 2009 to mark the bicentennial Lincoln's birth."

"Yes, I have a coin collection. A former history teacher encouraged it as a hobby and as a means of studying different eras in history." The boy paused. "For each new chapter in American history she would bring a coin from her personal collection as a reflection of the economy of the time. I became so enchanted with the coins my dad helped me start my own collection."

"Do you have a large one?" the captain inquired.

"It is growing," the Jason said with a smile. "Every month, with my allowance, I add one coin." The boy watched a calico cat come partially onto the porch and then quickly retreat. "I'm concentrating on pennies now. I have all the pennies from 1932 to the present. I have a few others, but my goal is to collect all of one set before tackling another." The boy watched as the cat meandered around the side of the porch. "I have a few silver dollars from the 1800s. My favorite coin is a large cent from 1793."

"I have quite a collection myself," the man boasted. "There are some coins that date to the mid 1700s. It may not be of interest to you, but I have a copy of every denomination that the Confederacy made."

"It sounds like you have an interesting assortment of coins," Carollyn mentioned.

"Do you have any here?" Nathaniel asked.

The captain smiled. "Most are at my house. I do have a few under the glass countertop inside. You are welcome to look at them later."

The waitress reappeared with drinks. She brought a frosted mug for the beer, but Carollyn chose to drink the beer out of the bottle. She gazed at the intriguing bottle. The label was onyx black with the likeness of a scarlet macaw in the center. The lettering was in thin silver tempus sans print. On the back of the label was printed 'a fine blend of colorful ingredients.' The boys eagerly started sipping the freshly squeezed lemonade.

"Family recipe since the beginning of the family tree," the old man boasted. "Came over on the Mayflower," he exaggerated, having no knowledge of his ancestors being on the historic vessel. "Hopefully it will be the beer of choice when we colonize space."

Carollyn took a small sip and acknowledged her approval. After the waitress took their order, the captain suggested they take their meal inside to avoid the mosquitoes and the Florida humidity. The old man politely held the door for his guests. Charkey, not wanting to miss the conversation, fluttered into the café side of his cage.

The inside of the restaurant was an anomaly in comparison to the outer. The oak floor was finely polished; the siding was a light red, closer to a rust orange, brick veneer, adorned by family and patron photographs and other mementos of the past. In the center of the wall was a beautiful painting of Charkey, sitting on a tree branch with a black background, the prototype for the bottle. Large pane windows led to the darkness outside that smothered the Atlantic. The shellacked golden oak stained picnic tables sparkled as if new. Shiny brass sea lanterns with pristine glass hung from the rafters to illuminate the room. Behind the bar in a glass encasement was the microbrewery where Charkey's was made and bottled. As promised, the glass countertop of the bar served as a display for numerous coins representing different eras of United States history. To the far left side was a finely polished banister and stairway leading to the Starlight Deck. A sign stated the romantic deck was reserved for adults only.

"Wow," an astonished Carollyn blurted.

The old man blushed with pride.

As Carollyn's eyes moved to look around the various walls, the boys' eyes fixated on the diverse collection of coins. The most impressive to Jason were the half-cent pieces and the two-cent pieces. Nathaniel's interest in the coins was an obvious attempt to mimic his older brother.

The old man whispered something in the waitress's ear prior to taking a seat with his guests.

"How old is the bird?" the inquisitive eight-year-old asked, oblivious to the change of surroundings as he returned to his seat.

"Well," the captain stammered, "Grandpappy did a lot of fishing in the Caribbean. He got his sea legs right after the war, and they never left him. On his last trip to Mexico in 1917, he brought Charkey back. He was just a chick then, so I guess he's about ninety-two years old."

"No way," Jason protested.

"Yes sir," the old man insisted. "Charkey is a scarlet macaw. According to records they live to be eighty or older. Old Charkey has kind of passed his expectancy. We're having a contest to see who is going to live longer. Anyway, Grandpappy willed the bird to Daddy, stating it was his quest for immortality."

Remembering Jason's previous question about Sergeant Charkey, he retraced the conversation. "Twice on that last trip to Mexico my grandfather found himself in peril. The first was when his fishing vessel was besieged by a hurricane. Grandpappy was in charge of lowering the sails to prevent the boat from capsizing. As he was pulling them in, a gust of wind blew him toward the raging sea. He held tightly to the rope hoping to keep the angry sea from swallowing him. As he was about to give up hope, a hand came from nowhere to pull him to safety. When safely on board he looked toward his angel. It was Sergeant Charkey. Grandpappy was so scared he fainted. When he came to, he told his mates about the experience, thinking that his eyes had played tricks on him. Not one of the men claimed to have rescued him."

Jason rolled his eyes. Nathaniel was too busy watching the bird to pay attention to the story.

Carollyn winced for a split second. An apparition suddenly appeared of two unshaven men garbed in confederate gray, sitting at a corner table, playing cards with a tattered deck while sipping beer from steins. Both had lit nonfiltered cigarettes dangling from their mouths. One had a hole in the left chest area of his jacket. The other man, who appeared a bit younger than the first, had a Lincolnesque mole on his right cheek.

Though neither looked away from their cards, she could feel the glacier stare emanating from their souls. In a blink of the eye the vision disappeared as quickly as it had materialized.

The man continued ignoring Jason's disbelief. "A few weeks later in the jungle of Mexico Grandpappy and a group of sailors were attacked by Indians. Gunfire was no match for the primitive weapons of the Indians, and they soon dispersed without a casualty on either side. Somehow Grandpappy got separated from the rest, perhaps because of a new flask of whiskey in his belly, and became lost in the jungle. He followed a labyrinth trail deeper into the forbidding jungle. The mysterious trail ended at the Indians' camp. In the middle of the encampment the men of the tribe were circling around a large wooden carving, dancing and chanting. In the background the women and children were busy meshing what looked like dough with their hands. Grandpappy was spellbound."

The captain paused as he sneezed into a handkerchief. "After the original dance stopped one warrior with a painted face and a hat of many colorful feathers continued chanting and dancing. The rest of tribe reverently knelt on their knees, hands folded behind their backs. It appeared as if they were preparing for a hunt or possibly a battle." The man took a deep breath. "Grandpappy was paralyzed with fright. He was not sure how to return to the ship, and knew night was quickly coming."

The captain paused to watch two cooks lift a glass pane from the bar. "A hand from behind him grabbed his left shoulder."

"Was it an Indian?" blurted Nathaniel, who now was intrigued with the conversation.

A sly, knowing smile appeared on the man's face. "Once again Charkey came to the rescue, leading him to safety. At one point they had to duck into the thicket as the warring party was marching toward the coast.

While in the copse Grandpappy found the chick bird, which had fallen out of a tree, and took it as an omen that Charkey would always be with him." The old man paused to sip on his frosty drink. "As the sun was settling into the amethyst mountains, Charkey led Grandpappy to the clearing and safety. Grandpappy said that there were several other times in his life when he was in grave danger that he felt Charkey saved him, although during those incidents he didn't actually see him."

"So all this time in the deep dark forest that they spent bonding," Jason asked sarcastically, "did the saintly sergeant impart any words of wisdom to your grandfather?"

Appreciating the young boy's disbelief, the old man disregarded the question.

For the first time Carollyn noticed the dark circles under his sunken eyes, a bluish purple tinge on the lips, the bruises on the paper-thin skin of the arms, and the wheezing of his breath. "I bet on you," she reassured softly, referring to the old man pondering on if he would outlive the bird.

Remembering an old James Bond movie, the old man quipped, "Only the good die young."

You have nothing to worry about, Jason thought but knew not to verbalize.

"What does Charkey eat?" Nathaniel asked.

"Mostly little boys," the captain joked, with a wink of his good eye.

Nathaniel laughed and said, "Not really?"

"Fruit, vegetables, and nuts," the man said, looking fondly at the bird. "Charkey seems to be partial to baked sweet potatoes with a touch of cinnamon and butter."

"Me too!" Nathaniel shouted, eyes wide open.

When he thought no one was looking, Jason threw a wadded up napkin toward the bird to startle it.

"Don't be a ron," Charkey chastised, "a moron."

"Charkey," the man protested, "these folks are our friends."

"That is all right," Carollyn interjected, "Jason is being a moron." Turning her attention to her eldest, she sternly warned, "Don't ever do that again. We are the guests here. You need to show some respect." Directing her attention to the captain, she apologized, "There is nothing wrong with your old friend's eyesight. He saw the moron throwing a piece of paper at him." Carollyn felt embarrassed by her son's behavior.

"I'm sorry," Jason mumbled without being prompted. The need of further direction was not necessary as he walked to the cage to pick up the paper.

"Don't be a ron, a moron," the bird once again chastised.

Nathaniel giggled. "Don't be a ron, a moron. My grandmother used to say that."

The waitress brought the order to the family. The old man motioned for the waitress to bend down so he could whisper that the meals were on the house; a gesture that he would often make when he felt he spent too much time bending patrons' ears.

"Can I share my sweet potato with Charkey?" Nathaniel asked the old man.

"If it is okay with your momma, after you eat everything, we will find a sweet potato for you to feed Charkey."

Carollyn smiled approvingly toward her son.

"Adolph was a goner," Charkey chirped, "should have been gone."

"Yes he should have," the old man whispered thoughtfully. Pointing to a picture of his father on the wall, next to an old rifle, he lamented, "Back in 1917 during WWI my daddy's platoon had just overtaken a farm house near Neuve Chapelle, Germany. After the battle, Daddy was scouring the area for survivors. He found a young German corporal hiding in a haystack. Daddy aimed the Springfield M1903 rifle straight between his eyes and demanded to know his name, so he could tell God whose soul to expect in heaven."

The man took a sip of lemonade, cleared his throat, and said, "The young corporal said, 'I am Corporal Adolph Hitler.' My daddy pulled the trigger of that gun," motioning toward the wall, "and the gun jammed. He told young Hitler that God must have intervened and that he had better be on his way before the Lord changed his mind. Hitler scurried off into the woods. A short time later my daddy had to return hostile fire and the gun worked perfectly."

"Yeah right," Jason mocked.

"My daddy was many things; but a liar he was not," the old man snapped irritably.

"So you're saying God spared Hitler so he could wipe out an entire race," the boy fired back, much to the dismay of his mother.

The man's trembling hand brought the now extinguished cigar to his mouth, and he inhaled. "Not at all," the man continued. "God intervened to save my daddy's life. When daddy needed his rifle to work, the good Lord unjammed it. Daddy only had one shell left."

Jason wanted to continue on the challenge of the prosperous tale of an encounter with Hitler that could have changed the world, but he could tell by the scowl on his mother's face that it was time to back down.

A young couple stopped briefly to say hello to the captain as they were exiting the restaurant. The young man looked at the trio of guests. "This man has some amazing stories," he mentioned with a smile. "The most unbelievable ones are always true."

Carollyn smiled and said, "They are definitely intriguing."

The captain stood and shook hands with the couple and thanked them for stopping by.

After the couple left he turned his attention to his guests and asked, "Where were we anyway?"

"We were talking about the war," Nathaniel quickly reminded him, ignoring his brother's stare to be quiet.

"Oh yeah. Anyway, after the war ended in 1918, Daddy returned here and reluctantly went to work for Uncle Luther and Grandpappy, who was now in the restaurant business. He had bigger plans for his life. He wanted to move to a big city and go into the housing industry. A feeling of obligation to family made him return to Daytona, he reasoned, if only on temporary basis." The man sipped his lemonade.

"Christmas Day, 1919, Uncle Luther died, and the next spring, oddly enough on April 14, my Grandpappy died."

"What did they die of?" Nathaniel wanted to know.

Rubbing his beard, the man quipped, "Not sure, but old Luther was eighty-one and Grandpappy was seventy-six." The old man cleared his throat. "Anyway, Daddy named the previously unnamed restaurant Charkey's."

"After the sergeant?" Nathaniel said, knowingly more than asking.

"Not sure if it was after the sergeant or the bird, but anyway he felt the name was fitting."

"Did your Uncle Luther have any children?" Carollyn inquired.

"Uncle Luther never married," the old man countered. "He was a bit shy around women. A nice evening for him was going out with his buddies." The man rubbed his beard. "Daddy said that Luther never wanted to be saddled with a wife. Said the women were too much bother."

Carollyn laughed. "That must have been lonely?"

"According to Daddy, Uncle Luther had several male friends that felt the same way. They would spend weekends together, even travel together."

"Rolling twenties," Charkey shouted.

"Yes, the twenties were a great time for Daddy. The world was at peace. Increasing number of tourists were flocking to Florida. These tourists needed a place to eat, which meant increased revenues for the restaurant. Most of the profits Daddy put into the booming stock market."

Oh no, Carollyn lamented to herself.

"During his time in the war he kept in touch with his high school sweetheart. He told me that she was the only girl he ever loved. According to Daddy, her long jet-black braided hair mesmerized him into a total bliss. She was an immigrant from Russia. Momma's family moved to America seeking new opportunities when she was just an infant. Immediately after Grandpappy's death, she started helping out at the restaurant." The man paused to watch a customer leave the store. "He always said that the immigrants were the backbone of America; they made our country strong."

"As long as they weren't black, Jewish, or non Anglo-Saxons," Jason mumbled under his breath, only audible enough for his mother to hear. Carollyn scowled at her eldest son.

"In March 1921 Momma and Daddy were married; in October my older brother Rufus was born. Four years later along came Allison, and in 1928 my parents were blessed with yours truly."

"Black Friday," the bird chimed in.

The old man took a deep breath and sighed. "Yes, Black Friday, one of the worse days in Daddy's life. October thirtieth of 1929 was indeed a godforsaken day."

"Did you father lose a lot in the crash?" Carollyn asked cautiously.

"What crash?" Nathaniel demanded. His mother motioned for him to be quiet so the captain could continue.

"Everything," the man said stoically. "You see, back in February my mother took sick with breast cancer. The cancer ate her up really fast. Though Daddy was praying for a miracle, he knew it was hopeless. At two o'clock in the afternoon on the thirtieth she went to sleep for the final time." The man stared out the window into the darkness with little emotion in his face. "While the rest of the country was grieving their financial loss Daddy was mourning something much more valuable. I don't how much money he lost in the crash; I just know it meant nothing to him."

Tears were forming in Carollyn's eyes. She felt compelled to reach over and touch the man's hand.

"You miss your mother?" Nathaniel asked.

"Sad part is I never really knew her," the man mumbled, before continuing. "The bleakness of 1929 drifted into the thirties. My sister was diagnosed with leukemia in the spring of 1931. By Christmas she was gone. My father was devastated."

"After Allison's death Daddy quit going to church, no longer believing in God." The man shook his head. "To be left alone to raise three kids by himself, then to have one die was more than he could comprehend. How could there be a loving merciful God?"

"But there is a God and Jesus," Nathaniel protested, "The Bible tells me so."

"We know," Carollyn reassured.

"I'm not sure Daddy would have been able to handle it if not for my grandmother Ruth," the old man sighed. "She was the iron rod that held our family together."

"That was Grandpappy's wife?" Carollyn asked for clarification.

The man smiled. "Probably the only woman that could put up with Grandpappy is what Daddy always said." He contemplated his words for a few seconds. "Grandpappy and Grandma Ruth probably only had the one child because he spent most of his time at sea."

Carollyn laughed.

"I believe that he may have married her because of her birthday." The captain laughed, "At least that was what Daddy always said."

"Her birthday?" a confused woman asked.

"She was born on April 14, 1865; the day that Lincoln was assassinated."

Carollyn shook her head. Jason turned his head to conceal a sneer.

"Anyway, she was the glue that held the family together. Grandma Ruth insisted that Rufus and I attend Sunday school and church. It didn't matter which church, just so it was church. One Sunday we told her we going to a different church with a friend. Instead we went fishing. Just as my pole was bowed with a big one, I felt a slap across my right leg. At first I thought it was Rufus playing around until the razor strap hit me again. I looked back and saw Grandma Ruth standing behind me. She didn't have to say a word, Rufus and I dropped our poles and rushed back to the house." The man smiled. "She told us that we were not old enough to make our own minds up about church, neither of us skipped again."

Carollyn smiled. "How old were you?"

"Probably around seven or eight."

"PT 109 … PT 109," Charkey called out, flapping his wings.

"What's a PT 109?" Nathaniel needed to know.

"It was a patrol boat used during WWII," Jason quickly interjected, demonstrating his knowledge of history.

"Not just any boat," the old man broke in. "PT 109 was Skipper John F. Kennedy's boat."

"The president?" Nathaniel asked.

"Yes sir, only he wasn't president at the time. He was an officer stationed on Base Rendova in the South Pacific. My brother Rufus had orders to report to the boat."

"Oh brother," Jason broke in, "You are like Shirley MacLaine. She has been reincarnated from famous people, and all your family have known famous people."

"Jason," an irritated mother snapped, "If you cannot show some respect for this gentleman you can sit in the car. You were not raised like this." She turned to the captain to apologize.

The old man waved her off. He pointed to a picture on the wall of his brother, who was leaning on a cane, standing with a young John Kennedy in front of PT 109.

"During a touch football game Kennedy tackled Rufus, causing him to twist his knee. The injury resulted in what was to be a temporary reassignment. This picture was taken on the afternoon of August 1, 1943. That night the PT 109 was patrolling the Solomon Islands; it was quite dark, no moon in sight. A Japanese destroyer appeared out of nowhere and cut right through the boat. Ironically," the man said, "by most accounts, the destroyer didn't even see PT 109. The entire crew was thrust into the cold Pacific." There was a pause. "If not for JFK they would have all perished."

"Was everyone killed?" Nathaniel blurted.

"At first everyone thought they were," the captain continued. "They even had a memorial service for the crew on the base. Rufus wrote home that it was very emotional, not a dry eye in attendance. Fortunately, Mr. Kennedy and his men had a bit of resolve and found their way to safety. Kennedy suffered from malaria and a back injury. The back injury followed him all the way to the White House."

"And your brother, Rufus?" a humbled Jason asked.

The old man sipped his lemonade while openly wiping a tear from his eye. "He was assigned to an aircraft carrier in the South Pacific. On October thirtieth of 1943 a Japanese kamikaze pilot flew into the starboard of the ship where Rufus was standing duty." The man peered out at the dark sea.

"I'm sorry," Jason mumbled.

"Your family has a long history of patriotism," Carollyn complimented.

The man smiled at the acknowledgment. "With Georgia being one of the original thirteen colonies I guess you could say we have served our country from the beginning."

There was a momentary lag in the conversation. The silence was interrupted with the banging of a waitress dropping a tray full of dirty dishes.

"Are you going to take that out of her pay?" Jason asked.

The man laughed, "Accidents will be accidents; no need to dock someone for that. Our customers love her; that is worth far more than a few glasses."

"Your ancestors served in the Georgia Regiment during the Revolutionary War?" Carollyn asked.

"My great-great grandfather and his brother both served," the captain boasted. "According to family history, one of their cousins was with Washington when he crossed the Delaware."

"That is impressive," Carollyn mused. "It is rare that a person can trace their lineage that far."

The man beamed with pride. "President Reagan once said, 'Freedom is never more than one generation away from extinction. We didn't pass it to our children in the bloodstream. It must be fought for, protected, and handed on for them to do the same, or one day we will spend our sunset years telling our children and our children's children what it was once like in the United States where men were free.'" The man stared as the waitress swept up the broken glass. "It is a great honor to know that my forefathers are partially responsible for making our country great."

"Strike three," Charkey chirped.

"I like baseball," both boys chimed in.

"I used to be a bit of a ball player," the old man reminisced. "Back in 1944 I signed to play for the Boston Red Sox farm team. I was a second baseman that had a knack for the long ball, which was a bit unusual back in those days."

"I'm a pitcher," Nathaniel interjected. "And sometimes I play third base."

"I roam the vast domain of centerfield," Jason added dramatically, temporarily forgetting he did not want to be there.

The man smiled in recognition of the boys' revelations. "My first at bat I hit a grand slam homerun over the centerfield fence." The captain stared out the window for a second. "Ironically, my last at bat, the results were the same," he lamented. "If I knew what the future held, I would have cherished those moments a little bit longer."

The sounds of an ambulance raced by outside.

"After my first year," the man continued, "I got an invitation from Uncle Sam to join WWII." He rubbed his nose. "Not having a choice I accepted the invitation."

"I have an Uncle Sam too," Nathaniel commented.

"He's talking about the government, dummy," Jason snapped sarcastically.

"Before leaving, I went on a church picnic with Emma, our first date. She made me promise to return alive. I asked her to marry me if I did. To my surprise, she accepted."

"How long were you in?" Jason asked.

The old man laughed. "Not long. After basic training, I was one of the lucky one hundred sixty thousand to be sent to England as the allied troops prepared for D-Day."

The waitress refilled the drinks. Then she walked to the door and turned the sign to indicate they were closed.

"I was in the first wave of the offensive. Right after we hit the beachhead, I felt a sharp pain on the right side of my face." He sighed. "Next thing I remembered, I was in an army hospital in England. The surgeons were unable to save my right eye. My baseball career was over. My souvenir for my stay in Europe was a glass eye and a limp in my left leg. The only things that kept my spirits up and gave me hope were letters from Emma. That sweet girl wrote me every day." The man took his hat off to wipe his forehead, revealing a receding hairline. "However, if given a chance to do it over I would in a second. Everyone should be willing to stand up for liberty."

"Amen," Carollyn acknowledged.

Jason thought, if your father would have killed Hitler, there would never have been a need for D-Day.

"Can I see your glass eye?" Nathaniel begged.

"Not now," his mother whispered, tapping him on the shoulder.

"When I returned to Florida in 1946, Emma was waiting for me at the train station. She did not seem to notice that I wasn't quite the man I once was."

"Who were you?" a puzzled Nathaniel asked.

His mother held his shoulder signaling him to listen more and talk less.

"She always told me that I went away a boy and came back a man. Emma was prouder of my service and commendations than I. She insisted that we hang my purple heart and other medals on the wall," he humbly said, pointing toward a display case.

"On Valentines Day in 1947 we were married at the First Methodist Church." The old man smiled broadly, revealing two missing teeth and one gold one. "Emma agreeing to marry me was the greatest honor of my life."

"Jackie ... Jackie," Charkey screeched.

"Who's Jackie?" Nathaniel asked.

"Jackie Robinson was the first black baseball player in the Major Leagues."

"Was not," Jason protested, "Hank Aaron was the first. I know my black history."

"Not well," the old man retorted. "It was Jackie Robinson. It was in 1947. Actually, Jackie breaking the color barrier wasn't easy. A lot of white players on his team, the Brooklyn Dodgers, signed a petition to keep him off the team. Many refused to talk with him in the locker room or the dugout. Not to mention the outraged fans that sent him hate mail. The unyielding fans at the ball park threw all kinds of garbage at him." The man coughed. "He carried the baton for his entire race. If he would have failed, Branch Ricky or any other general manager probably wouldn't have signed another black player for a decade."

"He was a courageous man," Carollyn agreed. Looking at her son she said, "The captain's right, he was the first African-American to play professional baseball. It wasn't easy; he was not allowed to eat in the same restaurant or sleep in the same hotel as his white teammates. Hank Aaron was not even out of school at the time. During his teen years Aaron attended a lecture by Robinson in Mobile in 1948. He later said that Jackie became a role model for him and gave Robinson much of the credit for his success. Aaron became a member of Milwaukee Braves in 1954. He was the last player to sign with the major leagues that had played in the negro league."

"You know your baseball," the old man quipped.

Carollyn smiled. "My husband is a jock, and all I hear is baseball. As you, he played a year in the minors."

"He would have been able to eat here," Nathaniel boasted proudly in defense of his new friend.

The captain shook his head. "No son, that is not true, not in 1947. Even if the community had been tolerant, my daddy wouldn't have. Actually, it is quite possible that he tried to eat here. The Dodgers trained here. Jackie was assigned to their minor league affiliate from Montreal. The Montreal team trained down the road in Sanford. There were many players that would stop by Charkey's during spring training. I remember vividly, like it was yesterday, a young black man coming in with a couple of white guys and my daddy turning them away." The old man sighed. "I believe those white guys were ball players, but I'm not positive. Of course if they were, that would mean the black man was Jackie."

"So, you're saying you conveniently don't know?" Jason asked.

The man let out a long sigh. "I don't know if it is a convenience of not knowing or a denial of the truth. To be honest, I am as guilty as my father. Though I was not the one demanding him to leave I supported the decision. Had I been in the restaurant alone the result would have been the same."

"I suppose confession makes the action right," Jason snapped mockingly.

The captain bit his tongue. "Daddy felt that if there were more black men in the armed services I would not have gone to war. If I didn't go to war I would have been playing second base in the majors."

"That's twisted rationale," Jason blurted.

"It was a bit misguided," the old man acknowledged. "It was how Daddy thought or rationalized his hatred. It didn't help that in an interview Branch Ricky was quoted as saying that the war had depleted the supply of good white players, so the Dodgers decided to expand their search by going to South America, Mexico, and non-white Americans. As for the war, I know there were just as many black soldiers as white. In that Uncle Sam did not discriminate."

"That's right; the black soldiers were human shields with inferior weapons. The white man got the rations, the right equipment, and the recognition. No discrimination there," an angry Jason declared. "Do you think your quote of Reagan applies to the African-American soldiers too?"

The man stared at Jason. "It applies to all American soldiers," he boasted. "Since the beginning of our country, African-American soldiers have shed their blood for this land of ours." The old man coughed. "Black blood has been spilled at Valley Forge, at Gettysburg, in France on D-Day, and in the Middle East."

"Name one African-American hero," Jason challenged.

"James Armistead was a double agent during the American Revolution," the captain was quick to point out. "Information he obtained while masquerading as a servant to General Cornwallis was vital to Americans."

Jason secretly was in awe of the answer. "Yet, when the war was over, slaves were still slaves."

"Actually, James Armistead, who took the surname of Lafayette, was granted his freedom as were many other slaves." The man hesitated. "Incidentally, Armistead himself became a slave holder."

"But not all African-Americans were set free."

Ignoring Jason's hostilities, switching back to baseball, the man continued. "Actually, Jackie Robinson's baseball career was delayed while he served in the army."

"Did his Uncle Sam give him an invitation too?" Nathaniel asked.

"The fire, the fire," Charkey blurted, changing the subject.

"The fire," the old man whispered barely audible, taking his wise friend's cue. "In 1948, the original Charkey's mysteriously burnt down. Fortunately, my feathered friend was living at Daddy's house at the time. It happened at 3 AM in the dead of winter. The fire inspector thought it was arson, although we never found the perpetrator." The man paused for a sip of lemonade. "With the insurance money Daddy took Emma and me on a cruise to Havana, Cuba. We spent two weeks there. Emma and I won several thousand dollars playing blackjack at the casino, which offset the loss of a thousand Daddy had at the roulette wheel. Of course we spent a lot of time on the beach too, some of the nicest beaches in the world. White powdered sand stretched along the coastline as far as the eyes could see. Many a night we spent spread out on a blanket, sipping Mai Tais and watching a romantic sunset. There were miles of teal-colored water with orange and violet rays bouncing off into the sweet night."

"With our winnings from blackjack, we rented a sail boat. We sailed to Bimini, which is known as the fishing capital of the world." Pointing to a giant blue marlin on the wall he said, "Emma hooked him and I reeled him in." The captained smiled at the memory.

"The people of Bimini are some of the friendliest people I have ever met." The old man stared at Jason. "The islanders' skin is darker than yours," he said, obviously wanting to make a point. "They will do anything to accommodate visitors to their island. Don't know if you know it but Ernest Hemingway spent many a day on the island drinking, writing, and fishing. The inspiration for *Old Man and the Sea*, Piccolo Pete, is from North Bimini." Pointing to a boat docked somewhere in the darkness, "Emma and I took our boat there almost every spring to take in the clear blue lagoon, the hospitality, and great fishing. Due to my health, I haven't been there for almost a decade."

"So you like the people of Bimini because they are subservient?" Jason asked, attempting to bait the old man.

"There's a big difference between hospitable and subservient," the captain sighed. "As I mentioned, the people of Bimini are hospitable."

Carollyn smiled at her eldest son, knowing the captain bested him.

"The trip to Havana and Bimini was the last vacation we would take with Daddy." The man paused for another sip. "When we returned Daddy and I built the present day Charkey's." Looking around at the walls he said, "It was Emma's idea to hang the mementos of the past on the walls."

"It was a nice idea," Carollyn mentioned.

A man and three children drifted past the table as they exited.

"Time for dessert," Charkey screamed, "time for dessert."

"Trudy," the old man shouted across the room, "three slices of key lime pie and a cappuccino for the lady." Then turning to Carollyn. "It's simply a must," he said, asserting his will.

"Is it an old family recipe?" Nathaniel asked gleefully.

The old man laughed, then his face saddened for a minute, a tear forming in his eye. "It's something that my wife Emma used to make. She baked it for me on our first date, the church picnic that I mentioned earlier."

"Then it must be exceptional," Carollyn said, softly reaching out and touching his trembling hand, knowing that Emma was no longer with him.

The man quickly regained his composure and continued the story. "As we were completing the restaurant Daddy started to complain of chest pain. Though he was not one for doctors, Emma convinced him to go. The doctor told us that he had lung cancer."

"Did he smoke?" Nathaniel asked.

"Like a chimney," the old man laughed in reflection. "Back in the 1930s and '40s we didn't know that cigarettes could cause cancer. Actually, some doctors even prescribed them for nerves and numerous other ailments. Daddy smoked three to four packs a day, and they were unfiltered too. Anyway, a week before his only grandchild was born he passed away."

"How sad," Carollyn sighed.

"Sweet Melissa," Charkey chirped.

The color drained out of the captain's face. He appeared to age ten years just with the mention of his daughter's name.

A momentary awkward stillness fell on the room. Carollyn, sensing the uneasiness, wondered if it was time to leave.

When he was ready the captain continued. "She was a sweet vibrant girl, intelligent and full of life. She was a cheerleader at her high school," he said, pointing toward an old faded black and white photo. The man cried a few tears. "The only real problem we had with her was her opposition to the war in Vietnam," the man mumbled. "It wasn't even her stance on the war that bothered us. It was her disrespect for all the men in uniform that made our country great." The man shook his head slowly. "One day a few GIs came in for dinner. Melissa sat down with them and started a conversation. When she found out they had just returned from Asia, she asked them how many women and children they had slaughtered."

Carollyn gasped, as she covered her mouth with a hand.

"They were horrified, as were Emma and I. No matter how much we apologized to the soldiers, it just wasn't adequate."

Carollyn nervously twirled her hair.

"After a good scolding and more than a few blisters on her butt, Melissa promised never to do that again."

"Those poor men," Carollyn mumbled in disbelief.

"We managed to survive that," he continued. "Then that godforsaken day …" the man's voice trailed as he sobbed openly.

Carollyn and her sons remained quiet to give the man a few minutes to regain composure. Nathaniel squirmed uncomfortably in his chair, unsure as to what to do.

"In 1966, the school nurse called Emma and me in for a conference. Naturally we were scared to death." The man paused for a second. "Our innocent Melissa was pregnant. We tried to stay calm. Actually, Emma did a better job than I. After talking to Melissa here at the restaurant that night, I'm not sure if I was angrier because she was pregnant or because the father was black. I asked myself, selfishly, what I did to deserve that."

"Are you a bigot?" Jason asked sternly.

The man ignored the question. "The first thing I did was to grab my .45 from behind the counter. I was going for blood. No boy was going to take advantage of my daughter and get away with it. As I loaded it, it misfired." He pointed toward a hole in the floor. "The shock of the gunfire gave Emma enough time to talk some sense into my head. Emma was right, it was just as much my daughter's fault as it was the boy's."

"What happened?" Carollyn encouraged the man to continue.

"I decided Melissa would have an abortion. Yes, that was awfully presumptuous, and my once obedient daughter refused. After several weeks of arguments Melissa ran away with her boyfriend. We never saw or heard from her again." The man began to sob. "We tried many times over the years to find her; we even hired a detective but never had any luck." The old man continued to sob. "Guess when someone doesn't want to be found they ain't gonna be found. The boy's parents always claimed they didn't know where they ran away to." He paused. "A few years later they moved away, I think to Jacksonville. If they knew their secret moved with them. Of course, I was behaving like a raging lunatic. There was no reason they should tell me."

Carollyn gave him an a comforting hug. Jason glared in his direction. Innocently, Nathaniel joined in the hug.

They all sat in silence for a few minutes. Trudy brought four slices of pie, a cappuccino, and two tall glasses of milk and a refill of lemonade for the captain.

After the brief reprieve, the bird broke the silence, "Memphis … MLK."

"1968 was a bad year," the man mumbled. "In the spring, I believe it was early April, Martin Luther King was killed. When I heard the news I prayed to God that it was a black man that had done it." The man paused to collect his thoughts. "We soon learned it was James Earl Ray, a white man. I think that is when the first realization of racial hatred occurred to me. It was wrong for any man to kill another because of the color of his skin or his ideas. I don't care what anyone says; King was a great man with solid ideas."

"Yes, he was," Carollyn agreed.

"The day after he died I took the sign down that Daddy and I had hung, 'No n_____allowed,'" the old man confessed. "Even though it was part of my heritage I also took down the confederate flag." He paused, staring nervously at his thick, overgrown yellow toenails protruding out of his sand-colored sandals. Self-conscious that his guests might notice them, he bent his leg under the table bench. "Daddy probably rolled over in his grave when that happened. Still, it was a few years before any black folks came to Charkey's."

"I wonder why," Jason mumbled.

The man continued, "Probably a good thing because it took some time to break Charkey from saying the 'n' word." The man moaned before continuing. "A few months after the death of King, Bobby Kennedy was killed by some insane assassin, in my opinion the first act of foreign terrorism in our country. I don't care what your politics are, but Bobby was a man that was willing to fight for what's right."

"Vote for George," the bird screeched.

"George?" Carollyn asked, puzzled.

"The 1968 presidential election featured three candidates," the man started. "Dick Nixon was the Republican nominee, tricky Dick, as his rivals rightfully called him. Hubert Humphrey received the Democrats' nomination. A discontented Democrat, Governor George Wallace of Alabama, ran as an independent."

"Why did you like Governor Wallace?" Carollyn asked.

"I had no trust in Nixon, who later as president proved me right. Humphrey appeared weak and indecisive. Of course he was the Democrats' third choice. If Bob Kennedy had not been assassinated, he would have received the nomination and would have won the presidency. President Johnson waited until the last possible moment to decide not to seek reelection. Vice President Humphrey, out of loyalty, was unable to declare his candidacy until Johnson made his announcement. His delay made him appear wishy-washy. George Wallace probably received my vote by default."

"'I draw a line in the dust and toss the gauntlet before the feet of tyranny, and I say: segregation now, segregation tomorrow, segregation forever,' are the words he used in his inauguration speech when elected governor," Jason recited. "Later he barricaded the admissions office at the University of Alabama to prevent African-Americans from entering. If not for the National Guard, we would never have been allowed in."

Carollyn stared in amazement at her historian son.

"I agree," the old man whispered. "He did those things. However, he said that the speech was written for him, and he was unaware of the content until it was read."

"His actions spoke louder than his words," Jason continued the debate. "What fool would not read a speech before delivering it?" The boy paused before returning to the deliberation. "Besides, if you listened to the passion in his diction, it is apparent that he was aware of the words and agreed with them."

"Governor Wallace was defending his beliefs; as an American it was his right to do so," the man countered. "It is the First Amendment."

"However, the speech was written for him?" the boy asked sarcastically.

"In the sixties, many people echoed his sentiments," the captain defended his position.

"It was also the right of every African-American citizen to have the same rights as the white. After all, we had the same responsibilities of taxes and going to war," Jason continued.

"The inferior neighborhood schools that were prevalent in the Negro communities were a travesty," the old man agreed. "Integration was not necessarily the only solution. Tax dollars could have been redirected to renovate those schools so that they would be up to the standards of the schools in the predominantly white neighborhoods. The restoration of these neighborhoods may have prevented some of the racial unrest of the mid-sixties to early seventies. How would you feel if you were sent from a poor, run-down neighborhood to a nicer one every day? At the end of the day you were sent back to your old run-down neighborhood. Wouldn't you feel angry? Wouldn't that make you feel there was a great divide between the races?"

Jason did not reply.

"It still doesn't make sense to me that a child—black or white—would spend three hours on a bus each day in the name of equality," the man paused. "If left alone, integration would have been a natural evolutionary process." The captain paused. "Many of the riots may never have occurred."

"So you are still defending Wallace?" Jason asked.

"I am providing an alternative viewpoint," the man quipped. "As for George Wallace, he did a lot of good for the state of Alabama, for all races. Late in his life, when it was not politically necessary to do so, he recanted many of his earlier stances on segregation, admitting that he was misguided. Even before he was elected governor in the early sixties, he was known to oppose the Ku Klux Klan. The fact is he lost his first election for governor because his opponent had the Klan's support."

There was a momentary silence as everyone reflected on the debate.

"Meathead," the bird shouted, as the tension broke.

Everyone laughed. "In January 1971, *All in the Family* made its debut. Emma and I loved the show. I think it had been on about a month when they had an episode concerning blood donation. Archie insisted there was a difference between white blood and black blood." The man paused to cough. "After the show, Emma looked at me and said 'You know, you are just like Archie.' Of course I denied it; after all, I did take the sign and flag down. After we sat in cold silence for what seemed like an hour she looked me square in the eye and said, 'His name is Laurence.' I stared at her in confusion; I had no clue what she was talking about. Then she continued, 'That boy that Melissa ran off with that you always refer to as Leroy—his name is Laurence.'"

"Oh my," Carollyn whispered.

"It is the only time I walked away from Emma angry." Pointing to the sea he continued, "I took my boat out and fished all night. Actually I did more thinking and talking to God. You know Emma was right; I was a bigot, an ignorant bigot. No disrespect intended but I did have good teachers in the way of bigotry. It is not an excuse, but racial prejudice is a learned behavior."

"Yes, it is," Carollyn agreed, "and it goes both ways."

"By happenstance a young black girl came into Charkey's the next day in response to my help wanted sign in the window. She was a student at Bethune-Cookman and needed money for tuition. Her daddy had been killed in the Korean War, and she had no one to help her. After asking her a few questions, which labor laws of today wouldn't allow, I took the sign from the window. Knowing that my regular patrons might be a bit skimpy on tips to a black girl, I started her at twenty-five cents an hour more than my regular girls."

"Vanessa was one of my best hires ever. It didn't take long before she was running Charkey's in the evenings and on weekends. A real sharp girl."

"So did you hire out of guilt or awareness?" Jason asked.

"I don't have the answer for that question," the captain said, rubbing his chin. "It is possible that I hired her for both reasons. The important thing is I gave myself an opportunity to open my eyes to all people."

"Where is she now?" a sleepy-eyed Nathaniel asked.

"Vanessa became like a daughter to us. Before she started dating her husband, she insisted on him getting our approval. He even asked me for my permission to marry her."

The man pointed toward a wedding picture on the wall. "I was given the honor of giving her away."

"That is a touching tribute," Carollyn smiled. Even Jason appeared to be touched.

The sounds of seagulls suddenly shrieked through the night, as they fought over food on the porch.

"Hammerin' Hank," Charkey blurted.

"Oh yes, old Hank," the man smiled at the memory. "Vanessa's husband, David, took me to Atlanta to see the Braves play against the Los Angeles Dodgers on April 8, 1974. It was in the fourth inning; I remember as if it was yesterday. Hank Aaron hit his historic home run 715, I believe off Al Downing. It was a bittersweet occasion for me. It was difficult to see Babe Ruth's record crumble."

"It bothered you because an African-American broke a white man's record?" Jason insisted.

"No, it was because I grew up in the era of Babe Ruth. The Babe was my idol, an American icon. He helped Americans survive a terrible time in history. We all relate to triumphs of our generation as if they were our own. It was nice, though, to see Aaron get the mark. He is a class act and continues to contribute to baseball and the city of Atlanta.

It is sad that he had to endure a lot of hate mail from bigoted people wanting him to fail. With ridiculous threats on his life he must have felt as though he was in hell." The man cleared his throat. "After the hit, a celebratory cannon sounded. His frantic mother raced to home plate to meet her son, not out of joy but because she thought Hank had been shot. No one should have to live through that, especially for a silly game. We, as a human race, need to rise above the color of our brother's skin and look into the eyes of his soul. Wanting someone to fail because they are different is ludicrous."

The old man picked up his stogie and stared at it. "Aaron broke the record that was supposed to be unbreakable." The man laughed. "Then Bonds broke Aaron's record that was supposed to be unbreakable."

"Hey, you didn't answer my question about Vanessa," the little boy whined.

The man smiled. "Vanessa and David live in Orlando. Vanessa is a clinical psychologist; she has her own practice. Recently, she has published her first book, some type of self-help guide. I am eagerly waiting for my autographed copy. David works as a physical therapist. He specializes in sports medicine. Some of his clients have included members of the Orlando Magic and the University of Central Florida sports teams. They have three grown children and two grandchildren. Kind of makes me feel like a great-grandfather. I spend every holiday with them and many weekends in between."

"And Emma," Carollyn asked, already knowing the answer.

The man shook his head slowly, staring at the ground. "Emma was my soul mate. Other than our disagreement in 1971 we never fought. We would take long walks on the beach, just the two of us, as if we were alone in the world. We managed the restaurant, went on picnics, fabulous fishing trips, and taught Sunday school. We laughed a lot. She was my best friend." The man paused to maintain his composure. "In the summer of 1976 she found a lump in her breast. It was cancer. Emma moved into heaven on our thirtieth wedding anniversary in 1977. She is God's now; guess she always was and always will be. Having her as my wife for thirty years was a sign of God's love. I don't know that I ever did anything to be blessed with a treasure like my Emma." Surprisingly, the man maintained his composure. "I do miss the touch of her lips. Waking up next to her in the morning gave me the courage to face each new day. I tried to contact Melissa when Emma got sick, but we still couldn't locate her. I figured if she knew her mother was dying she would come home. After she died I stopped trying to find Melissa. I don't know how I would have told her about her momma."

"I'm sure she would have come if she knew," Carollyn reassured, placing her hand on his. "I know it is rough to lose anyone to cancer. You must have felt helpless during the ordeal of her illness. I recently lost my mother to cancer." She paused for a second. "I decided to go to medical school because of all the members of my family that have been afflicted by cancer. Even as an oncologist, knowing what was going on in my mother's body, I was rendered totally powerless."

"I am sorry for your loss," the man said thoughtfully, sincerity resonating in his voice. He turned his attention to the boys. "I'm sorry for the loss of your grandmother. By getting to know the three of you, I can tell she was a wonderful person."

For a few seconds, the old man fidgeted with his empty lemonade glass. Carollyn stared nervously at the wall.

"I think the hardest part of the ordeal was the doctors keeping us in the dark," the captain continued. "On our first trip to the oncologist, the doctor looked at us as if we were imposing on his day. 'You have cancer,' he said in a monotone voice without even looking at Emma. 'We'll run some tests to see if it spread and start chemo and radiation.' Before we could ask any questions he was out of the examine room."

Carollyn shook her head sadly. "Sometimes we physicians get so wrapped up in our lives we fail to consider the patients' needs. Somewhere on our journey we forget the basic compassion that drove us into the profession. When Momma was first diagnosed with cancer I was a partner in a practice in Denver." She paused to collect her thoughts. "I still remember receiving the phone call in my office from my daddy." She stared out the window to the dark sea as tears welled in her almond eyes.

The old man reached out and touched her hand. The boys instinctively remained quiet. "Daddy's voice cracked, and he couldn't even get it out. After he stopped sobbing, he was able to relay that Momma was diagnosed with colon cancer."

The man squeezed her hand tightly. Nathaniel flung his arms around her neck.

"The doctor said that the tumor had been there for nearly seven years. There were no signs or symptoms, nothing." Carollyn paused and shook her head. "Momma had a colonoscopy when she turned fifty, just as it is recommended. Everything was clean. Then one day she started bleeding, and there it was. When they removed the tumor they discovered that it had metastasized to her liver." The woman wept openly. "There were too many lesions on the liver to do any type of resection. The only option of treatment was chemotherapy."

The captain looked at the boys. "Why don't you ask Trudy to take you guys to the upstairs balcony so you can get a better look at the ocean?"

The boys scurried off. The man made eye contact with Trudy to indicate that it was okay. After the boys started up the stairs the captain nodded for Carollyn to continue.

"Even as a physician I had great difficulty accessing information from Momma's doctors. Finally, we decided to relocate back to Chicago, so I could help Momma and Daddy navigate through the health-care system. Even practicing in Chicago, communications with the doctor wasn't always clear and precise. If not for my own knowledge we would have been lost in the quandaries of treatment."

The man returned his hand to hers.

"I remember the apprehension my parents had when they put the port in so they could administer the chemotherapy. Even though I was familiar with the procedure, I couldn't help biting my nails." She gasped. "This wasn't just another patient, this was my mother."

"I know that had to be difficult," the man said softly.

"The hardest part for Momma was the distortion of her body image. The once radiant woman now had an unnatural object protruding from just above her right breast." Carollyn moaned. "Even though her clothes concealed it, she always knew it was there. A menacing reminder that she was no longer herself."

"That had to be a terrible ordeal for your entire family."

"It was, especially for Momma. The rest of us adapted to her condition, knowing that we were being given some extra time with her. We prayed nightly that a miracle would happen."

"Your father was able to be supportive?"

"He was the best," Carollyn smiled. "Every other week Momma would have to spend the day in an outpatient clinic hooked up to chemo. Daddy did not miss a session. Together they sat in agony watching other hopeful patients receiving the same treatment, then eventually fall prey to the killer. After each treatment, she started wondering when her chair would become the empty one." Carollyn sighed. "The physicians did nothing to alleviate her fears; their only answers were to cite statistics. I kept saying to them 'she is not a statistic, she is my momma.' But it did no good."

Jason and Nathaniel raced back to the table.

"I've been told that when battling a serious illness a large part of the battle is maintaining a positive attitude," the old man continued. "It was hard for us to be positive when the doctors treated us like statistics part of the time; and the rest of the time as illiterate imbeciles. If they would have been honest, provided options or just some encouraging words, dying would have been easier for Emma. The last several months of her life she was busy dying, largely caused by the attitude from the doctors. With a more positive attitude, I believe that we could have spent our time celebrating life instead."

The man paused to cough. "You should only have to die on the appointed day of the Savior; the rest of the time should be spent relishing each breath."

"I agree, a positive attitude is imperative to being well," Carollyn agreed. "As physicians, we have an obligation to encourage our patients to continue to live even when death appears imminent. I have seen many patients with poor prognosis, without a valid medical explanation, go into total remission. I give credit to God and the human spirit." The physician paused briefly. "Since the experience with my mother, I have been much more conscientious on how I treat my patients."

Turning to the boys the captain changed the subject. "Did you see anything?"

"I saw the moon," Nathaniel shouted. "It is right over the middle of the ocean."

"I believe I saw Mars," Jason boasted, "but it may have been Saturn."

"I think he saw stars," Nathaniel laughed.

The man scratched his left ear. "Both the planets should be in the sky this time of year. If I have my facts straight, I believe that Saturn would be slightly to the southeast."

"Then it was Saturn," Jason declared.

The captain looked at Nathaniel. "The planets are so far away that they appear to be stars. The big difference is that they don't twinkle like the stars."

"That's because they are reflecting the sun's rays, whereas stars create their own light," Jason pointed out.

"So, it is nice to hear the fog has lifted," Carollyn mentioned.

"It's still pretty foggy," Jason volunteered. "There are some patches where we can see the sky."

"Marissa ... where's Marissa?" Charkey chirped.

"Marissa is the manager of the restaurant," the captain explained. "She came looking for a job back in 1992. She had just moved from Seattle and was looking for a fresh start. She had some type of boy trouble out there." He continued, revealing more than he should. "Think a boyfriend got her pregnant and left her. In her desperation she had an abortion. It must have been real difficult for her."

Trudy interrupted, "Captain, the boys have cleaned the kitchen and we're ready to go; is there anything you need?"

Carollyn pulled out her purse to pay.

"Ma'am," Trudy looked at her, "Captain says it is on the house. Don't try to protest, it ain't gonna do any good."

The man looked at his guest and said, "Please, I spent the entire meal monopolizing your time."

Realizing she wasn't going to win, she put her purse away and softly thanked the man.

"Trudy, if there is a sweet potato left can you bring it to me on your way out?"

"I swear," the waitress laughed, "you do spoil Charkey."

"Anyway," the man continued, "Marissa came in for an interview with a ring stuck in her nose and one in her eyebrow; the right side of her head was shaved. She talked to me about peace and 'The Universal God's' love. It was her mission to come work for me. Some weird-sounding spirit guide directed her in a dream or some type of meditation to move to Daytona and work at a restaurant on a serene beach. I thought she was really out there, a real moonbeam type person. I was looking for the men and white jackets and nets. There was not a chance on earth that I was going to hire her."

"But you hired her anyway," Carollyn mused.

Trudy set a sweet potato in front of the man, hugged him good-bye, and left for the night.

The cook stopped by and placed something in the old man's hand as he prepared to leave.

"Fortunately, Vanessa and David were visiting for the day. Vanessa helped me interview Marissa. Somehow she convinced me to hire her, minus the rings. Vanessa always was a champion for the underdog."

"Since she has been around since 1992 that must mean she is your girlfriend?" Jason teased.

"Absolutely not," the man protested. "There has never been anyone except Emma."

"I'm sorry," the boy apologized.

"Marissa is like another daughter. She looks after Charkey and me. Her spiritual beliefs are a bit different ... some would even say odd. Actually, they are odd. There are all kinds of crystals in her office that she claims have special powers of healing, serenity, wisdom, and compassion." He pulled a sterling silver necklace from beneath his shirt. The necklace had a medallion made of an oblong piece of polished rose quartz with a small circle of topaz attached to its top. "Marissa said this is supposed to bring me serenity." He chuckled. "Must work because since I've had it I've been much calmer. She is constantly burning incense and doing weird meditations. Seems as if every month she is running to Cassadaga to have a medium talk to the dead. She has stopped trying to lure me into that part of her world. But despite her eccentricities she is genuinely a good person. I love her dearly. Along with Vanessa and David she is my family."

"Cassadaga," Carollyn laughed. "Is that some type of new age shop?"

The man shook his head and grinned. "No, it's a town of psychics about forty minutes west of us. Allegedly it is the vortex for psychic energy. Legend says it has more energy than any other area in this hemisphere. Not sure whose legend it is; maybe theirs."

"You aren't even curious?" Carollyn asked.

"Well," the man stammered, sounding a bit embarrassed, "I went once. This guy told me he felt or saw a spirit of a lady that had died of something related to the chest area. He said her name started with a 'M' sound. He talked about her liking to bake pies. Said she was happy now and wanted me to go on with my life. He told me things about us that no one knows." The man paused. "He said a lot of things that sounded as if he was communicating with Emma." The old man hesitated. "But he couldn't bring Emma back. I couldn't hear the softness of her voice or feel the gentleness of her touch. I'm not certain if he was legitimate or just a good guesser. It doesn't matter; I still don't have Emma. I've never been back and don't have any need to go."

"Sounds interesting," Carollyn mused.

He pointed to the inside of the restaurant. "Her boyfriend or husband or whatever remodeled the inside of this place. His next project will be the porch."

There was a brief moment of peaceful silence. The only sound was of the Atlantic beating the beach as it had for millenniums.

The old man turned his attention to the very sleepy Nathaniel. "I suppose I'm going to need your help to feed Charkey." The man let out a dry cough. "Before we feed the bird, I have a souvenir of your visit." Looking at Jason, he said, "from one numismatist to another," as he handed Jason a 1864 two-cent piece.

Jason's eyes lit up and he exclaimed, "Thank you."

Carollyn was flabbergasted but knew not to protest.

The little boy perked up immediately. The captain looked at him strangely. "I believe you have something sticking out of your ear." The man reached to his right ear and produced another 1864 two-cent piece. "You better place this in a safe place," the old man said in a serious tone before bursting into laughter.

The wide-eyed boy stared in disbelief. "Thank you," he shyly mumbled.

Jason studied the odd copper coin, which was a bit smaller than a quarter. The obverse was a striped shield with a ribbon flowing above it with the motto, "In God We Trust." To each side of the shield were olive branches. On the reverse, inscribed in bold print was "United States of America" circling the outer parameter of the coin; "2 Cents" was engraved in the middle surrounded by wreaths.

"This was the first coin that had the motto, 'In God We Trust' engraved on it," the man said, as if teaching. "It was minted due to the high demand for small change during the Civil war. I'm not sure my facts are straight, but I believe they stopped making them somewhere around 1872."

"Thank you," both boys repeated.

"Now for payment," the man continued to Nathaniel, "I will require your assistance to give Charkey a bedtime snack."

The two walked to the cage together, the old man using the young boy's left shoulder as a cane. Though not officially invited, Jason followed them.

Carollyn watched with pride as her boys talked with the man as they were feeding the bird. Nervously, she pulled a legal-size envelope out of her Louis Vuitton purse. Her long slender fingers glided over the seal, as she continued to watch the interaction between the old southern gentleman and her Yankee sons. Staring at the envelope, she was confused as to why she pulled it out and stuffed it back in the purse. Realizing it was late, she slowly started toward the cage to say good-bye.

She noticed a faded black and white picture of a bearded rugged Confederate soldier on the wall. "Grandpappy," she mused. The same strong jawbone and prominent cheeks of the captain were evident in the picture. The man in the antique picture had the same mole of the earlier vision. Even the faded eyes in a century-and-a-half-old portrait were piercing and brutally cold. Apparently, hatred finds a way to survive death.

There were definite dominant traits that were passed down to future generations. She was pleased that some traits could be changed. Unsure as to why she reached and touched the face on the picture, a gripping wintry chill rippled down her spine. Immediately, her arm bolted back. Momentarily she glanced at the table where the apparitions had previously made their acquaintance, but they remained unseen. In the air there was the aroma of stale tobacco, though no one had been smoking.

Her eyes shifted quickly to the old man. Behind him, out the window, the moon was forcing its way through the mist to illuminate the dark sea. In the distance she heard thunder, warning of an impending storm. She casually glanced at the various ornaments that adorned the walls. There were numerous photographs and hand-painted pictures along with souvenirs from a century gone by. Carollyn felt that the restaurant, minus the picture of Grandpappy, was warm and inviting. She was happy that she and the boys had stopped by.

The captain and the boys stood at the cage engaging the bird in idle conversation.

Carollyn slowly walked up behind them. "Thanks for a delightful evening," she said to the man, kissing him on the cheek. "Are you going to be able to get home okay?" Carollyn peered through the clouds of the cataract to the genuine love in the captain's soul.

The man was touched by her concern. "I just live next door. A short jaunt is good for the heart."

"You have been good for my heart," the lady said as she smiled. "Hope you don't mind if we stop by again."

Before the captain could answer, Nathaniel interrupted. "Hey Mom, I thought you said we were going to meet my great-grandfather tonight?"

"We did," Carollyn smiled as tears streamed freely down her high cheeks.

Chapter II

Wednesday

Do not underestimate good, thinking it will not affect you. Dripping water can fill a pitcher, drop by drop; one who is wise is filled with good, even if one accumulates it little by little.

—Dhammapada 9.7

At precisely 3:00 AM a wicked bolt of lightning ripped horizontally across the starless night. As the remnants of the first began to fade, the heavens sent a second jagged vertical bolt as a reminder of her fury. Seconds after the flash dimmed a roar of thunder resonated off the earth as it competed to be heard above the howling wind. Then there was silence. The still was soon shattered by a colossal mountain of the Atlantic slamming against the sea wall, followed by a downpour. Not to be defeated the wind, thunder, and lightning resumed their chorus.

The smell of freshly brewed coffee blending with frying eggs and bacon met Carollyn as she opened her eyes. She smiled slightly, lying still for a moment, reflecting on the aroma of her childhood. The rejuvenated woman tiptoed into the kitchen where the old man was cooking breakfast with delight. She glanced out the window to a yard decorated with tree limbs and a portion of a tin roof blown from an old storage shed.

"Good morning," she whispered. "Breakfast smells just like Momma used to cook it."

The man flipped an egg without looking at his granddaughter. "Why don't you pour yourself a cup of coffee," he said, motioning toward the mugs with his free hand, "and take a seat out on the porch. We can have breakfast out there and enjoy the cool breeze, while it lasts." As if reading her mind he continued, "Let the boys sleep in; we will tend to their breakfast when they get up."

Hugging the man from behind she kissed his grisly cheek. "Thank you, captain," she whispered. She then poured two cups of coffee. After splashing a thimbleful of cream in hers, she knowingly stirred a teaspoon of sugar in his. The man glanced at her as she walked to the porch, saddened slightly that she had not addressed him as Grandpappy.

Carollyn brushed the debris of the night from an aqua and white lounge chair and then did the same to a more comfortable looking padded chair. As she settled into the seat her eyes fixated on the purple rays majestically bouncing off the waveless ocean, highlighting the awakening crimson ball from which they came. While she nervously waited for her breakfast, Carollyn momentarily studied the coffee cups. The one she was drinking from was a blue cup with the picture of The Ryman Auditorium in Nashville. The other cup was olive green with a replica of the Twin Towers on it.

The man quietly placed the eggs beside her on an old wicker table with a cracked Plexiglas top. Without a word he settled into the pale green padded chair. The mesmerized physician continued to stare at the spectacular array of colors unfolding in front of her. After a few moments she raised the coffee to her lips, turning slightly to the old man, but keeping one eye trained on the sea as she smiled.

The man nodded in acknowledgment. "I'm not much of a decorator," he laughed, referring to the furnishings on the porch. "But the artist that created this view sure knew what he was doing."

Carollyn took another sip of the strong Columbian brewed beverage. "This coffee is good, but the sunrise has really opened my eyes to the beauty of nature." She took another sip. "I am so thankful that you are sharing it with me." She paused for a moment of silent reflection. "I'm used to waking up to the view of the clichéd cement jungle staring menacingly through my window. It is so much more picturesque than Momma described it to be."

The two sat in silence, enjoying the breeze and marveling as the sun leisurely took its place in the cerulean sky. Carollyn sprinkled Tabasco sauce on her eggs, something the man thought was odd for a northerner. She eagerly spread the homemade pumpkin butter, sent to the captain by a distant cousin from Savannah, on the piping hot fresh buttermilk biscuits. As a child she envied her friends' tales of going to their grandmothers' homes for good down-to-earth cooking. Her mind drifted back to the quiet kitchen at her parents' home in Chicago. Her mother struggled in the kitchen to make the ordinary meal. Cooking just was not something she enjoyed. Melissa would often reflect on the artistry of her father in the kitchen. "Unfortunately," she would complain, "the chef gene skipped a generation."

Returning her attention to the coffee cups, she continued. "Did you and Emma travel a lot?"

The man smiled at the memories. "We would go as often as possible. Being in the restaurant business, it wasn't always easy to get away, but we would take at least one long trip a year." The old man paused for a few seconds. "We used to be closed every Sunday and Monday, so we would get to take small trips year round. Every winter we would go to Plant City, which is over near Tampa, for the Strawberry Festival. We would find a motel, and the next morning go out to the strawberry fields and pick berries." A broad smile came over the man's face at the memory. "When we returned home Emma would make the best strawberry jam you ever tasted. We would always pick enough to freeze for the whole year. Somewhere there is a picture of your mother in the middle of a strawberry field with berries smeared all over her face."

"Strawberries always brought Momma pleasure," Carollyn mused. "Now I understand why."

"In late spring or early summer we would drive to Georgia to pick peaches. We would always bring back a truckload and put them up just the way we did the strawberries."

"What about your big trips?"

"Every fall we would go to Bimini or other Caribbean islands to fish. We would spend time fishing and visiting with the locals. Most nights we would sleep on the boat, but we would always spend at least one night in a hotel. Emma and I would walk the quaint cities and just listen to the sounds of the island. Late at night we would sit on the terrace and enjoy a nice bottle of wine and melt into each other."

"Then every couple of years we would go to sites around the states. We went to Nashville several times. Emma loved the Grand Ole Opry, so naturally we had to go to see it live. Truthfully, it was worth the drive." The old man smiled at the reflection.

"I have been told that it is a spectacular show."

"It is the longest running radio show in the nation," the man quipped. "It always has a live audience."

"I did not know that," Carollyn acknowledged.

"All of Nashville is worth seeing," the man volunteered. "Being a bit of a history buff, there are a lot of things to visit." The old man paused in reflection. "Andrew Jackson's home, the Hermitage, is still there. It is amazing that the wallpaper from the 1700s, without any restoration, remain so vibrant. It was interesting to see the carriage he rode in to Washington; it was so small I can't imagine it being comfortable. I was intrigued to read about the political scandals of those days." The man paused. "Andrew Jackson's wife, Rachael, was accused of bigamy, of which she was unwittingly guilty. It seems as that her first husband was insanely jealous, so she left him. The divorce decree was on the docket but never heard. Believing she was divorced, several years later she met Jackson and they were married. Her first husband heard of this and accused her of adultery. Once everything was straightened out, she and Jackson got remarried. Jackson's political rivals used this to campaign against him. The harassment became so severe and Rachael Jackson got so worked up that she died of a heart attack several months prior to Jackson taking the oath of office. Lines from her epitaph read, 'A being so gentle and so virtuous slander might wound, but could not dishonor.'"

"It sounds fascinating."

"Emma and I would always take a horse and buggy ride through downtown, always stopping by Printers Alley. That was an old hang-out for aspiring stars back in the 1920s. The local legend is that in the wee hours of the morning you can still hear the echoes of some of the legends strumming and singing."

The man bent down to pet a black cat with a white diamond on its forehead that wandered onto the porch. "Can't feed you," he whispered. "If I did you would forget where your home is."

Carollyn smiled at the cat.

"The most humbling place in Nashville is an old cemetery near downtown, on Nolensville Pike."

"Oh?" Carollyn raised her eyebrows.

"In the midst of the cemetery there is a marker that reads, 'Here lies the first white man born in Nashville.'"

Carollyn looked puzzled at the relevance of the tombstone.

"Sometimes we forget that we were not the first settlers of this continent," her grandfather mused. "We were the messy houseguests that forgot to go home."

There was a momentary lapse in conversation. Carollyn stared at the clouds that were lazily floating by.

"Sometimes your momma would travel with us; other times she would stay home with a friend. Of course when she came, we always allowed her to bring a friend."

"So Momma caught the travel bug from you?"

"In 1972, Emma and I went to visit an old army buddy of mine in your city, Chicago. If only we had known Melissa was there."

Carollyn looked surprised. "What was your favorite thing about Chicago?"

"We enjoyed the Lincoln Park Zoo," the man mentioned without hesitation. "Being a baseball fan, going to historic Wrigley Field may have been the highlight of the trip."

There was a long, awkward silence. The sun continued its ascent to the top of the sky.

Pointing toward the side of the porch with a finger that had plastered egg on the fingernail the man broke the silence. "Melissa … er … your mother used to sit there for hours painting. She was quite an accomplished artist. I was real proud of her work. The painting of Charkey that hangs in the restaurant was done by your momma."

Carollyn smiled, "I know." She took her last sip of coffee. "My favorite painting is of this beach; it was, done in acrylics, I believe. The waves are aqua blue with whitecaps rising to the surface. The sun is much like it is today, crimson red sneaking through the lightly clouded sky. On the left there is a discolored orange crab, with a tad of green algae on its shell, edging back into the water. There is a shadow cast upon the water of a man fishing." She paused and looked directly at the man, with a twinkle in her almond eyes. "The silhouette is yours, standing knee deep in the water with blue overalls rolled up, one strap undone, revealing an olive shirt. An old wide-brim straw hat shades your head. Charkey is perched proudly on a tree behind you." Carollyn's eyes clouded with tears. "Momma had the painting above the mantle of her fireplace. Now I have it hanging in the lobby of my office. Every time I look at it, my mind drifts to her."

The captain stared in disbelief. Melissa must have done that painting after she left; she still cared about her family.

"Momma had such an eye for details," she laughed, "she even remembered to put the intricate details of the fish hooks stuck in your hat."

The man could conceal the tears no longer as they freely flowed from his eyes. "I really loved your momma. We really loved her." He paused to wipe a crinkled handkerchief across his cheeks. "I still regret chasing her away. I obviously didn't know what I was doing. I only wanted what I thought was best for her." He paused to regain composure. Carollyn softly held his hand, but did not speak. "It would have been a bit wiser if I would have considered what Melissa felt was best," he said. Staring off into the depth of the sea he quietly lamented the consequences of his actions as he had done many a lonely morning.

"We all do what we feel is best for our children," she reassured. "Your reaction was out of love, not malice."

"Still," the old man said, "I chased my precious girl out of our lives." He put his head into the fingertips of his left hand and sadly shook it.

Carollyn rubbed his neck gently with both her hands. Sensing his need for meditation, she quietly cleared the table and washed the dishes. Leaving her grandfather alone also allowed Carollyn to avoid feelings of loss deep in her heart.

The boys eventually rose from their slumber. After bidding their great-grandfather good morning, they settled in front of the television set with bowls of cereal with fresh peaches diced into them. As soon as Carollyn discovered them sitting on the couch with their breakfast, she gently reminded them that meals were to be eaten at the table.

Carollyn returned to the porch; the old man gave her a warm smile.

"Did your father date after your mother died?" Carollyn wasn't sure if she was interested in her great-grandfather as much as she was interested in what her own father might do.

Her granfather shook his head. "Over the years he had numerous women he would call on. Daddy was the type of man that didn't like being alone."

"Was there anyone special?" Carollyn asked.

The captain frowned. There was silence for a few minutes as he pondered whether to reveal the family scandal. "There was this woman, Zelda. He kept company with her off and on ever since I can remember. Neither Rufus nor I could stand her. Daddy always thought it was because we didn't want anyone taking Momma's place."

"Do you think he was right?" Carollyn said, raising her eyebrows.

"No, at least that wasn't the case with me. I don't remember objecting to any of the other women Daddy would bring around. I just didn't trust her. Zelda was tall and rail thin. Long stringy black hair with white streaks like a skunk flowed to her waist. A bump the size of a pea sat on the ridge of her curled-up snout. Five crooked boney sticks protruded from each hand. When she laughed, it sounded more like a hyena cackling. The ugliest pale green cat eyes bulged from her head."

"Was her skin green?" Carollyn teased.

"That is exactly what Emma used to say," the man smiled. "She always referred to Zelda as the old witch." The old man paused. "That was odd, because my Emma never had a bad word to say about anyone."

"What happened to her?"

The frown returned to the man's face. "Over the years she would come in and help out at Charkey's from time to time. She would wait tables or cook, whatever Daddy needed her to do. Of course there were long spells, sometimes a few years, when they weren't seeing each other and she would stay away." The man paused to think if he wanted to reveal the rest of the story. Finally, he decided to forge onward. "Shortly after the fire, Daddy and Zelda had one of their big fights. She stormed away, stating that she would never return."

"What did they fight about?" Carollyn inquired, curiously.

"With them, we were never certain. However, this time I believe Zelda wanted to go on our Cuban vacation." The captain paused to wipe his nose. "Daddy never took her on any family trips. He knew that we did not like her and would not subject us to the stress." The man slipped his sandals on. "I think he knew that Emma and I would stay in Florida if she was going to tag along."

"He made the right choice," Carollyn defended him.

"We didn't see Zelda until a couple months after Daddy died. She didn't even have enough decency to come to his funeral."

Nathaniel interrupted to ask if they could watch television now that they had finished their breakfast. Carollyn instructed him that they could do so after they washed their dishes.

"One day Zelda showed up at Charkey's to announce that Daddy had intended for her to have half of the restaurant upon his death."

"Oh no!" Carollyn exclaimed.

"I told her in no uncertain terms that she was out of her mind. She said it was in a legal document that was in Daddy's desk, which must have burned in the fire." The man's face became tense.

"Of course," Carollyn cut in sarcastically.

"It was supposed to have been a repayment for all the work that she had put in at Charkey's over the years." The man paused to sip some cold coffee. "Besides, she continued, Daddy was the father of her illegitimate daughter."

"Oh no," Carollyn exclaimed again. "What did you say?"

"I didn't have a chance to utter a word. Grandma Ruth was sitting in her rocking chair taking all this in. Quietly, but faster than I believed she ever moved, Grandma sneaked up behind Zelda and started whacking her with a broom. The last time I seen Zelda, she was running down the street with Grandma Ruth chasing behind."

They both laughed.

"So was that the end of it?" Carollyn asked.

The old man put on the straw hat that was sitting on the table. "Not quite. A few days later a policeman came to talk with me. He said that he received an anonymous tip that Daddy had burned down the original restaurant and that I was an accomplice."

Carollyn stared in disbelief.

"Having nothing to hide, I answered his questions." The man wiped a bead of sweat off his forehead. "A couple of days later the officer returned to tell me the case had been closed."

"That must have been a relief." Carollyn whispered. Secretly, she wondered if her great-grandfather was the culprit in the fire.

"It was a big relief." There was another awkward pause. "About a month had passed since the incident when I received a letter from an attorney. Zelda decided to threaten to have a paternity suit if I did not relinquish half my interest in Charkey's." The man cleared his throat. "This letter had indicated the suit could get really nasty if we did not settle it quietly."

"That sounds like a threat," Carollyn said.

"Exactly; some attorneys will do anything if they smell money," the man sighed.

"How did you handle it?" Carollyn asked.

"My attorney sent a letter to her lawyer, stating that we would welcome a suit to clear my daddy's good name. He further stated that we would ask the court, when we won, to order her to pay our attorneys fees. I never heard from her again."

"That must have made you happy." Before she could stop herself, Carollyn blurted out, "Do you think there could be any truth to the paternity claim?"

The man pondered the question. "Anything is possible," he confessed. "As you might have guessed, Daddy was not a choir boy. However, I honestly believe he was not the father. If he had been, he would have made provisions for the child. It is unlikely Zelda would have kept paternity a secret from Daddy." The old man looked out at the sea. "Looking back on the whole situation is a bit sad. Zelda did spend a lot of time at the restaurant, for which she was well paid. Trying to claim half may have been her way of trying to hold onto Daddy. As for the father of her daughter, I doubt that she even knew the identity." The man scratched his nose. "Too bad they didn't have DNA testing back then. I'm sure Zelda's daughter, I don't even recall her name, would have liked to have known the truth. Most likely, Zelda convinced her it was Daddy."

"What happened to her?"

"The gossip tree has it that Zelda and her daughter moved to South Carolina soon after my attorney wrote to hers. I believe she was from there." The man laughed to himself. "Another rumor has it that she became fish bait."

Carollyn looked at her grandfather in horror.

"If that is true, I had nothing to do with it or knowledge of the deed. Who knows, it is possible that she attempted to blackmail someone that wasn't as ethical and law abiding as I."

"What do you think your father saw in her?" Carollyn said, trying to identify what her father may do in a future relationship.

"That's a difficult question," her grandfather said as he rubbed his beard. "Emma and I theorized that it was possible that Daddy picked such a homely girlfriend so he wouldn't fall in love with her. By not being overly committed he would not tarnish my mother's memory." The man took another sip of cold coffee.

"Okay," Carollyn replied, attempting to decipher the logic.

"You know," the captain said wryly, "in some ways I feel bad for her. She was devoted to my father in her own way. It must have been difficult that he died while they were on the outs."

Carollyn decided to change the subject. "When did Grandma Ruth die?"

"Grandma Ruth lived to be almost a hundred," the man quipped. "On November 22, 1963, she was sitting in her rocking chair entrenched in the news about President Kennedy's assassination. I went to ask for an update, and she was gone." The old man paused. "She was a fascinating lady, was never sick a day in her life."

"She sounds wonderful."

Her grandfather stood and started toward the stairs and motioned for her to join him for a stroll on the beach. Before he hit the sand, the old man removed his sandals. "Salt air is good for all that ails you," he said in between coughs.

Carollyn put her arms around him, leaning in as they walked side by side. Shouting into the house, she instructed the boys to remain close to the house and for Jason to watch his younger brother. The boys were too captivated by *The Professor of Science Show* to care where their great-grandfather and mother were strolling to. The seagulls clamoring and diving for food chaperoned them as they made their way down the white sandy beach.

"We always wondered if Melissa kept up with her artwork," the old man mentioned.

Carollyn smiled and said, "She had a passion for it," pride resonating from her heart. "In our house Daddy turned the garage into a studio. We always knew when Momma was feeling blue because she would get lost in her studio for days, almost as if she was hibernating. Momma would paint the sea, the mountains, sunsets and sunrises. She would paint places where we visited and places she wished we could see. There was always something magical about her art; it was as if her soul vibrated onto the canvas."

There was a pause for a second, as a tear began forming in her eye, more of joy than sadness. "When Momma was told the cancer was terminal, she secluded herself in the studio for almost a month. Upon emerging, she presented us with an illustrious garden with a juxtaposition of all types and colors of flowers wrapped around a serene, seven-tiered marble fountain with crystal clear water flowing evenly. Three monarch butterflies fluttered gently around the top tier." Carollyn paused for a brief moment, allowing a nervous giggle to escape. "Momma was a butterfly enthusiast; although she never collected them, except on canvas."

"On the lower six tiers there are several atala butterflies characterized by their navy blue iridescent wings with large red-orange spots and three rows of irregular glistening gold spots." Carollyn closed her eyes to enhance the visualization. "The atala butterflies are joined by black swallowtails. They have jet black wings, with a sun in the middle of each wing, revealing a partial lunar eclipse."

A volley ball bounced in front of the couple, hitting the old man in the knee. A chubby teenager scurried to pick it up, apologized for the stray ball, and then quickly returned to the game.

Carollyn continued her description, "Emerald swallowtails with lime green wings, and a vertical light green band on each wing, hover near the base. Black with pale yellow striped wings zebra swallowtails are positioned on the outer periphery, of the fountain, to provide just the right contrast. Bees are busily pollinating the foliage as cardinals, bluebirds, robins, and a large parrot serenades her Eden." She paused to laugh. "A radiant gold brick walkway encircles the cascade. True to form, the bricks were created with elaborate detail even down to the grouting that holds them together. Next to the fountain is a comfortable golden oak bench with red and green plaid cushions. On the right side of the bench beautiful jacarandas curl up the arm. Soft peach-colored roses elegantly ascend the left arm."

Carollyn paused for a breath. "She told Daddy and me when we miss her to look at this painting and remember where she is, and then we can celebrate the life she lived." She started to sob. "I look at the painting every day, I miss her so much. There was nothing I could do to save her; my medical knowledge was useless. I miss Momma so much." Carollyn buried her head into the old man's chest as they stood still listening to the waves roar to the shore.

The old man patted the back of her head, feeling more helpless than he had ever felt. Guilt lingered in his soul for not being there when his little girl needed him most.

The two soon continued the barefoot journey as the sand turned into pebbles. Occasionally, they drifted knee deep in the cool water, then returned to shore. They talked of Carollyn's father and her husband and what it was like growing up as an only child. She remarked that being an only child inspired her to have two, but she was sure there would not be a third. After a long stroll they came upon a Hobie Cat resting on the shore. More at the insistence of Carollyn than the tired old man they sat and viewed the sea. In the horizon a school of dolphins playing under the white animal-shaped clouds entertained them.

For a few minutes they superficially discussed the clouds and the meaning of their shapes. They giggled lightheartedly.

"This reminds me of the Rorschach test I had to take in my psych rotation," she laughed. "After the professor interpreted my answers it was apparent that I was not going to become a psychiatrist." Carollyn laughed and shook her head. "I don't think that was an option anyway."

There was an awkward silence for a few minutes.

"Tell me about your father?" the old man asked hesitantly, unsure if he was about to tear open a scar that would have been better off untouched.

"Daddy is doing fine," she sighed. "After Daddy and Momma left Daytona they moved to Savannah."

"You mean after the grumpy old man chased them away?" the man interrupted.

"No," Carollyn insisted, putting her hand on his knee, "they chose to leave. Another choice would have been to stay and deal with the issues." She smiled at the old man and embraced him. "Anyway, Daddy worked in the rail yard at night and attended the University of Savannah during the day. During the evenings Daddy stayed with me while Momma made extra money waitressing." She paused and then caustically added, "I wonder where she obtained that skill?" They both chuckled. "The first few years they didn't see much of each other. Momma said it laid a foundation for a strong marriage."

"In the late sixties and early seventies Savannah wasn't a city that was ready to embrace biracial couples, so after Daddy graduated they decided to move to Chicago." She paused and touched the man's right shoulder reassuringly. "Unfortunately, you weren't alone in your objections to biracial unions. I think, at the time, the majority of the country was on your side. Anyway, Daddy received an offer to work for the First National Bank of Chicago, where he stayed until he retired. Along the way he picked up an MBA and then a PhD in business management. Now he is a part-time professor at City College, as he puts it, for his fun money. However, I think it's the need to feel useful. Since Momma passed it gives him something to do to survive the long, lonely days."

"After we settled into an apartment in the city Daddy insisted that Momma return to school. She eventually received a masters in education." Carollyn smiled and said, "I thought that my mother being a teacher was pretty cool, until she started teaching at my junior high school. Teaching a benign subject like art helped us manage to survive those three years of sharing the campus." She laughed again and said, "But it wasn't easy having my mother's colleagues scrutinizing my every move. The first time I kissed a boy there was a clamor of teachers scurrying to tell Momma."

"You must be very proud of your parents," the man said, feeling proud himself.

"Yes," Carollyn answered in a soft voice, "but not for their education or the material things they accumulated. I'm proud of them for the love they shared with each other every day of their time together. A love that started out as a speck of sand and the pressure of the clam forced it into a pearl." She paused. "I stole that phrase from Momma. Who undoubtedly was plagiarizing you? Just as important as the love they showed me were the values they taught me to live by. I learned early that race, nationality, and religion were mere outer dressings, that the real person came from inside."

The man shook his head. "Love is more important than money, isn't it?" he asked rhetorically. "You were indeed fortunate to have been raised by parents who embraced diversity."

"And the greatest of all is love," Carollyn said as she once again hugged the old man.

"Did you see your other grandparents often?"

Carollyn frowned. "Rarely," she hesitated for a second, as she watched a hermit crab return to the water that had chased it to shore. "Their thoughts on biracial marriages weren't much different than yours. Actually, they may have been worse. They were given an opportunity to adjust, but chose not to."

The man appeared surprised. "I'm sorry."

"They attempted to convince Daddy that he wasn't my father, that Momma was just using him. Not sure for what, because his parents were dirt poor." She shook her head. "They visited a few times in Savannah, though I was really too young to remember. According to Daddy, the only reason they would come is because of the free rail passes."

"When they visited they ignored Momma and me, which infuriated Daddy. They would spend several weeks, at my parent's expense. They would insist to be taken to the beach and to nice restaurants. There was never a thank you or a please; just do. I think it was hard on Daddy to realize his parents' only interest in him was a free vacation. Even though Momma loathed their visits she always encouraged Daddy to invite them back. Momma would insist that sometimes people change. Daddy's answer was always the same: 'Just because rattlesnakes shed their skin it doesn't change the fact that they are a rattlesnake.'"

"When we moved to Chicago, they would call from time to time to ask for money. They thought Daddy was rich because he worked in a bank. On my sixteenth birthday, they called, and I answered the phone. They did not acknowledge me or my birthday. Daddy was so incensed that he asked them never to call again. Even though it hurt him deeply, he is happy that they complied with his request."

The man was speechless. He reflected to the last time he had spoken to Melissa. His eyes rolled to pieces of broken shell scattered throughout the sand. Over forty years before, after weeks of arguing over the pregnancy and his insistence on her having an abortion or giving the 'bastard' child for adoption, she left home. On Christmas Eve 1966, two weeks after running away, Melissa called home for help. The man kicked at the dirt, barely scuffing it. Emma was taking a walk on the cold moonless beach by herself trying to come to grip with a Christmas without their daughter. The phone rang the old man answered it on the first ring.

"Hello, Daddy?" a weak whimpering voice met him on the other end.

"Well the prodigal daughter returns," he remembers snapping angrily.

"Daddy," she continued, though it was obviously difficult, "I'm scared and I want to come home. We don't have any money and are living out of Laurence's pick-up."

"Do you?" The man had replied, attempting to keep his voice from revealing vulnerability.

"Please, Daddy, can we come back to Daytona?" Melissa pleaded.

Feeling he had the upper hand, the man made his rules and said, "Of course dear, I will come get you tonight. But, there are some conditions we need to discuss."

"Okay," she relented.

"You have to stay in school."

"Okay," Melissa agreed, probably because she had every intention of doing so.

"You have to give your baby up for adoption."

"Okay," she whimpered, hoping that after her father saw the baby he would change his mind.

"And beyond any doubt you are forbidden to see Leroy again."

The final straw broke, and instantly Melissa's determination returned. "I will not stop seeing Laurence; I am in love with him. I will stay in school; I will be open to giving your grandchild up for adoption if Laurence and I decide that is what is best for our baby. But I will not stop seeing Laurence. Do you understand?"

"Fine," the man snapped. "If you aren't willing to play by my rules, never call this house again. Just don't call again!"

The man heard the click of the phone and then the forever haunting sound of the dial tone. He screamed into the phone demanding to know where his daughter was; but the sentence had been passed. The old man had banished Melissa forever. Emma never learned of the conversation or even that there was a call. If she had, she would have never forgiven her husband. Instead the agony was his alone. The shame of this action prevented him from revealing the dark secret to anyone.

Oblivious to the captain's pain, Carollyn continued, "It was strange growing up. All my friends talked about visiting their grandparents and the presents they would receive on holidays. I always felt a little left out, a bit envious."

"I'm sorry," the captain mumbled, barely audible.

"I'm so grateful to God that my children were blessed to know their grandmother, my mother, before she died. And Daddy really relishes the role of the great spoiler."

"And your husband's parents?"

"Steve's parents live in Cincinnati, so we don't see them as often. Maybe twice a year; but they love to spoil the boys too." There was a slight pause, as if a random thought had entered her mind before she continued. "Last summer we sent them by plane for a visit. We were both scared with it being the boys' first trip away from home. But the boys acted as if it was a common routine. Grandpa and Grandma Bowers took them to Kings Island and to a Reds game; thankfully they were playing the Cubs." She let out a nervous giggle. "Just as importantly, the Cubs beat the home town team. The boys had a great time. Steve and I had a nice time, too, having a bit of quiet in our normally boisterous house. It was right after Momma died, and the quiet allowed me to be reflective of all that she meant to me. It was the best therapy I could have. Hopefully, flying to Cincinnati will become a yearly ritual." Carollyn sighed, shaking her head and said, "They seem to be growing up so quickly."

The old man clumsily stooped to pick up a starfish that the fervent tide had thrown to shore. He looked at Carollyn with a bashful grin and said, "You know, by studying the starfish I have learned the keys to happiness."

His granddaughter smiled back but did not speak.

Pointing toward the first leg, the man continued, "This leg represents love. That is, all the people that we have loved and those that have loved us." The man paused for a second. "In the movie the *Wizard of Oz* the surprisingly wise wizard said to the Tin Man, 'A heart is not measured by how much it loves rather by how it is loved.'" The captain coughed. "I am fortunate to have been loved by some very special people; Emma, Vanessa, David, Marissa, and countless more." He hesitated for a second. "And I know now, by my Melissa."

Touching the second leg of the starfish, he continued, "This leg is for honesty. It is important to be honest with others and with yourself. Until the frog looks at the total reflection in the pond he cannot change into a prince. Until a frog becomes a prince, or in some cases a princess," he said with a wink, "he cannot fully appreciate life."

"The third leg is for memories." The old man started singing in a gruff, slightly out of tune voice the song 'Memories,' that years earlier had become famous by Barbara Streisand. Carollyn smiled slightly and felt compelled to join in the singing, with the voice inherited from her grandfather.

Visions of the past flowed freely through the man's mind. For a moment he relived family picnics, parties and vacations. The laughter of Emma and Melissa resonated in his mind. Then as had happened before he felt the tenderness of Melissa's hug around his neck. Instantly his thoughts darted to the memories that were not to be. The memories lost because of his hatred. His voice quivered ever so slightly. A tear formed in his eyes for the loss of what might have been.

Carollyn did not notice the sudden shift in her grandfather; because she was lost in the bliss of childhood memories. Gratitude filled her soul for the love that her parents had given her. They had a love that wasn't only spoken but was demonstrated everyday. Her heart saddened with the thought of never seeing her mother again, but the joy of her mother's love encouraged her to sing louder and stronger.

An elderly couple walked slowly past, stopping for a brief moment to listen to the duet. "You're singing our tune," the man shouted in a shaky voice while squeezing his wife's hand. The captain and Carollyn smiled broadly.

When finished they sat for a few minutes in quiet reflection. Before they burst into laughter.

The captain smiled at his granddaughter. "Melissa used to write poetry," he said. "Shortly after Emma passed on I was looking through some old scrap books." There was a brief pause, as he looked down the beach, concealing his emotions.

Carollyn causally patted his knee.

After regaining composure he continued, "Emma pasted one of Melissa's poems in one of the books." The captain hesitated for a second. "If it is alright I would like to recite it to you."

Carollyn smiled. "I am flattered," she said.

The man stared at the sand for a few seconds concentrating on the words, before starting the recital.

Memories

Memories, memories
The golden past
Lighthearted moments
    shared with friends
Tears of joy
Laughter shared by all
Kind words spoken
    and those received
These precious memories
Those golden memories

"That is a testimony that Momma had some good memories," Carollyn said. "I assure you that she relived those memories everyday of her life." Momma loved you and Emma very much."

The captain's mind drifted to Emma. "I wouldn't trade all the laughter Emma and I shared for another twenty years of life." The man took off his hat and wiped his brow with his forearm. "Emma was my beacon of light; she demonstrated to me how to make sense out of this senseless world. Memories of friends and family warm my heart, but memories of

Emma give me hope for tomorrow. I know she is in heaven waiting for me with a fresh hot pie." He chuckled and patted his stomach. "And it won't have any calories. Of course, I have many memories of my Melissa too. She was a free spirit with an infectious laugh that could ignite a room full of angry sailors." The man hesitated and said, "Hopefully, she'll be waiting to see me as soon as I receive my call to heaven."

Carollyn gave him a reassuring smile. "She's waiting there now, with Emma. Momma will be holding an easel and anticipating your first fishing trip."

The two watched as a pelican elegantly swooped into the water, emerging with a fish.

"The fourth leg is for regrets. Without regrets we cannot appreciate the good things in life. Without appreciation of the good we cannot change the things we have done wrong. My many regrets have become learning experiences that have hopefully enabled me to become a better man." The old man dusted sand off his knees, as he continued, "even though there are more than a few regrets I wish I didn't have. Sometimes, we are the authors of our own destruction and thankfully of our own resurrection."

"This brings us to the fifth leg." The old man paused to wet his dry lips with his tongue. "The psalmist commands us, 'I acknowledge my sin unto thee, and mine iniquity I have not hid. I said, I will confess my transgressions unto the Lord; and thou forgaveth the iniquity of my sin.'" The man looked up at his granddaughter, saying, "In order to achieve happiness, a man has to forgive others as well as himself. And the Bible instructs a man to acknowledge his sins to his brother."

The old man slowly hobbled to his feet, steadying himself with a cane, and gently tossed the starfish back to its home, quietly pondering if the unforgiving sea would regurgitate the helpless creature again. He turned back to his granddaughter. "Carollyn, I have sinned against your mother and father. In doing so I have robbed you of the joy of knowing your grandmother and me of the pleasure of watching you grow. I deprived you of the ability to brag to your friends about visits to your grandparents' kitchen. The sins of the father truly transcend to the children for generations. Today my sins must cease casting that shadow."

He paused, watching as two children splashed in the waves. "In our youth we at times make single rash decisions that have consequences that alter our lives forever. I can only ask your mother's forgiveness in prayer; but when I have a chance I will beg your father's." He looked squarely into his granddaughter's eyes. "Now I am asking for yours?"

Carollyn lunged into her grandfather's arm and started to sob. "Oh Granddaddy," she cried, "I forgave you before I ever met you." She let out a deeper sob. "Momma talked about you before she died and told me of the starfish. She said that although it was difficult she too had forgiven you."

The two embraced as the tears and fears of their souls flowed purely out of them like the fountain in Melissa's painting.

"Thank you," the old man whispered, "for having the strength to find me, for forgiving me, and for calling me Granddaddy." That was the easy part, he thought; he was not certain that he would ever be able to forgive himself.

Carollyn gushed, "How could I not find you or forgive you? You are my Granddaddy."

The sun stared directly down on them as they started the trek back to the house, contently listening to the serenade of the seashore. In the distance they could see two boys playing tag with the flowing and receding tide. The faint gleeful laughter tickled their ears; soon the invigorating noise turned into a symphony of newfound harmony.

They stopped momentarily to watch a man wading in the water knee deep. He carried a long broom handle like stick, with a basket attached to the end. Carefully he would dip it in the water, then quickly pull it out full of small fish. Systematically, he would walk out of the water and dump the catch into the bait bucket, then return to do the same.

The two were upon the boys before Jason and Nathaniel realized that they had returned. Jason quickly hugged his mother as Nathaniel dove into the old man's outstretched arms, knocking him off balance as they both plummeted to the earth. A horrified physician raced to the man's side, only to have him playfully splash water in her face. The captain and Nathaniel laid in the wet sand as the waves rolled over them, laughing, as Carollyn and Jason joined in the folly.

"Charkey's here," Nathaniel finally announced over the laughter.

The man looked puzzled.

"Yes," Jason confirmed, "Marissa brought him over."

"Miss Marissa to you," the mother scolded.

"She said she was too young to be a miss," Jason insisted.

"It's still Miss Marissa to you."

"Yes ma'am," the boy agreed. "Anyway, she came to check on Grandpa and found us. We told her we were your great-grandchildren and she started to cry." Barely taking enough time to breathe he continued, "She said she had been asking her spirit guides to help us find you, and here we are! She said 'Praise be to the Universe.'"

"Yeah," Nathaniel broke in, "and she called you a knucklehead," he said, looking at his great-grandfather.

"A knucklehead?" Carollyn laughed.

"Miss Marissa said if she was a moonbeam then Grandpa was a knucklehead," the youngster said innocently.

"Guess I should be careful what I say in front of impressionable ears," the man joked.

"Then we went to the restaurant for coconut ice cream and to bring Charkey back," Jason interrupted, "Miss Marissa said it wouldn't be a family reunion without him."

The boys helped their great-grandfather to his feet, and the four of them hurried to greet their feathered friend. Charkey, who had free roam of the house, was perched valiantly on the kitchen table, staring at the back door, impatiently waiting for their return.

"Welcome to Charkey's," he squawked, ruffling his feathers. "Welcome to Charkey's, let's eat." Everyone laughed.

"Marissa, I mean Miss Marissa brought us a seafood casserole," Jason volunteered, running to the refrigerator.

"Yeah, it is microwavable," Nathaniel added, "but she said not to tell the customers."

The old man gave a half frown, saying, "We don't microwave anything."

"Bake it at four hundred twenty-five degrees," Charkey advised.

Carollyn accepted the bird's wisdom and placed the casserole into the oven. Forty minutes later they all sat around the antique oblong oak table enjoying one of Granddaddy's specialties with a nice refreshing glass of lemonade. After lunch Carollyn and Jason cleaned the table as the old man and Nathaniel set up the checker board.

Charkey flew onto the checker board and plucked one of the old man's black pieces and dropped it on the floor. "He's a cheater, he's a cheater," the bird alerted. After the amusement, the checker game continued.

After Carollyn and Jason finished cleaning the kitchen, Carollyn excused herself to the porch to phone home.

After a conversation with her husband, Carollyn called her father to tell him about the adventure the threesome were experiencing. Overhearing the conversation, the old man excused himself, just when he was on the verge of losing his fourth game, and shuffled to the porch. Carollyn looked at him knowingly and said to her father, "Daddy, there is someone here that really wants to speak with you." She handed the phone to the nervous captain.

"Hello," the old man said before the receiver of the cell phone reached his mouth.

"Hello," a reluctant voice responded.

"It's good to hear your voice, Laurence," the man continued. "You and Melissa have a fine daughter and some mighty handsome grandsons. I think Jason has your chin and Nathaniel has your eyes," not really remembering what Laurence looked like.

The man on the other end wanted to remind the intruder that he had suggested rather strongly that Carollyn be aborted but decided to be polite. "Thank you," he responded. "I am proud of them." He paused for an uncomfortable moment. "Think they both have Melissa's nose."

There was silence for a few seconds, but it seemed an eternity. "Laurence," the man stuttered, "thank you for taking such good care of my little girl. You did her right. Even though I didn't give you a chance, you were a fine son-in-law."

"Melissa was a special girl," Laurence acknowledged. "Even though we were not a part of your life, you were always a part of ours. Melissa adored you; she constantly recited your wisdom. The loss of your love and approval wounded her more than she would ever admit. She was your little girl. Even though we had years of happiness, I could never replace you in her heart. I resented you for that. Maybe if I did not hold that hate I would have encouraged her to contact you and Emma. I was wrong. Please, forgive me."

"It was I that was wrong," the old man confessed. "That Christmas Eve night when Melissa begged for help I allowed my prejudice to deny her the solace she deserved. I judged you because of the color of your skin, not the size of your heart." The old man coughed. "If time could rewrite itself, my memories would be of the times we shared, the laughter we created. Laurence, I am truly sorry, forgive me."

"Forgiveness is difficult," Laurence replied. "The pain you caused me is forgettable. The shear agony you caused to Melissa will be etched in my soul long after my death."

Again there was an eerie silence. The old man felt as though he had been stabbed with a much deserved ice dagger.

"But," the man on the other end of the phone continued, "The love I hold for Melissa demands that I forgive. She would have it no other way."

"Thank you," the grateful father acknowledged.

"I hope you are treating my daughter right."

"Yes," the old man reassured. "I will do all I can to make her and your grandchildren comfortable. As I said before, you have a fine family."

"You know they are all I have," Laurence continued, his voice breaking.

"I understand," the man reaffirmed. "I would never do anything to make them uncomfortable. I am just thankful the Lord has given me a second opportunity with my family."

There was silence then the two men exchanged pleasantries and the old man invited Laurence to visit, and then, feeling a little less empty, he handed the phone to Carollyn.

After the phone conversations, Carollyn gave her grandfather a big hug and for the first time told him that she loved him. Feeling tired, she retired to her room for a late afternoon nap.

The captain and the boys sat on the porch, relaxing to the sounds of the waves and the calling of the seagulls. Nathaniel, having difficulty sitting still, decided to explore the beach.

"Don't go off too far," the great-grandfather cautioned. "Make sure you stay within eye distance." Then he looked at Jason, smiled and mumbled, "With my eyesight that is not very far."

"I'll keep my eyes on him," Jason reassured.

The captain retreated for a few minutes into the house and then returned with a pitcher of lemonade and three glasses. "Emma and I would sit here for hours sipping lemonade, just watching the day go by," he said.

"It is pretty," Jason agreed. "Have you ever thought about living anywhere else?"

"When I was a young man, probably about your age, I fantasized about living anywhere but here." The man coughed, then drank a sip of lemonade to get the tickle out of his throat. "I dreamt of far off lands, great mountains to climb, new adventures. Truthfully, I hated the beach and Daytona."

"What happened?" Jason asked. "Why did you stay here?"

Nathaniel scampered up to the porch to show off some seashells that he discovered. After his great-grandfather and brother showed the proper amount of admiration, he placed them on the table, gulped down a glass of lemonade, and returned to the beach.

The man took a deep breath of salt air. "The summer I played minor league ball for the Boston Red Sox, I got a little homesick. At the time I wasn't sure whether I missed my pappy or the beach."

"Or Charkey," Jason cut in.

"Or Charkey," the old man laughed. "Anyway, after I was drafted and spent some time in Europe—about got my head blown off—I never had a desire to be anywhere else but here."

"Do you think it was Grandma Emma that changed your mind?"

The man smiled at the thought of Emma. "No, I believe Emma would have followed me anywhere." The man lit his stogie. "I learned to appreciate this piece of the world once I was away from it for a while. I missed Daddy, the restaurant, and my friends. Once I got off that train, returning from the hospital in Europe, I knew this is where I belong." The man chuckled as he put the stogie in the ashtray. "It is kind of like Dorothy in *The Wizard of Oz*. In Kansas everything is dark and dreary. Her family didn't understand her. She knew the only way she would truly be happy was to run away from home. Happiness was just a short escape over the rainbow. When Dorothy arrived at her destination, at first it was new and exciting. After being away for a short time, it occurred to her that where she came from was where she belonged. She was right: 'there is no place like home.'"

"I may change my mind when I am older; but I can't visualize living in Chicago all my life. I want to live where it doesn't snow in the winter and that I can fish year round."

"Do you have a place in mind?"

"A couple of years ago we took a vacation to Hawaii. The beach was pretty, the waves nice. I think it would be fun to live there."

"If you still feel that way when you are old enough, to set out on your own, you should go for it." The man paused. "Just because I decided that staying close to home was right for me; it isn't right for everyone."

"That's true."

They sat in silence, watching Nathaniel chase the seagulls.

"Can I ask you a question?" Jason asked.

"Jason," the captain replied earnestly, "I want you to feel comfortable asking me anything. I give you my word I will always be honest."

The boy smiled. "Last night at the restaurant, why did you give us those two-cent pieces? You didn't know we were family. It just seems that it was an expensive gift for two strangers."

The man pondered the question while he took a drag from his cigar. He twirled the smoke around his mouth and gently exhaled.

"You should really try to quit smoking," Jason said, sounding somewhat self-righteous.

The captain put the cigar out, making a mental note to avoid smoking while the children were visiting. Actually, he thought, maybe he should quit altogether. "I don't know," he said. "Maybe because the conversation the four of us were having made me feel close to Melissa. Looking at you and Nathaniel made me reflect on how many children she had, if they were boys or girls. In many ways your spunk and the way you carry yourself reminds me of Melissa." He paused to wipe a tear from his eye. "I haven't shared my family history with anyone in years. I guess it just felt like the right thing to do." The man paused for a second. "When I found out who you were, it made the night one of the most spectacular nights of my life." The old man paused to collect his thoughts and continued, "It is as though God had finally answered my prayers. A peace has come over me that I never thought possible."

"The night did turn out special," Jason agreed. "I'm really glad that I met you."

Nathaniel stormed back to the porch. "What's for dinner?"

"Dinner?" the old man joked. "What makes you think I am going to serve you dinner?"

"Because," the young boy laughed.

"Come with me," the man demanded. "I'll show you what we do on the beach for dinner." He looked at Jason. "You need to come too," he coaxed. The captain guided Nathaniel into the house with his hand as Jason followed. "You need to keep your voices down," he reminded. "Your momma is sleeping."

A cool Florida breeze swept off the Atlantic through the window, brushing against Carollyn's face. She gently smacked her lips, the taste of salt a reminder as she woke that she was not in her home. The darkness slowly covering the room gave hint that the sun was bedding for the night. There was stillness in the house, no boys, no grandfather, no Charkey fluttering about. Curiously she walked out on the porch. In the sky there was a faint star beginning to flicker slightly above the rising crescent moon.

"Star light, star bright the first star I see tonight," she recited to herself. Her eyes became fixated on the beach. In the water the old man, dressed in faded blue overalls with one strap undone, was busily casting a line into the calm turquoise sea. An oversized straw hat covered his head. An orange feather saluted from the side with three hooks stuck in the brim. Behind him Charkey was perched on a tree, with an anklet reminding him not to fly away. As expected, the bird was coaching the old man. To the left of the captain were two boys, both wearing straw hats, with lines in the water, the youngest boy's fishing pole bowed. Carollyn smiled toward the heavens. "Momma, I hope you have your easel ready."

Chapter III

Thursday

Never confuse movement with action.
—Ernest Hemingway

The crescent moon cast its reigning beam upon the tranquil water as the multitude of stars twinkled in praise of their nighttime king. Carollyn stood on the porch marveling at the tide and questioning why she was awake at 4:00 AM on a night she was not on call. Briefly her mind drifted back to her fifth birthday. It was her only real remembrance of life in Savannah. Her parents had taken her to Tybee Island for a picnic. The day had been full of laughter and splashing in the water and wedging slushy wet sand through her toes.

She could clearly remember a multitude of jellyfish floating in the water, venturing wherever the waves chose to guide them. Near the picnic area an eloquent five-walled sand castle emerged from the earth surrounded by treasures she had collected from the sea. Seagulls were frantically feasting on leftovers from the party. The sun had just set, and the moon and all its stars were starting to infest the satin blue heavens. A small fire kept them warm from the chilling spring breeze.

They were all stretched out on a blanket listening to music on a transistor radio, not that it was important, but she thought it was "Joy to the World" by Three Dog Night. She had just started to dance in time with the waves when the shadows of four or five large men hovered over her father. "Boy," she remembered hearing an angry voice. "Don't you know the likes of you don't belong here?" The man spat, "Especially with a white whore after dark." The man then stomped the radio with his left foot. Her mother grabbed her tightly, pulling her to her bosom. All the muscles in her father's face were drawn tight, as he knelt on one knee, prepared to spring into action.

"Boy, ain't you gonna answer the question?" another man blurted. "Or ya too yellow to speak?" Her father remained silent.

"He ain't yellow, Frank," another man snapped snidely. " 'Cause he is black. Black boys don't belong in these parts, especially with a white whore." In unison the men let out a sinister laugh. "If you ain't gone by the time my boys and I get our hoods, your pretty little daughter will be missing her daddy," the ring leader slurred. Once again the men laughed and stormed off in a drunken stupor, directly through the castle.

Without a word her parents packed up the blanket and picnic basket, leaving the busted radio behind. They drove back to Savannah in their old VW van without the benefit of headlights, which had been smashed out. A week later they packed the van and moved to Chicago. It took years for the confused girl to understand the night that her parents always refused to talk about. That was the last she had seen of the Atlantic until this week. A week of healing for her that she hoped could be transferred to her father and transcend to her children.

Carollyn's thoughts quickly shifted to the outline of two young men and their great-grandfather loading a boat for a day of fishing. Wishing her mother could see this; instinctively she dialed her father's number.

"Ah, hello," came a drowsy rumble.

"Daddy," she exclaimed, "the boys are getting ready to go fishing with Granddaddy."

"What?" a confused sigh resonated over the phone. "What time is it?"

"About four," she giggled, as she leaned on the post of the porch.

"Your time or mine?" Laurence mumbled, trying to wake up.

"Isn't it exciting?" an animated Carollyn said.

The father was now sitting in bed, his eyes fixated on his clock. "It would have been more exciting at eight or nine AM"

"But it couldn't be as exciting then," a lady sounding more like a teenager continued, "because it is happening now."

"I thought you had a husband to wake up for things like this."

"It wouldn't be the same. Besides, he has to get up early for work; I couldn't disturb him."

"Yet, I get the honors."

"Don't you wish you were here to go on the trip?" Carollyn asked with glee in her voice.

The grandfatherly instinct took over. "Hey, can that blind old sea goat see well enough to take a boat out?"

"Of course. He's my grandfather; he can do anything," Carollyn laughed. "Oh Daddy, he has changed from the way you described him. He's loving, thoughtful, and gentle. He wouldn't harm anyone. He simple adores the boys. Sometimes rattlesnakes can shed their old skin."

"So he's drugging you?" the man mumbled sarcastically. "Be sure those white sheets you're sleeping on don't have eyeholes in them."

"Sheets," she protested, "he's not allowing me to use any sheets. They might get ruined on the ground under that old hickory I'm sleeping under."

"Seriously," her father cautioned, "is the boat seaworthy and is he able to captain the boat?"

"Daddy, they'll be fine," she said, trying to reassure herself as much as her father.

"Hey, I have to go; they are getting ready to cast off." She hung up the phone and started toward the dock.

The purring of the engine interrupted the calm of the night. Carollyn reached the boat just as the boys were settling onto the red and green plaid cushions of the boat, firmly snuggled into life jackets. "Boys, have a good time," she shouted. "Behave, listen to your great-grandfather, and catch a lot of fish." Her voice faded as the vessel headed north-northeast out to the venturesome sea.

"Remember the Titanic," Charkey chirped, sitting on the usual perch behind the captain.

"Silly bird," the man mumbled. "Neither of us were around when the Titanic set sail." He coughed and looked at the boys. "Besides, with the crew we have, we're unsinkable."

"S.S. Minnow," the bird mocked.

The captain laughed and then started singing the theme song for Gilligan's Island. He gyrated his hips back and forth as if dancing. Charkey frantically flapped his wings as the man sang, occasionally repeating parts of the lyrics. During the dance routine the captain pantomimed the words, turning to the boys with five fingers in the air to indicate that there were five passengers. He pointed to the clouds and then used a downward swooping motion of his arms to indicate lightning. As the old man's right arm plunged towards the ground he almost lost balance and fell. Jason quickly grabbed his arms to help him regain balance. Even with the near mishap the captain insisted on finishing the song.

The boys bursted into hysterical laughter as the song concluded. They had no recollection of the historic journey of Gilligan; the catalyst of their laughter was the out-of-tune gruff old voice and the hula swaying of the old man's hips.

The boat throttled down as the land slowly faded into the horizon. Occasionally, they would pass another boat anchored or moving out to sea. With each passing boat, the captain would politely wave his hand; a gesture the boys would mimic. The old man motioned for Jason to take the wheel so he could sit and enjoy the coming day.

"But I've never driven," Jason protested.

"Ever ride a bicycle?" the man queried, stepping away from the wheel.

Cautiously placing both hands on the wheel, Jason answered, "Well yes, but ..."

"Same thing," the man quipped as he plopped into the seat next to Nathaniel, "only no wheels. You don't need to keep in between the lines, either," he laughed.

Jason took steady hold of the wheel, keeping his eyes straight ahead into the landless horizon. Gradually, he became more relaxed and began to enjoy the chore. Occasionally the captain would shout directional changes that were usually disputed by Charkey.

Looking quizzically at the cushions, Nathaniel declared, "These are just like the ones in my grandma's picture."

The old man laughed. "When I bought my first new boat, years ago, your great-grandmother wanted to do something special to celebrate.

So she decided to make me some special cushions. She took your grandmother to the cloth store to pick out the material." The man cleared his throat. "Emma, er, your great-grandmother, picked out a nice shade of sea blue; but your grandmother had a different idea. She insisted on red and green plaid." The man laughed. "I think she was probably about your age. So at the christening of our new boat they presented me with green and red plaid cushions."

"Are those the same ones?" Jason asked, peering back from the captain's nest.

"No," the man smiled. "Over the years Emma and I wore out many a cushion. We always replaced them with the trademark pattern. Even when we bought a bigger boat, it was green and red plaid." Patting the seat, he said "Marissa made this set last fall, probably the last I will ever need."

"Hey, are we going to catch a marlin?" Nathaniel asked.

"Possibly … but not likely, it is not really the season for marlins," the captain coughed.

He stood up to shut the boat down. "Let's stop here for a bit, see how hungry the fish are."

The sun was responding to its wake-up call spreading a magnificent array of colors over the ocean as the moon fell to the other side of the earth. All but a few stars had vanished from the sky. Daybreak had arrived.

Looking in the cockpit, Nathaniel looked puzzled. "Where's the depth finder?"

"Depth finder?" the old man snapped defensively. "Why would I need one of those new technical gadgets when I have my keen sense for the awareness? I've been fishing these waters all my life. If I can't find where they're biting I shouldn't be fishing. Besides, that's like cheating; it's not giving the fish a sporting chance."

Nathaniel looked perplexed. "My Grandfather Laurence uses one."

"Oh," the man stuttered. "Ah, depth finders are, ah, necessary for lake fishing like your Grandfather Laurence does; but for ocean fishing it's best to go on instinct."

"Why?"

"Ah, because the currents of the oceans are different than that of the lake and, ah, in the lake you need the depth finder to locate the good spot." There was an awkward pause. "There are always a lot of old tree limbs in lakes that you have to steer clear of."

Jason smiled in sudden admiration at the old man's fumbling attempt at diplomacy.

"What are we fishing with?" Jason asked, reaching for the bait bucket, feeling the need to rescue his grandfather.

"Got some squid and some shrimp," the man was quick to respond. "Also got some new lures the kid at the bait store claims are foolproof." The man chuckled. "Heard that one before, but the kid believed it, so it didn't hurt me to ante up a bit of money."

The man patiently helped Nathaniel wrap a piece of squid around the barb part of the hook. Jason, a more experienced fisherman, had already baited his hook and cast in the water.

"Hey, Grandpa," Jason protested, "There's no bobber on mine."

"Don't use bobbers in salt water; just watch your line. Be careful that you don't yank too soon or the thief of the fish will rob you blind." The man assisted Nathaniel to toss his line to the starboard side. Before he could bait his line, he heard the shrill of excitement from his youngest grandson who had the first catch of the day. The sound of the reel buzzed as Nathaniel struggled to bring it in. The old man grabbed the line as the fish was flopping in the air and pulled it the rest of the way.

"What is it?" Nathaniel asked.

"Certainly not a marlin," Jason teased.

The old man smiled. "You caught a beautiful red grouper, one of my favorite fish. We'll put this on the grill tonight, add some lemon pepper, a dash of garlic, and a squeeze of lime, and my secret ingredient, a bit of freshly ground ginger. You're taste buds are in for a succulent treat."

"How can you tell it's a grouper?" Jason quizzed.

"Good question," an excited Charkey chirped in.

"Yeah?" Nathaniel joined in on the chorus.

The man held the fish up for the boys to see. "Groupers are brownish red with the lining of their mouth a scarlet orange." Pointing towards the dorsal fins he continued the education. "This back fin is smaller than the second back fin. Groupers always have black spots around their eyes." The man dropped the fish into the cooler. "This one is definitely a keeper."

No sooner had Nathaniel dropped his line in the water than he received another tug. The screeching of the reel could be heard above the squawks of the seagulls as he pulled in another fish. For the next thirty minutes the three men took turns pulling in fish as fast as they could drop their lines in the water. They were catching a wide variety of fish: grouper, red snapper, amberjack, African pompano, and cobia. Some were legal sizes; others the captain graciously returned to the sea for another day. As quickly as the hit had arrived it faded away, as if the fish had figured out that they were being led into a trap.

Jason reached into a cooler for a bottle of water. Without asking, he handed one to the captain and to his brother. "Do you really believe in ghosts?" he asked, partially because of curiosity, partially because he didn't know what else to talk about.

The old man wiped the perspiration off his brow. "Can't say; I haven't ever seen one, at least not to my recollection. A lot of folks seem to believe in them." There was silence for ten minutes before the captain spoke again, pointing north towards St. Augustine. "Folks say St. Augustine is one of the most haunted cities in the United States. I used to think it was a ploy to lure tourists to the city. I'm not sure anymore."

"Why not?" Jason queried.

"Terisita and Dominick," Charkey reminded.

"Terisita and Dominick?" Nathaniel chirped questioning.

The man sighed. "There's an old family legend that I think is based in some truth, not sure as to how much. Back in the 1760s in Boston there was a man by the name of Raphael Gonzalez that was betrothed to a beautiful senorita by the name of Terisita." The man paused to take a small sip of water. "Boston was a very turbulent city; there was a great unrest due to what was considered unjust rule from England. There were many splinter groups of rebels that met regularly to discuss ways of overthrowing rule from the Mother Country. One of these groups was led by young Raphael and a patriot by the name of Isaiah Hamilton." The man stopped as a fish played with his line, continuing after the fish decided to move on. "Despite frequent warnings by soldiers of the crown to cease, the young zealots continued their pursuit of a revolution. If not a revolution, a kinder government where taxes were fair and the peoples' voices could be heard."

"Sounds like present day America," Jason joked.

"Several days prior to the date Isaiah was to be married he was shot by Colonel Alexander Lynch in front of a local store. Isaiah was unarmed and had his back to Lynch. The owner of the store was coerced into signing documentation that the colonel acted in self defense. Word soon spread on the street the next target was to be Raphael." The old man paused as he watched Nathaniel reel in an amberjack. "A group of locals, should I say, escort ladies, helped smuggled Raphael on a ship heading south. The plan was for Terisita to follow when it was safe." The man stopped for a gulp of water. "This particular vessel was captained by my great-great-great grandfather." The man glistened with pride. "The year was 1762; the destination was St. Augustine, which was property of the Spanish government and a safe haven for Raphael. When he landed he immediately made plans for Terisita to join him."

"Unfortunately, 1763 changed the luck of the young couple. In a treaty, Spain and England traded colonies; Spain gave St Augustine to Britain in exchange for Cuba. In the fall of 1763, Terisita arrived dressed in a wedding gown, with her faithful dog, Dominick., Eagerly disembarking from the ship, she expected to find her future husband waiting. Instead she was met by a young boy Raphael had befriended. The lad was charged with telling her the agonizing news of Raphael's demise. According to the boy, her fiancé was hung in the middle of the town by British soldiers for treason. One week earlier, to the day, he had been buried in the Huguenot Cemetery just outside the city."

The man paused, looking at both boys, and then continued. "After the terrifying revelation, the boy mysteriously disappeared. Later that day, people in the city revealed that a boy matching the description to the one she was talking to was executed with Raphael for treason to the crown."

"No way," Jason protested.

The captain held his right hand in the air as if on a witness stand. "It's not my story; I'm just repeating the account of my ancestors … our ancestors. Terisita and Dominick went to the cemetery to find her beloved. It was late at night, and the winter wind had begun to chill. As they searched the graveyard a brutal storm rolled off the Atlantic.

Terisita refused to give up the search, even though she was soaked and cold. In the morning the groundskeeper found her curled up under a tree, dead. The coroner said she froze to death, but we all know she died of a broken heart. A few days later Dominick joined her on the other side. To this day they are searching for Raphael."

Jason reeled in a red snapper and put it in the box. "So what makes you think this might be true?"

"Several months ago, a couple came to eat at Charkey's. They claimed to be ghost hunters. According to the lady they took a picture at the Huguenot Cemetery of a bride and a dog."

Nathaniel looked at him, puzzled as to why a bride would be at a cemetery.

"And the picture?" Jason pondered.

"Never saw it," the captain laughed. "The guy promised to send me copies; but as of yet they haven't arrived. I suppose he forgot. Guess I can make up my mind if they come."

"Maybe the ghost stole them," Jason teased.

The man laughed.

"I'm not trying to be disrespectful; but isn't it strange that Terisita would put her wedding gown on prior to getting off the ship?" Jason asked.

"It is a bit peculiar," the man quipped. "Remember, I'm just repeating the story passed down to me. I'm not even sure there was a Terisita."

"Maybe she put it on before she went to the cemetery," Jason suggested.

"Perhaps," the man agreed. "That would make more sense. Maybe we should take some literary license and change it for future generations."

"What about the guy in that psychic town that told you things about Emma?"

The old man stared at his line without a word.

"How do you think he knew?" Jason continued.

"Don't know," the captain started in a monotone voice. "It is strange that he would come up with accurate information that no one else knew." The man cleared his throat. "It is possible that our society closes our minds to the supernatural. Since we refuse to believe, the spirits choose not to reveal themselves." The man shook his head as he pondered the discussion.

"So you're saying a closed mind shuts out the truth about our ancestors from the other side?" Jason said, paraphrasing. "Kind of like when our forefathers advocated for the continuation of slavery? They closed their mind to brutality of slavery so they could not see the truth."

The man chuckled. "Strange analogy, but I think you're on the right track."

"And if Terisita and Dominick are ghosts, why are they still searching for Raphael? Wouldn't he already be on the other side?"

"That is an excellent point to ponder. When I get to the other side it will be my first question," the old man boasted.

"So you are saying you don't know?"

The old man peered in the cooler at their catch. "Yes, I am saying I don't know. The truth of the matter is I'm not sure that I want to know. Sometimes speculation is much more tantalizing than truth."

Jason laughed.

"What are we taking about?" Nathaniel asked.

"Just stuff," Jason retorted. "It is kind of grown up talk."

"When are we going catch some more fish?" Nathaniel asked, changing the subject.

"In just a few minutes we will move to a new spot," the old man said.

"Hey, can I try one of the new lures?" Jason asked his great-grandfather.

"Don't think they will work, but why not give it a try?" the captain quipped.

"Ah, but you should keep a positive attitude," Jason shot back with a smirk on his face.

"I am positive; positive that it will be a waste of time."

There was a tug on Nathaniel's line, and the buzzing of the reel signaled the drought was over. Over the next ten minutes while Jason and his great-grandfather were preparing the pole with the lure, Nathaniel brought in a fish each time he dropped his line in the water. His boredom was overtaken by the thrill of the catch. Nathaniel was particularly gleeful that because Jason was struggling with the lure, his own numbers were exceeding his brother's. It wasn't often he bested his older brother in anything.

The old man stopped working on the lure to watch a boat approaching. When the boat was closer, he heard over a loudspeaker a request to pull up beside his boat.

"Who is that?" Jason asked.

"I believe it is an old friend of mine, Steve Knox," the man replied.

Nathaniel dropped his pole to watch the boat approach.

"Grab his line," the captain commanded to Jason, "and help pull her into us."

Jason grabbed the line and assisted in aligning the two boats.

"Steve," the old man mumbled, "what you doing out here midweek?"

"Just a little vacation," the bronzed man laughed.

The old man looked at his grandchildren. "Steve is one of the salesmen that supply us with our seafood."

"I should be the only salesman," he responded. Looking at the boys, he continued, "These must be your great-grandchildren. I heard they were in town. I'm sorry to hear about Melissa."

"Thank you," the old man whispered, staring at the sea. "This is Jason and Nathaniel," he said, recovering from the moment of grief.

"Nice to meet you," Steve said to the boys. Hugging the model-like woman standing beside him, he said, "This is my wife, Jackie."

Jackie reached over and kissed the captain on the cheek. "Good to see you; you are looking well." She had a seductive sweetness in her voice that sounded sincere.

Steve looked at the boys. "When I was a kid your grandmother used to babysit me."

He looked towards the captain. "Actually I believe she even spanked me on several occasions."

The old man laughed. "You were a rowdy child."

"This old sea dog," Steve said, patting the man on the shoulder, "taught me how to fish."

"Now he cheats, though," the old man moaned, motioning to Steve's boat. "He uses a depth finder."

"You should only use those in fresh water," Nathaniel said knowingly.

Everyone laughed.

Motioning to his passengers, Steve introduced them. "This is Carlos and his fiancée, Lauren."

The captain nodded. Nathaniel, bored with the conversation, returned to fishing.

"Are they biting for you?" Steve asked as he stretched his neck and peered toward the cooler.

"We are getting our limit," the captained offered. He did not ask Steve about his catch, figuring that most fisherman lie about what they are really bringing in.

The waves picked up a bit, almost knocking the captain off balance.

"I was going to bring Carlos and Lauren by Charkey's later this week and introduce you. They are going to get married in the fall, and I suggested they do it at your place."

The old man looked long and hard at Carlos, trying to determine if he knew him. Carlos was of stocky build with a military haircut and a neatly groomed goatee. "What you sell, son?" he asked suspiciously.

Everyone laughed.

"I sell hogs in Orlando. Once I get married, we will be moving to Daytona."

"Well, my days of riding have been over for several decades. So, I guess you won't be trying to sell me anything."

"No, sir," Carlos replied with a warm grin.

A pelican landed on the roof of the captain's boat.

"Get out of here," Charkey squawked.

"Tell me about this wedding," the captain asked. "How many people are coming?"

Carlos looked at Steve and motioned for him to lay out the plan.

"They are looking at about a hundred people," Steve started explaining. "The plan is to have the ceremony on the beach and the reception in the restaurant."

"When is this going to be?" the captain asked.

"The middle of October," Carlos revealed.

"Hurricane season," Charkey shouted.

The man shook his head. "Charkey is right, that is right in the thick of hurricane season. There is a chance that you could get rained out. What is your contingency plan?"

"Then we would move the ceremony inside," Steve offered.

"The plan is to have all the chairs lined up on the moonlit beach. The bridal party will be launched on a pontoon, so we are completely surrounded by water," Lauren said with stars in her eyes.

The old man laughed. "I can't promise the moon or dry weather, but I can promise you Charkey's if you want it." The man coughed. "Any friends of Steve are friends of mine. Steve, why don't you bring them by the restaurant Saturday evening around seven, we will eat and make the plans," the captain suggested.

"Sounds like a plan." Steve watched as Nathaniel reeled in a grouper. "By the way, we are getting a shipment of South American langoustines in on Monday. Are you interested?"

The old man stared at the salesman. "So, now, you are going to count your outing as a business expense, aren't you?"

"Hey, I always go to where the customers are," Steve said with a broad smile on his face.

"What type of discount are you going to give me for interrupting my day of fishing?" the captain said, trying to appear somber but finding it difficult to mask his smile.

"I'm sure we can work something out," Steve laughed. "We always do."

Jason stood by, listening to the conversation, gaining great respect for his great-grandfather.

After a lengthy chat and the sharing of lemonade, Steve pushed off and away from the captain's boat. His boat started motoring toward shore.

The captain looked at Jason and winked. "Don't tell Steve, but I get most of my seafood from him. We use a few other minor suppliers, just in case we need something different. But Steve has the best."

Jason nodded in acknowledgment, and then he returned his attention briefly to his fishing rod. After a few minutes Jason looked quizzically at his great-grandfather. "I didn't know you could ride hogs."

The man tried to conceal his laughter. "He was talking about Harley Davidson motorcycles. They are called hogs."

"Oh," Jason said, feeling a little embarrassed for not knowing that.

"You rode a motorcycle?" Nathaniel joined the conversation.

"Years ago, before the war, I had a little bike. Then after the war I bought a bigger one. Emma and I would love to take rides in the country." The man sighed. "But that was a long time ago. My riding days are now just a faded memory."

Jason tossed his line twenty feet in back of the boat and sat down, resting the pole in a holder, to wait for a nibble.

"Strange-looking lure," the old man laughed. "I'm not sure that the fish can distinguish purple from green."

"I think the fish will be attracted to the red feathers," Jason laughed. "The shiny silver beads will probably arouse their curiosity."

"If you want to believe that, feel free," the old man said, shaking his head.

"Grandpa," Nathaniel started slowly, "Why do you like fishing?"

The man smiled knowingly. "I guess because my pappy did and my grandpappy before him. It is something our family has done for generations. For us it is a means of relaxation, but for our ancestors it was a means of survival." He reflected on his answer before going forward. "Some of the most romantic times I shared with Emma were in the middle of the Atlantic under a full moon being serenaded by the waves gently tapping the boat as if it were a piano keyboard. Our lines would lie limp in the water and we would bask in each other's company." The man smiled. "I'm glad I have the opportunity to share it with you boys … my great-grandchildren." A tear formed in his eye.

"I like fishing too," Nathaniel smiled, revealing a missing right molar.

"Uh oh," Charkey called.

The old man immediately looked at the sea over the starboard side.

Jason's line went taut, and he swiftly started reeling in the line. Grandfather was wrong; the lure was effective in snagging a big one, and it wasn't going to give up without a fight. Jason stood firmly bracing his knees on the back of the boat. The fish started pulling to the left and then unpredictably changed to the right.

Keeping his eye on the line, Grandpa tapped Nathaniel on the shoulder. "Need to reel your line in, son."

"Why?" Nathaniel whined.

"Think your brother has hooked a shark," he responded calmly. "If I'm right he could get tangled up in your line." The old man paused as he stared at Jason's line. "Sharks have been known to go after other bait while fighting for their life. We don't want to risk having it snared on two lines. Good way to lose it."

Jason stared over his right shoulder and said, "What makes you think it's a shark?"

"Two things." The captain glanced at the youngest to make sure he was complying with the request. "First, Charkey called out a warning; he has a sort of sixth sense when it comes to sharks. I have never hooked one that he didn't know about before my line was hit."

"Okay?" Jason said in a questioning voice.

"Second, the fish you have is fighting like a shark; it starts in one direction and then quickly reverses its path." Nathaniel dropped his pole on the floor and ran to his brother's side. "Next," the man continued, "it will start trying to circle the boat." He motioned Nathaniel to step back to give Jason room to work. "Sharks have a tendency to work the fisherman. Instead of panicking, like most fish, they methodically attempt to remove the hook."

"Should I give it a bit of slack to play with? I read in *The Old Man and the Sea* that the man let his line out to play with the great blue marlin," Jason asked, feeling a tinge of apprehension.

The man's mind faded back to 1948 in Bimini. The crystal clear blue water was as smooth as glass. A cool fall breeze was slowly following the Gulf Stream. Emma's rod was lazily resting in its holder. Pappy was below deck sleeping off a wild day of sun and beer, mainly beer. The two sat counting the stars as they appeared in the purple haze, making a wish on each one. The sun was submerging into the depth of the quiet sea. Suddenly there was a tug on Emma's line. The battle of wills was on. The man knew in an instant that Emma had hooked a marlin.

Together they battled with the great warrior all night, taking turns with the rod. Finally as the sun was raising its fiery head, the giant fish leaped from the water as if trying to hurdle the giant ball and then dove into its home for the final time.

"Grandpa, should I give it some line?" Jason asked again, snapping the old man out of the reunion with his beloved Emma.

"No keep it taut; show him who's boss," the captain said in a steady voice.

"Maybe it's a marlin," Nathaniel suggested.

The old man ignored him, concentrating on Jason's challenge.

Jason's biceps began bulging as he slowly struggled with reeling in the line. The shark started its circle of the boat, as predicted, moving in jagged swoops up and down. Suddenly a fin appeared on the horizon. Sweat formed around Jason's spine and quickly fanned outwards until his shirt was drenched, his eyes keen on the prey.

"Try to keep him toward the front of the boat," the experienced fisherman cautioned. "Sharks will attempt to go after the rudders when they get close. The metallic metal attracts them. Besides, at the bow you will have less space to cover, keep you from getting tired." He tapped Nathaniel's right shoulder, who was getting too close to his brother, almost tripping him. "I need you to grab hold of the wheel and keep the boat steady. Don't turn it; just hold her steady. Nathaniel rushed to obey the skipper's order. The man's attention returned to Jason. "Try to keep him away from the anchor while I pull her up; don't want the beast to wrap your line around the chain. That's not a way to end the battle." The man slowly raised the anchor. He handed some leather gloves to Jason and held the line while he slipped them on. Turning his head toward Nathaniel, the captain shouted, "Hold the wheel steady!"

The gray blue fin appeared again, somewhat closer to the boat, and then submerged back into its hideaway. The great warrior stopped the fight, and Jason relaxed his overextended muscles, allowing the line to go slightly flaccid. A horrified look came over the old man's face. Before he could utter a warning, the line stretched, almost pulling Jason overboard with the thrust, as the wise warrior leaped from the water, revealing its entire body, heading towards the open sea. With his great-grandfather's help they were able to salvage the catch and redirect it toward its captors. Nathaniel swiftly abandoned his post, reappearing at his brother's side. "Jason, did you see that?" he exclaimed, eyes focused on the sea, waiting for a second leap.

"Wow," Jason screamed.

"Boys, we have a fight on our hand," the captain said, his voice quivering as his eyes widened.

"I want to help," Nathaniel begged.

"Nathaniel, get back to your post," the skipper gently encouraged. "We can't get her in unless you hold the boat steady."

With renewed purpose Nathaniel returned to his assigned post.

"I didn't know sharks could jump," Jason continued, exhaustion showing in his voice. "That thing must have been ten-foot long."

"They can jump if they're makos," the man said, almost out of breath, as he leaned on the cabin. Knowing that law prohibited the catching of mako sharks he wanted to call the battle a truce, but he knew that Jason would be disappointed. It would be much better to allow him to be the victor and then turn the shark loose. The captain was also relieved that Jason's skills of measurement were a bit exaggerated. The shark could not have been more than five feet, if that, six at the most. Still it was a vicious and worthy opponent.

The shark plunged from the water again, though barely lifting itself totally out of the water. Jason muscles flexed as his back arched, attempting to pull the fish back toward the boat. Nature took pity on the boy, shielding him from the blazing rays of the sun with large white clouds. A pelican dove into the water not more than ten feet from the shark, returning to the air with a fish hanging from its mouth.

Nathaniel returned to his great-grandfather's side, wrapping his arms around his waist. "Are we going to put the shark on the grill too?" he asked.

"We'll see," the old man whispered, already knowing the answer.

"It really looks mean," the boy continued.

The man felt increasingly out of breath as he continued to lean against the cabin. "Please, get your brother some water," he instructed Nathaniel.

Nathaniel raced to the cooler in the back of the boat. He quickly gulped a bottle of water before providing some relief for Jason. The tired boy placed the rod in a holder, steadying the rod with one hand and pouring the water into his mouth with the other. After drinking half the bottle, he poured the remaining portion over his head. Before being directed back to his post, Nathaniel brought his great-grandfather water as well.

The mako maneuvered Jason from one side of the boat to the other. Jason temporarily lost the grip on the pole as he stumbled over the pole Nathaniel had carelessly left on the floor.

Again the mighty warrior went limp; the wise fisherman awaited the assault. As the shark once again leaped for the sun, Jason snapped it back into the water. "Get over here," he commanded the prey.

There wasn't a muscle in Jason's body that didn't ache, but his adrenaline begged for the quest to continue. The old man periodically gave the boy a reprieve, but for only a few precious seconds. With much prompting Nathaniel maintained his post at the helm.

The fish was being slowly and grudgingly inched toward the boat. "Careful he doesn't try to go under the boat and abate the line," the man puffed, leaning on the rails.

Jason nodded in agreement while watching the blood form around the shark's mouth. The fight for life could still be seen in the deep, dark pupil of the shark. The fourteen year old was mesmerized by the countless oversized teeth on the mako. Before he could react, the hunted bolted under the boat, ramming its head into the underside. The boat rocked, and Jason used his knees against the side to remain steady. The old man kneeled at the side, knife ready to snap the line. An overeager Nathaniel appeared at his side. The shark reappeared from its hiding place. Not willing to surrender the fight, it jerked away from the boat as it attempted to submerge. There wasn't enough line for it to play with. Jason's reflexes brought it back toward the vessel.

"Is he going to eat the boat?" Nathaniel asked, already knowing the answer.

"Nathaniel," the man snapped without patience in his voice, "Go under the captain's seat and get my camera, and do it quickly." The boy scurried to the task.

Jason looked at the man, saying, "How are we going to get her in the boat?"

The man, keeping a steady eye on the prey, said, "Son, we don't have a choice; we are going to have to cut her loose."

"Is it too big?" Jason asked.

"Not too big for the boat," he huffed. "It's against the law to capture makos. But if we could take her in, you are the man to do it. You are the victor."

The shark was barely fighting, dangling a few feet from the boat as his captor kept the line taut; perhaps conserving its energy for one last jaunt. The battle scars on its fin and sides were a testament to past battles with rudders of boats and larger sharks. In its right eye, an old fish hook was the only reminder of a fight won with another fisherman. It had not been an easy life for this great predator, daily successfully fighting off attackers. This day, the shark was finally defeated as a fourteen-year-old boy became a man.

"Here's the camera," Nathaniel whispered, holding the camera toward his great-grandfather.

"Can you take a good picture?" the man asked Nathaniel, looking toward Jason.

The older brother smiled and nodded.

For a brief moment, the old man thought about getting the Hoyer crane from the back of the boat so they could hoist the monster out of the sea. But he decided that would be a daunting if not dangerous task for a mere picture.

"Sure I can," Nathaniel reassured, pulling the camera from the case.

"Be careful. Lean a bit over the rail, but keep your feet on the ground and snap a couple of pictures." The man snugly held the young boy's waist as he stood carefully and snapped five pictures. "Now go up on top and snap a few pictures with your brother holding the line. If we're lucky you can capture both your brother and the mako." The man took a deep breath. "Jason, see if you can pull her up a little higher."

Jason pulled the five-foot shark halfway up the side of the boat. Nathaniel quickly snapped several pictures. Nathaniel quickly dropped the camera on the seat, and then he scurried to take a closer look at the catch.

"You want to set her free?" the old man asked Jason.

The newly anointed man rested the rod in the holder, took the knife from the man, and cut the line. The shark remained still for a few minutes, as if wanting to get a last look at its master, and then dashed under the boat into the depth of the sea, preparing for the continual battle for survival. Slightly disappointed that he didn't have a trophy for his two-hour endeavor, Jason smiled, knowing that his prey put up a mighty battle and deserved to be spared. Two tired men slumped to the floor and leaned against the railing with an enthusiastic and full of energy first mate at their side to attend to their needs.

"The predator is always the prey," the old man moaned. "For the sharks it's been that way since prehistoric times."

The boys stared at the old man, pondering the meaning of his words.

"How about getting some sandwiches and lemonade from the cooler?" the captain begged, looking at Nathaniel. "Lunchtime passed us by a few hours ago."

The old man stared at the light blue trim peeling from the boat. Then he quietly gazed at the mystic sea. The Atlantic was a large part of his life and remained his closest friend. There had been many victories at sea; he couldn't help but wonder if this was his last.

The sun decided to break through the clouds to witness the tired warriors. The two sat in silence for a few minutes before Jason spoke. "Thought you said those lures were a waste of time?"

They both shared a laugh.

After a long rest and some tall tales of wild fishing adventures that sounded too made up to be fiction, it was time to head for home. The captain took the wheel and headed toward shore with Charkey barking orders from behind. The sea was calm; the air fresh as the four fishermen basked in the glory of the catch. In the horizon they could see the sun slowly inching its way out of the sky.

Nathaniel, never tired of fishing, threw a line off the starboard as the boat made a slow trip toward land. Every few minutes he reeled the line in, revealing the effort was futile. Persistently, he cast back to the sea repeating the ritual. Jason sat by his grandfather, enjoying the serenity of the sunset.

"What is your philosophy on life?" Jason asked.

The old man did not respond immediately, trapped in the memories of his life. He reflected on Emma and Melissa and the many friends he had made. He remembered the stories by his father about Grandpappy and Uncle Luther. For a second he was in his yard with Rufus, tossing the baseball around. It all seemed like yesterday, yet so distant.

"Imagine that you want to build a house," he started, "that is going to cost two hundred and fifty thousand dollars." He paused to look back toward Nathaniel to see how much luck he was having.

"Don't worry, he hasn't fallen out yet," Jason joked.

"I agree to give you the money to build the house," the man continued. "The only caveat is that it has to be completed in two hundred and fifty days, and you may only use a thousand dollars per day. If you don't use a thousand dollars on one particular day you lose it."

"What if it rains one day?" Jason asked.

"You still lose it," the man said.

"That's not fair," Jason protested.

"Why isn't it fair? The agreement was a thousand dollars per day."

"Shouldn't there be an exception?" Jason asked.

"God gives us each so many days to live. Once those days are gone, they are gone," the old man continued. "He doesn't give us extra time because we had the flu or we were feeling blue. When our time is up, that is it."

"Okay," the boy agreed.

"When you first start the house, you start with a footer, which leads to the foundation." The man blew into a handkerchief. "The foundation for life is our childhood. Of course, the architect is our parents." The man paused to point at dolphins gliding carefree over the ocean. "As we grow we build the walls during our teen years. In our twenties we start putting a roof over it."

"So, what if a person has a bad childhood?" Jason asked.

The old man reflected on the way he treated Melissa the last several months she lived at home. "The time remains the same," he said sadly. "You may need to restructure the house to a design that is more suitable, but the time remains the same. The money spent can't be given back." The captain turned the boat slightly. "The money spent today is for the tools we will use tomorrow. Sometimes those tools won't seem useful until later. There are some tools that will never be of use."

"You're talking about things like school work?" Jason asked.

"School work and other life lessons," the old man mused. "The memories of events of our lives never escape us. Some are good; others aren't as pleasant."

"Land ho," Charkey cackled.

Jason stood to see the faint outline of the coastline ahead. The beach remained active with beachcombers. Young lovers walked hand in hand through the sand. Children scurried around playing in the waves. College students busied themselves with volleyball or Frisbee.

The sounds of fun rang through the air. Nathaniel dropped his pole, scurrying to the front of the boat.

"Jason," the captain ordered. "we're getting in cell range. Why don't you call your mother to let her know we're on the way. It will probably be another hour before we dock. We're coming in a bit to the north so we can take the scenic route home."

Jason was quick to obey the order.

"Hello," Carollyn answered on the first ring, a slight hint of worry in her voice.

"Momma," came a sound of a boy wanting to be a man, "Get the frying pan ready; we're heading home with a boatload."

Her bright relieved smile radiated over the phone. "And just who do you think will be frying those fish?"

"Of course the best cook in the world," he teased, "my great-grandfather. But you are in charge of cleaning them."

She laughed. "I'm afraid you dialed the wrong number." There was a brief pause. "Did you men have a good time?"

"The best," Jason sounded sure. "I even caught a shark."

"A shark?" she exclaimed, not truly believing her ears.

"Yes," he boasted. "Must have been twelve-feet long; it took me several hours of hard reeling to land her. We had to cut it loose because the law doesn't allow this type to be caught."

"Oh, the big one that got away." She was privy to tall fish stories.

"But, Momma," he continued, "we got pictures to prove it."

"I'll believe it when I see it," she reassured. "How's your brother?"

"Fine, he caught the most fish. We all did well. Grandpa says we will be docking in an hour or so."

"May I talk to your brother?" Carollyn asked.

Nathaniel and his mother talked as the boat made her way into shore. He told of the great shark adventure and his role of keeping the boat steady and being in charge of refreshments. According to Nathaniel, the shark was almost twenty-feet long. He told his mother that is came real close to eating the boat.

The boat skirted the shore, heading south to Daytona, being escorted in the sunset by a noble bald eagle. The old man turned on the radio.

"This is WGFT Jacksonville," came the announcer, "bringing you the best country to enjoy the sunset with. Our gift to you." There was a pause. "Alan Jackson … 'When Daddy Let Me Drive' … brings back some sweet memories for me."

The captain motioned for Nathaniel to take the wheel.

"Oh no," Charkey declared.

The captain looked at Jason and patted him on the shoulder. "I think it is time for some lemonade," he said as he fell onto the cushioned bench.

Jason was quick to comply with the request, grabbing three lemonades out of the cooler. He opened the first and gave it to his brother, then opened the next for his great-grandfather. After sitting on the bench next to the man he opened his.

"Thank you," the old man said, his voice sounding tired.

"It was my pleasure," Jason replied. He was going to make a caustic remark about his brother steering the boat, but felt it would be better off not to.

The captain rotated his vision from Nathaniel to the sea to Jason. He pointed towards the radio and said, "This song reminds me of your grandmother."

Jason nodded to acknowledge that he heard his great-grandfather but did not reply.

"When Melissa was eight years old I bought an old red flatbed ford truck from old man Guthrie. It wasn't much to look at; it had more rust on it than paint. The engine sputtered and stalled at every stop sign."

Jason took a small sip of lemonade and asked, "So why did you buy it?"

The man took a drink of his lemonade and coached Nathaniel to go a bit more to the left before replying to Jason. "Mrs. Guthrie had just put her husband into a home. She had no use for the truck and needed the money." The captain coughed. "So I decided that I would buy it."

"That was a nice thing to do," Jason commented.

"Guthrie," the man continued, "was a World War I veteran. While in Germany he stepped on a land mine and lost both of his legs." The man stopped to wipe his brow. "He had hand controls on the truck that controlled the gas and the brakes."

Jason nodded in response.

The old man pointed toward the shore where there was an area roped off. "They found sea turtle eggs in the area, so it is blocked off so people don't disturb the nesting area," he instructed.

Jason peered at the area and asked, "How long will the area be restricted?"

The man replied, "Until the Wildlife protection agency determines that all the eggs are either hatched or infertile."

Jason turned his attention briefly to Nathaniel to make sure he was doing alright.

"Back to the truck," the captain said. "Because of the hand controls it was easy for Melissa to drive it. I would allow her to drive down the beach every Sunday night." He laughed; "of course Emma wasn't too thrilled with the idea."

Jason smiled, thinking about his mother's reaction if his father would allow Nathaniel or him to drive before they were old enough.

"We would go a few miles or so," the man said. "Then we would stop and sit in the back of the truck to talk and look at the heavens."

"Did Grandma Emma go with you?" Jason asked.

The old man laughed. "She would not miss it. Afterwards she always scolded me for allowing Melissa to drive." The man shook his head.

"It sounds like you had a good time."

"It was fun," the man sighed. "In the darkness of night we were all allowed to be whom we wanted to be. I did not have to be the responsible restaurant owner. Melissa was free to be a child." The old man looked towards the shore and then returned his attention to Jason. "Our favorite game was to count the stars."

"What happened to the truck?" Jason asked.

The captain laughed so loud that Nathaniel turned to see what the commotion was about. The great-grandfather apologized for the noise and then instructed Nathaniel to keep an eye on his driving. "The truck," he began the explanation, "always had an oil leak. As I said before, the motor wasn't in great shape when I bought it." He stood to get a cramp out of his leg. "I was never one for checking the oil. One rainy night Emma and I took it into the town to run some errands." The man stopped to gather his thoughts. "Our car was in the shop for some routine maintenance." The captain shook his head and smiled. "It started raining really hard. We were probably two miles away from the house and the engine died."

"What did you do?" Jason asked.

"I had two choices," the man said as he sat back down. "I could have sat there and listened to Emma complain until the rain stopped, or I walk to get help."

Jason smiled and said knowingly, "You walked for help."

They both laughed.

"Doing just fine," the old man said to Nathaniel, "just like your grandmother used to do."

Momentarily he flashed back to when Melissa first drove a boat, snickering at the thought of her grounding it on a sandbar. Her face was so pitiful it was hysterical; he and Emma were unable to contain their laughter. The poor girl thought she had damaged her father's boat, and yet her deranged parents couldn't keep a straight face. Oh, he missed the innocence of Melissa's youth. Hopefully Nathaniel wouldn't inherit her luck.

The old man looked over his shoulder to Jason. "Look at the shoreline; the rosy sand stretches for miles. I wouldn't live any other place on earth."

"It is unbelievably beautiful. Just like Grandma's paintings."

As the sun continued its nightly descent into the ground, the bald eagle continued escorting the crew safely home.

Chapter IV

Friday

*One small grain of sand seems quite insignificant. If
you fuse the grain in a handful of sand you will create a
pebble. If you throw the pebble into a lake it will form a
ripple. If permitted, this ripple will continue throughout
eternity.*

*A single birth may seem quite insignificant. If you
fuse the deeds of that one person into a lifetime you create
a wave of memories. If permitted the wave of memories
will transcend to all generations.*

The sun peeked through the window, creating a prism from the reflection
off the mirror attached to the dresser. Two young cardinals were perched
on a limb directly outside the window, practicing a new melody. All the
clouds in the sky were absent.

Carollyn awakened to the sound of children's laughter resonating
through the house.

Naturally, she thought it was their grandfather that was entertaining
them, but she was wrong; it was Charkey. The bird was in a clowning
mood, cackling some nonsense towards the boys then quickly fluttering
to another side of the room, usually making a vain attempt to hide from
them, sending the boys into hysteria.

Carollyn watched in amusement for several minutes and then became suddenly alarmed. It was strange that Grandpa wasn't out of bed. He prided himself in always being up before the crack of dawn. Not that it was necessary, but Carollyn expected to be greeted by her grandfather standing with a frying pan over the hot stove. She left the boys and slowly walked to his room.

Carefully she eased the door open. A humming sound of a nocturnal oxygen concentrator greeted her. Grandpa was lying flat on his back, jaw wide open with one snore following another, the nasal cannulla half out of his nostrils. Carollyn gently reinserted the tubing and stood watching the old man comfortably sleeping on the antique brass bed. "The mattress should be elevated a bit," the physician said to herself.

The pale green room was a shrine to the life shared with Emma. Their wedding picture stood proudly on the cluttered dresser, next to the picture of Emma and the newborn Melissa. On the walls were memories of fishing trips and walks in exotic places. Above the bed was a painting, most likely done by her mother. The captain and Emma were standing beside a boat, with a bottle of champagne, preparing to christen it. Perched on the bow looking on approvingly was Charkey.

On the bedside table was a well-read brown leather King James Bible, undoubtedly from the captain's wedding day. Curious, she flipped it to where the book marker protruded from the pages. *To every thing there is a season, and a time for purpose under the heavens.* Ecclesiastes 3. In the margin of the page was scribbled in red ink "Today is a day of reconciliation. Praise be to God." It was dated the night they had arrived.

Carollyn smiled and quietly left the room. After making the boys blueberry pancakes she sent them out to play. As soon as she heard the old man begin to rustle, about a quarter to noon, she started making his breakfast. Soon he came stumbling from the bedroom.

"Thought you were going to sleep the day away," she said sweetly, kissing his cheek. "Your coffee is poured, and I'll have some pancakes and bacon for you in just a second."

"Guess sleeping to noon was a good ploy," the grandfather mumbled.

"Ploy?" Carollyn said, raising her eyebrows.

"It got you to fix breakfast," the man said, laughing. He then sat down hard in the chair.

Carollyn laughed. "And I thought you were sleeping in because the boys tired you on your fishing excursion."

The captain stared at the beach, but did not answer.

Carollyn put the pancakes and bacon on the table and sat down; they both ate in silence, taking in the quietude of belonging.

"How long have you been on oxygen?" Carollyn asked, as they were almost finished eating.

"Are you asking as a physician or my granddaughter?"

"I don't know, maybe both," Carollyn said, with a slight hesitation in her voice.

The man stared longingly at the Atlantic for a few minutes before answering. "Guess it's been a couple of years," he finally said.

"Has your doctor talked to you about using it during the daytime?"

"Just as I suspected," the old man snapped, "you're playing doctor."

Carollyn put her hand on his. "Does that mean yes?"

He glared at her scornfully, and then a tear formed in his eye. "Doctor Richter strongly suggests that I wear it in the daytime if I need it." The man took the final bite of the pancake. "It's a bit dry," he mumbled.

"And?" Carollyn continued, ignoring his attempt to change the subject.

"And it is too inconvenient," he quipped. "If I'm tied to a tank I can't work, I can't fish, I can't walk on the beach."

"There are lightweight tanks," she encouraged.

"Can we change the subject?" her grandfather huffed. "You're only going to be here a few more days; let's talk about something more pleasant."

Carollyn smiled. "Will you promise to talk to your doctor about alternative tanks? Or if you would like I can talk to him."

"Then can we change the subject?" the man insisted irritably.

"If you promise," Carollyn stated firmly.

"Scout's honor," the old man relented, knowing that he was not going to follow through on the request.

"Hey, you received some pictures in the mail yesterday!" Carollyn said, somewhat relieved that the subject has been discussed.

"Pictures?" the man asked, "who would be sending me pictures?"

Carollyn handed him a large envelope addressed to him and Charkey from Ocala, Florida. Just then a wet and sandy Jason came running into the house.

"Can I have some orange juice?" he said out of breath.

"Excuse me," Carollyn scolded. "First of all you are wet and sandy. Secondly, don't you know how to say good morning?"

"Good morning," the boy said sheepishly to his great-grandfather.

"Good morning," the old man said, studying the envelope. "Don't worry about being wet, that's why we have this tile down; cleans up easy. The housekeeper will be here this afternoon, anyway. She needs to earn her keep. The cost to keep this place neat is unbelievable." The captain groaned. "Which reminds me, I better tidy up a bit; we don't want the housekeeper thinking I'm a slob."

Carollyn stared at her grandfather. "The proper response would be: listen to your mother."

The man ignored the retort as Jason rushed to the refrigerator to pour some orange juice. He reached for a letter opener that looked like a pirate's dagger with a ruby in the middle of its handle. Awkwardly, he broke the seal and retrieved a letter and two pictures.

> *"Dear Captain and Charkey,*
> *We're sorry it has taken so long to send you these pictures, but we misplaced your address. Hopefully they are suitable to hang in the restaurant. It was great hearing the story about Terisita and Dominick. Both of these pictures were snapped at the Huguenot cemetery. They match the description of the ghosts in your story. Having legends to go with the pictures make our adventures that much more interesting. We will be returning to St Augustine on another ghost hunt within a few weeks or possibly sooner, and will try to take the long way home again and stop by Charkey's. If we are lucky we will have some new pictures. We're taking a laptop and a portable printer so we won't have to wait for the pictures. Your place is a must for anyone visiting Daytona. It was the best seafood we have ever eaten. Giving us our meal on the house was too generous. Personally we think you should have charged extra for the history lesson! Hope all is well.*

Kind regards,
John & Lori"

The trembling hands held the pictures with amazement. The first was of a silhouette of a dog, kind of like a greyhound or hunting hound, standing erect. It was easy to make out the head, body, and legs. It was indisputably a dog, but it was peculiar in that it appeared a bit one dimensional. The second was a side view of what appeared to be a woman carrying a bouquet of flowers. This picture wasn't as distinguishable, but it was a woman. It almost looked as if it was a flame of fire taking the shape of a bride, but it was too well defined to be a flame or a reflection of light. Both pictures had pitch black backgrounds. Toward the bottom of the pictures were the faint outlines of tombstones.

Carollyn, looking over the old man's shoulder, deliberated on the pictures. "Who are Dominick and Terisita?"

The man pushed his chair out from the table to stand up. "I believe that is a story that Jason can best enlighten you with," he quipped. "I'm going out to the porch for a breath of fresh air and the taste of a good cigar."

"Smoking isn't good for your lungs," Carollyn scolded him.

"And nagging isn't good for my ears," the old man mumbled.

The man hobbled out on the porch and fell into his favorite chair, as Jason began to recant the fable to his mother. White marshmallow clouds crowded the light blue sky, deceiving beachcombers of the brutality of the sun. The captain started to light the cigar but remembered his promise not to smoke in front of the children. Instead he resolved to relax in his paradise and enjoy the fresh air. He watched as a few treasure hunters carefully surveyed the beach with metal detectors, realizing that they would never retrieve enough booty to pay for their devices. A middle-aged man and a young boy were attempting to launch a box kite in the distance. Suddenly a pair of legs poked out from behind a palm tree. The man glanced down at the unlit cigar, mumbled under his breath, picked up an oversized straw hat from the table, and struggled down the stairs to investigate.

Gingerly, with his cane leading, he circled around the palm tree until he was staring directly at the back of his youngest grandson.

"So what are you up to?" he snapped, playfully.

Nathaniel, somewhat jolted by the sneak attack, looked up at the old man. "Trying to make a sand castle, but it's not coming out too well."

The man mused, "It is hard to make a proper castle without the right tools."

"But I don't have any tools," the boy whined.

"Go into the garage," the engineer commanded, pointing toward the house. "You will find two plastic buckets and a plastic shovel." He avoided using the word toy. "Bring them out here."

"Yes, sir," Nathaniel's voice faded as he dashed on the mission.

Using his cane for leverage, the old man slowly lowered himself to the sand, knowing from the other day when he was toppled over; he would not be able to rise on his own accord.

Soon the eager student returned with a fluorescent green and a hot pink bucket with matching shovels.

"I don't think I can use this one," he said bashfully holding out the pink. "It's made for a girl."

"Nonsense," the man protested, "it's the perfect bucket for gathering water." He coughed loudly. "Now go fill it to the top with sea water, and be quick about it. We have a castle to create."

"Yes, sir," the boy giggled, starting toward the ocean only to retrace his steps to drop the green bucket at his great-grandfather's side. Soon he was back, splashing water every which way. "Now what?" he asked eagerly.

The captain's mind was instantly transported back to younger years with Melissa. There were many mornings they would sit on the beach for hours, playing in the sand, getting muddy just to build the perfect castle. The morning would end with Emma scolding them for getting sand over her freshly vacuumed carpet. The man would always respond with, "If you knew we were making sandcastles why didn't you wait until we finished before vacuuming?" As Melissa grew older she gave up making the castles for painting them on canvas, sometimes with paint and a few times experimenting with charcoal.

"What do I do now?" Nathaniel impatiently pleaded.

"Put the water bucket by the tree," the captain demanded, "then come sit beside me."

The boy quickly complied with the command.

"Fill the green bucket with sand about three quarters to the top." The man paused as the boy started on the mission. "After the sand is in, fill the rest with water."

"Why?" Nathaniel asked.

"The water will help the sand stick together. Once you pour the water, mix it in well."

As Nathaniel worked on the mortar the man contently watched the young surfers battle the waves for supremacy.

"Finished," the willing pupil shouted.

"Good," the old man said with a smile, tapping his right shoulder. Pointing toward an area of sand he continued, "We're going to carefully turn the bucket upside down here. Then we will lift it slowly." The man watched as Nathaniel followed the direction. "This will form our first tower." As predicted it was so. The first tower was formed. "Now take the shovel and start sculpting the top of the tower so it looks like a chess castle."

Nathaniel started the structuring of the first tower as instructed, carefully making the top ridged. With minimal intervention he was able to mold the top into the shape of a rook on a chess set. The captain started scooping and forming the sand for the wall that would lead to the next tower.

"Grandpa," the boy asked, staring at the masonry, "Grandpa Laurence says if you had it your way all black people would still be slaves or sent away to Africa."

The man was stunned to silence, haunted by his past actions.

"That isn't true, is it?" Nathaniel asked earnestly.

"President Lincoln said, 'Whenever I hear anyone arguing for slavery, I feel a strong impulse to see it tried on him personally.'"

"What does that mean?" Nathaniel asked, obviously confused by the quote.

The man chuckled, wondering why he was starting an intellectual conversation with an eight-year-old. "It means if a man feels that slavery is okay, he should try being a slave." There was a brief pause. "It is wrong now and it was wrong a hundred and fifty years ago for one man to own another."

"Then why did they do it?" the boy asked.

The captain shook his head. "Because the people from Africa were of different skin color and of different religious beliefs, the white men in this country and other parts of the world rationalized that they were not human. Since they were less than human it was okay to own them like a mule."

"But I'm black and I believe in Jesus," the boy said.

"I know," the man reassured. "But many of your ancestors didn't. Christianity had not reached Africa." He paused to try to gather the right wording. "It is all right their beliefs were different. Just because a person's beliefs are not the same as yours, it doesn't mean they are wrong."

The two artists continued contently, without words, concentrating on the sand castle. As Nathaniel finished designing the first tower, the old man continued building the wall toward the tower-to-be. When the boy was satisfied with the first, he ran to the ocean for more water to start the second. The man watched as he hurried back with the pink bucket, spilling as much water as he retained.

Two young ladies clad in barely enough cloth to call a bikini leisurely splashed through the water.

"You know, Nathaniel, there are different forms of slavery," the man said, finally breaking the silence, after the boy returned. "A person that is captured by false beliefs or fears is enslaving himself from being truly free."

"I don't understand," Nathaniel said, looking directly at his great-grandfather.

"If you are afraid of water, you avoid doing anything around water; your fears are keeping you from enjoying that aspect of life."

"But I'm not afraid of water." Nathaniel was not understanding the conversation.

"Bad example." The man wondered why he chose this avenue of discussion. "If I don't like someone because of their skin color, I am preventing myself from the joy of knowing them."

"You mean like you not liking Grandpa Laurence?"

The old man let out a huge sigh, almost a moan. "Precisely. When your grandmother and grandfather first got married, I thought it was wrong because of the color of his skin. By doing that I alienated myself from my daughter and cheated myself of the joy of a family."

"But I'm black and you love me?" the boy asked.

"Yes, I do very much love you and your brother and mother."

"And Grandpa Laurence?" the boy whispered, staring into the old man's eyes.

"And Grandpa Laurence." The captain gave a reassuring smile. "I have let go of my fears about him being black. I am no longer a slave to my prejudice."

Nathaniel thought for a minute. "I think Grandpa Laurence should stop being a slave to his prejudices too." The boy hugged his great-grandfather around the neck.

The captain reflected on words he had just read from the writings of Henry David Thoreau: "It is never too late to give up your prejudices." Many great men throughout the history of the world had preached those sentiments; too few seemed wise enough to heed the advice. But now it seemed as if people were changing for the better.

The two craftsmen bridged the gap between the two towers before Nathaniel went for more water. The man relaxed in the cool breeze waiting for the water boy to return. Before he returned, Jason appeared with two glasses of lemonade.

"Mom and I saw you out here and thought you could use some refreshments."

The tired man reached for the glass. "Thank you, I sure need this."

Jason knelt down beside him. "Can I help?"

"If you don't mind, can this be Nathaniel's and my special time?"

"Sure," the boy responded understandingly. "I told Mom about the ghosts; not sure that she believed the story."

Nathaniel came running back, splashing water. "Hey, Jason, look at our castle!" He grabbed the lemonade from his brother and started gulping it. "Want to help?"

Jason looked at his great-grandfather knowingly. "No thanks, Mom and I are going to take a walk. But your castle is killer."

Jason turned and jogged slowly back to the house, his muscles bulging from his tank top, feeling good about himself in allowing his brother to be in the spotlight.

Handing the empty cup to Nathaniel, the man continued the tutelage. "Fill this with sand and water, and then gently dump it on the top of the second tower."

The boy eagerly followed the instruction.

"Now cup your hands and form the new top into a dome."

The boy listened and began molding the top. "Kind of like making a snowball?" he asked.

The captain chuckled. "Never really seen snow, but I think you have the right idea."

The two paused for a few minutes to watch Jason and Carollyn start their stroll down the beach. The man marveled at the physical resemblance Carollyn had to Melissa.

"Grandpa," Nathaniel started in a whiny tone while forming the dome, "Do you believe in God?"

"'If God did not exist, it would be necessary to invent him;' so says the great philosopher Voltaire," the old man said, gazing at the heavens.

"Invent him?" the boy asked.

"No, we don't need to invent him," the man laughed, for a second time, having forgotten for a brief moment he was talking to an eight-year-old. "Look at the beach and the birds and the beautiful sky, the moon and stars at night. It is obvious there is a God."

"So do you believe?" the boy asked, trying to solve the riddle of his great-grandfather's quote.

"Yes," the old man relented. "Do you believe?" The man reflected on another of Voltaire's sayings: "God is a circle whose center is everywhere and circumference nowhere."

"Oh yes," Nathaniel exclaimed, "I just wanted to be sure you were going to heaven."

The captain smiled as his great-grandson returned to their masterpiece. Looking above, he recognized the genesis of a storm in the blackening clouds. Slowly, he crawled to the second tower so he could start building the wall to the third tower.

"Is God black or white?" Nathaniel asked.

The old man laughed to himself, recalling earlier years when even considering God to be anything but white would be blasphemy. "I don't think God has any particular color. Since he is the Almighty, I believe he is different colors to different people."

"Do you mean he can change colors?"

"Not necessarily," the man said, not really knowing how to proceed. "I believe that people see him differently, in the image they expect."

The boy looked at him perplexed.

"God is like a rainbow," the man finally said. "He is of many different colors."

Somewhat satisfied with the answer, Nathaniel scurried off to the sea for his third bucket of water. The seagulls circled overhead calling out warning of the pending storm. The importance of completing the castle superseded the need to seek shelter. The captain gazed down the beach, hoping that Carollyn and Jason had not walked too far.

"How should we make the third tower?" the boy asked as he knelt down beside his great-grandfather.

"Let's do it like the last, except instead of making the top rounded we will use the shovel to scrape the sides to make a point." The man sneezed. "When it's finished it will look like a church steeple."

"Are you afraid of anything, Grandpa?" the boy quizzed.

The man looked south toward where the others had walked. To his relief they were returning. His eyes returned to the gray mass above; he felt that they had a good half hour, maybe even forty-five minutes before the rain would come. With luck there would be no early lightning to force them to abandon their project.

"Grandpa," the Nathaniel snapped a bit impatiently, "Are you scared of anything?"

The old man laughed at the intolerance. "I haven't really given it much thought. When you live as long as I, you outlive most of your fears." He considered the question as his great-granson skillfully whittled the sides of the tower into a steeple. "What are you afraid of?"

"Snakes and wild bears when we go hiking and ... ah ... ah ... girls."

A broad smile came over the man's face. "Is there a particular girl that scares you more than others?'

The boy turned bashful. "Ah ... ah, Amy Sue Murphy." He giggled a little, turning his head away from his great-grandfather.

"What so scary about Amy Sue?" the old man asked calmly.

"She wants to kiss me," Nathaniel laughed.

"She does!"

"And Jason sings, 'Nathaniel and Amy Sue sitting in a tree. K.I.S.S.I.N.G. First comes love, then comes marriage and then comes Nathaniel with a baby carriage.'"

"Well, for now it is okay to be a little afraid of Amy Sue." Somehow the man avoided laughing. "But one day your fear will become fascination."

"No it won't," the boy scolded.

The only response from the man was a knowing smile.

"Where do babies come from?" Nathaniel asked, stopping his work and looking directly at his great-grandfather.

The words echoing in his ears, he flashed back to Melissa asking him the same question when she was around eight or nine. Being dumbfounded then and uneasy talking about the forbidden fruit, he informed her in no uncertain terms that mermaids set babies afloat on rafts. Under a full blue moon, deserving mortals would wait for the infants to arrive on shore. When they found their treasure they would take them home and shower them with love. Now, the fable, once thought to be wise, was a memory he wished could be erased. If he and Emma would have been open about sex, maybe they could have prevented Melissa from becoming pregnant. "Well," he started, "there are some subjects that an old man like me isn't really good at explaining." There was a pause. "I believe the best person to talk to you about that would be your mother or father. If you like I could mention it to her."

The boy took a moment to contemplate his great-grandfather's offer. "Is that because Momma's a doctor?"

The discomfort continued. "Well, yes, that's one of the reasons. However, the best reason is that most important topics like this should always be discussed with your parents. They care enough about you to give you the right answers."

"You can't give me the right answers?"

"Of course," the man stumbled, "but you live with your parents and they will be able to answer questions about babies that you will think of later."

"Okay," Nathaniel agreed and was off with the pink bucket for a dip into the sea.

Carollyn stopped by to admire the architecture. "Don't you think you should call it quits? It's getting ready to storm." She peered closely at the fort; a chill ran up her spine. "It's getting a bit breezy out here, too."

"We have at least another half hour before we'll have to run for cover."

The lady skeptically looked at the sky. "Not sure that you are in running shape."

"We'll be fine," the man encouraged. "It's important for both of us to finish."

"Okay, you're the stubborn old expert," Carollyn said, a half frown on her face.

"Did Jason tell you the story of Terisita and Dominick?" the captain asked, even though he knew the answer.

Carollyn rolled her eyes. "Interesting family lore, I think Momma told me about them once." Carollyn smiled. "She passed on many stories from Daytona. It was as if part of her never left."

"Now we have pictures that collaborate the story," the man said, trying to continue the conversation.

"My scientific mind has a bit of difficulty validating them," Carollyn said.

"So, you think it some sort of trick photography?"

"The thought has crossed my mind." The woman stared nervously at the gray sky before glancing toward the water to see Nathaniel. "I find it difficult to believe something that I can't see or have some type of verifiable proof that it exists."

"How do you explain God?" the man queried, trying not to sound condescending.

Carollyn sighed. "The Bible reveals that God is love. Though I cannot see him in the physical sense, I am surrounded by the warmth of his touch." She paused for a second, realizing the unrelenting intellect in her grandfather that had been present in her mother. "In the alleged ghost pictures there is nothing definitive."

"There are many mysterious things in the universe," the old man philosophized. "Some we can see, and some, such as an atom, we can't. Sometimes we need to take things on faith."

"I will agree there was something there," Carollyn reluctantly relented. "But I will not categorically profess that it is evidence of the existence of ghosts."

"Hi, Momma," Nathaniel greeted on his return. "You like our castle?"

"Yes, it is beautiful," she mumbled politely, not appearing to be overly thrilled.

The old man interpreted her nonchalant answer as her desire for the project to be finished so they could avoid the rain. "Don't worry," he reassured, "we will be in before the storm."

"Grandpa says you are going to tell me where babies come from!"

Carollyn's jaw dropped toward the earth.

"We will talk about this later," the wise old sage reassured. "It's really okay."

Still stunned, Carollyn acknowledged the forthcoming discussion and started to the house. Turning back briefly toward the dynamic duo she shouted, "Is it okay if Jason puts some fish on the grill?"

The old man nodded.

"How are we going to make the fourth tower?" Nathaniel asked.

"Why don't we duplicate the first?" the man suggested as he crawled to start the fourth wall, wheezing sounds coming through his mouth.

"The other night when we were looking at your coins," Nathaniel said in almost a whisper.

The old man nodded for him to continue.

"I saw one with an Indian on it."

"Okay," the great-grandfather said, not clear as to where the conversation was headed.

"Jason said it was a nickel. I think he is wrong, because that other guy is on the nickel."

The man smiled at the innocence. "Actually your brother is right. That is an Indian head nickel or some folks call it a buffalo nickel. They were minted before the Jefferson nickel."

"Buffalo nickel?" Nathaniel pondered. "I thought they just made them."

The man laughed. "They did, to commemorate the original one."

"Oh?" Nathaniel said, a bewildered expression on his face.

"President Theodore Roosevelt ordered the first ones to be minted as a tribute to the Indians and the great buffalo, in the early 1900s." The man paused for a second to be sure he had his facts straight. "I believe it was in 1913."

"Who is the Indian?" Nathaniel asked. "I think it might be Geronimo."

A seagull landed in the middle of the castle, looked at Nathaniel's surprised face, and flew away.

"That is a pretty good guess," the man said. "However the profile is a composite of three Indian Chiefs: Iron Tail, Big Tree, and Two Moons."

"That is probably why I thought it was Geronimo," Nathaniel said earnestly. "Is the buffalo a combination of three too?"

The captain could not contain his laughter. "I suppose that all buffalos look pretty much the same," he mused. "The one portrayed on this coin was a black diamond bison from the Bronx Zoo."

The inquisitive young boy ran out of questions and refocused on the fortress.

The captain's vision took him to Caribbean Charkey's. This was only the second time since Emma's death he had stayed away from the restaurant for this long. He looked at the upstairs veranda with the white railing. When he and his daddy designed the restaurant they decided to put a two-bedroom apartment and porch upstairs. This was to be his and Emma's living space. His father thought that the young couple needed to have some privacy. However, since he became ill before the restaurant was completed, the couple never had an opportunity to move in.

When Melissa was young, they turned one of the rooms into a playroom for days that Emma was at the restaurant. Then when Emma became ill, she used a room to rest in when the days became too long.

Marissa suggested that they convert it into an "adult only" dining area, which had turned out to be popular with young couples. Though the laughter and friends produced so much happiness over the years, they had been so much like his family, he was happy to have this brief sabbatical.

At first he thought the restaurant wouldn't be able to function without him. Now he knew that he couldn't function without the restaurant. That had changed this week.

The captain's focus took him to the porch of the house. A bare-chested Jason was starting the gas grill in preparation of cooking the catch from the day before. Carollyn was sitting in his favorite chair chatting with the chef. Charkey was oblivious to it all, as he was fretting over the coming rain.

"Grandpa, do you like baseball?" Nathaniel asked without looking up from his project.

"My favorite sport," the man quipped. "I used to be a pretty good player."

"Mine too!" the boy said with excitement in his voice, concentrating on the tower. "I bleed Cubbies blue."

The man watched as the boy sculpted the wet sand. "I grew up a Yankees fan," the man started. "Probably because Babe Ruth helped ease my father's pain during the Great Depression; actually he eased many a folks' pain." He paused for a second to study the clouds. "After Ruth, Jolt'n Joe DiMaggio stole America's heart, giving us something to hope for as we moved into WWII."

"You like the Yankees?" Nathaniel asked.

"I gave my love affair up with the Yanks in 1944 when I played that year of minor league ball for the Bosox. I changed from hoping to play along side DiMaggio to being in the lineup with Ted Williams. Of course D-Day ended my hopes of that, but it didn't squelch my love for the Red Sox." The old man admired the fort forming before him. It was a basic fort design he had been teaching children for years. "Who's your favorite player?"

"Aramis Ramirez," the boy answered without thinking. "He's a third baseman."

"Oh, the hot corner; need someone quick there," the man replied.

"Hot corner," Nathaniel giggled. "My daddy calls it that."

"They call third base the hot corner," the man began to teach, "because most right-handed hitters drive the ball in that direction. The player has to be fast or the ball will get by him."

"That's why I play the hot corner," Nathaniel boasted, because I'm really fast. When we finish do you want to see how fast I run?"

The man smiled. "Yes, I would like that." The captain paused. "I thought you said you were a pitcher?"

The boy looked at him quizzically, "Didn't you know I could play two positions?" Nathaniel gave his great-grandfather a stern, but playful scowl. "I thought I told you I played third base."

The man gave the boy a loving smile.

There was a pause in the conversation as the two concentrated on the sand. Gray clouds were slowly surrounding them, preparing for their outburst.

"So how are the Cubs doing this year?" the captain quizzed.

"About as well as they do any year. I think next year may be their year."

That brought a smile to the old man's face. "We Red Sox fans said that for years; then in 2004 we finally had our year." The man smiled broadly, "Then in 2007 we repeated the feat."

"Do you collect baseball cards?" Nathaniel asked, still not looking up from his creation.

"I have a big collection of many of the stars of yesterday: Ruth, Dean, Ted Williams, and Joe DiMaggio. The list goes on and on. Even today I catch myself buying a pack once in awhile."

"Jason and I collect them too," the boy said proudly.

"I think I have an old Jackie Robinson or two, and I know I have a Hank Aaron and Willie Mays. Tonight, we will look for them. You and Jason can pick out a few that you like to take home."

"For keeps?" the boy looked at his great-grandfather.

"For keeps," the delighted old man repeated.

Nathaniel noticed a mother putting a shell to her young daughter's ear near the shoreline. He watched as the girl giggled in delight. "Why's that lady putting the shell in that girl's ear?"

The man peered at the mother and daughter, smiling at the memories. "Legend says that you can hear the sea in some shells," the man replied.

Nathaniel looked puzzled. "Is that true?"

The old man laughed. "If you listen carefully, you can hear a rumbling sound that sounds like waves rushing to the shore." He paused to catch his breath. "Would you like to get a shell and try?"

"No," Nathaniel quickly responded, "I want to finish our castle."

Jason appeared at his great-grandfather's side. "I remembered the lemon pepper, the lime juice, and the garlic, but I forgot the secret ingredient."

"How do you like our castle?" his brother interrupted.

"Looks good," Jason said, smiling at his younger brother.

"Freshly ground ginger," the captain reminded him. "You will find some wrapped in foil in the bottom of the refrigerator."

"Grandpa is going to give us some old baseball cards," Nathaniel continued, ignoring the other conversation.

"That's nice," Jason replied as he started back to the house. "I need to get back to the grill." He stopped after taking a few steps toward the house and turned back toward the playmates. "Mom wants to know if you're going to be much longer?"

"Tell her not to worry about the storm. It will have some patience and wait for us. Besides, a bit of water has never hurt anyone."

"Hey, Jason," Nathaniel shouted, "you were right; it is an Indian head nickel."

Jason smiled and nodded.

"The Indian on the front are three different Indians posing as one," he continued.

His older brother smiled at the them as he backed toward the house.

"When I grow up I am going to play baseball for a team called the Buffalos, so I can honor the Indians," Nathaniel said, continuing to try to engage his brother in conversation.

"That's good," Jason acknowledged, then turned and trotted back to the house.

"I'm going for more water," the boy shouted as he was off running to the sea in zigzags so he could make the seagulls fly.

The captain used shells to form a drawbridge and windows along the castle's walls and towers. When he arrived at the fourth tower, he carefully flattened the rounded ridges so they would not look identical to the first. Then he started building the wall from the first to where it would connect with the fifth. Peering into the heavens he was sure they would have enough time to finish the castle. When Nathaniel had tired of chasing the seagulls and pelicans he returned from his mission.

"What took you so long?" the great-granfather asked, though he already knew the answer.

"I was chasing the birds," the boy laughed as he poured the final tower.

"Why would you want to do that?"

"I wanted to catch two of them," he said rather seriously.

"Two?" the man said, eager to hear the rationale.

"Yes," Nathaniel exclaimed, expecting his great-grandfather to already know the reason why. "One so Charkey can have a friend. The second Jason and I could take home."

"Oh," the old man pondered. "Do you think a seagull or pelican would like to be that far from the sea?"

Changing the subject, the boy's attention returned to the castle. "How do you want to make this one?"

"Take the shovel and split the tower down the center until the head of the shovel is covered with sand." He took a deep breath while Nathaniel followed the direction. "Now push all the sand that is on the outside of the castle off." The boy followed the instruction. "Now smooth out the side and the bottom where you just scooped it out." The man finished the wall as Nathaniel finished the task. "Take two handfuls of sand and place them on the base, and make it into a half circle…this will form shoulders." The captain waited patiently as Nathaniel completed the task. "Fill the plastic cup with sand; put another tower on top of the shoulders you just made." The old man used the tree and cane to help keep his balance as he stood up. "Now round the sand into an oblong circle." The man stood hovering over his grandson. "We're going to make this into a face. Use two fingers and create his eyes."

Nathaniel laughed. "This is fun, Grandpa."

A smile of approval came over the captain's face. "Under the eyes, pinch some sand into a ridge so you can shape a nose." He handed a stick to the boy. "Use the stick to draw a mouth and eyebrows." The man paused. "Now we have a king to look over the castle and guard it against evil spirits."

"What's the king's name?" the boy asked.

"I believe his name should be King Nathaniel!" the man said with a smile on his face.

"Yes!" The boy shouted. "I am King Nathaniel, the greatest king in the world."

"Put some shells on your castle for windows and doors." The man brushed the sand off his clothes the best he could. "Now it is time for us to admire our handiwork."

"Not yet," Nathaniel cautioned. Stooping by the head he reached into the wet sand, where water had splashed out of the bucket, and retrieved enough sand to form ears on each side of the head. Around the mouth he worked the sand into protruding lips.

The stick that carved the mouth became a comb to give the mannequin hairlines. Nathaniel stood up and wiped his hands together. "Now we are finished!"

"Can't deny your grandmother's blood in you," the man mused with pride.

The two stood in front of the castle smiling at what they had accomplished. Nathaniel walked around it several times, stopping to rearrange the shells or add new ones.

Water started falling lightly to the earth as a bolt of lightning flashed across the ocean, followed swiftly by an atmospheric clap.

"That is our signal to go in," the man said. "If we're lucky we can get some of this good sand on the carpet."

"Yes, I guess it is time to go in." The boy lamented that the special moment was ending. "I hope the castle will be here after the rain so Jason and Momma can look at it."

"I hope so too," the man said, realizing if it was a typical storm only a vestige would remain.

The two started walking toward the smell of fish on the grill with the old man using Nathaniel's shoulder as a cane. Jason left his post, running quickly to join them.

The cool rain increased its descent. Carollyn stood on the porch; hand on hip in an "I told you so" stance.

Charkey's voice was barely audible above the howling wind. "Down the hatch it's going to be a bad one."

"Do you know what I want to be when I grow up?" Nathaniel asked, his arm around his grandfather's waist, Jason supporting the other side.

"No, what?"

"Just like you," the boy said with a smile looking up at his great-grandfather.

"You know people say that rain is tears of joy coming from the angels in heaven." The man hesitated as he wiped his eye. "Today at this very moment you proved them right."

Chapter V

Saturday

*Then shall the King say unto them on his right hand,
Come, ye blessed of my Father, inherit the kingdom
prepared for you from the foundations of the world: For
I was an hungered, and ye gave me meat: I was thirsty,
and ye gave me drink; I was a stranger, and ye took me
in: Naked, and ye clothed me: I was sick, and ye visited
me: I was in prison, and ye came unto me. Then shall the
righteous answer him, saying, Lord, when saw we thee
an hungered, and we fed thee? Or thirsty, and gave thee
drink? When we saw thee a stranger, and took thee in? or
naked, and clothed thee? Or when saw we thee sick, or in
prison, and came unto thee? And the King shall answer
and say unto them, Verily I say unto you, Inasmuch as ye
have done it unto one of the least of these my brethren, ye
have done it unto me.*

—Matthew 25: 34-40

Scarlet and purple intertwined with orange rays peacefully glided off a
rippling sea as the new day approached. Carollyn was quietly pouring
a cup of coffee, trying not to wake her grandfather and sons, all of
whom stayed up way too late watching an *Andy Griffith Show* marathon

on TV. Her last memory was of Barney gallantly criticizing Andy for allowing Opie to have an imaginary friend, Mr. McBeevee. That was around 1:30 AM.

There was a light tap on the porch door, and then the door slowly opened.

"Hello," she heard a whisper as Marissa stepped in.

"Good morning," Carollyn said, smiling.

"The light was on so I thought I would stop to say good morning."

"I'm glad you did. Can I pour you a cup of coffee?" Carollyn asked as she presumptuously pulled a cup from the cupboard.

"Usually I don't drink any, but maybe just a half of cup. Is Daddy still in bed?"

"Still in bed?" Carollyn asked in a mocking tone. "He and the boys stayed up watching TV until I don't know when." Carollyn handed the cup to Marissa. "Let's visit on the porch so we don't wake them up."

The two women quietly moved to the porch and sat at the table overlooking the beach. There was silence for a few minutes as they breathed in the essence of nature. A rainbow mimicking the colors of Charkey spread across the fresh sunrise. On the far horizon they could barely see the fins of dolphins rejoicing in the new day.

"So are you ready for the party tonight?" Marissa asked, not quite knowing what to say. Nervously, she twirled the ends of her hair.

"Yes, I am looking forward to meeting Vanessa and David and their children and getting to know you better. Granddaddy is much more excited than he is letting on. Is there anything I can do to help?"

"Nothing; we're bringing an extra cook in to help with the preparation and Trudy has volunteered to work on her day off. After my morning walk I'm going to go set up the Sand Castle Room. Trudy and I decided to make it a buffet. When Daddy has one of our family reunions, there's no telling who will pop in. It's always smart to have plenty of food."

"Has anyone else been invited?" Carollyn asked.

"I believe Daddy invited Uncle Gus, but I'm not sure. It's kind of like phone tag; one person gets invited and then they invite another. It really doesn't matter; before the evening is over you will feel as if you have met half of Daytona. There are always a lot of unexpected guests."

"Who's Uncle Gus?"

"Gus is one of Daddy's oldest and dearest friends. He was the best man at Daddy's wedding. And Daddy was best man at Gus's weddings … all six of them." Marissa let out a small giggle. "He has a touch of Alzheimer's now, so they don't get together like they used to. Some days he remembers Daddy, and sometimes he doesn't."

"He doesn't live alone?" The physician in Carollyn surfaced.

"No, he has lived in a nursing home for about a year. For a while he was living with his daughter, but he became too difficult to handle. Daddy was going to take him in until Vanessa and I convinced him that he was better off in a home. If he would have moved in here they would both be totally incapacitated." She paused briefly to sip her coffee. "Gus probably is happier in the home anyway. There are a lot of activities for him to enjoy specifically designed for the people living with dementia. His daughter and granddaughter visit on a regular basis, so there is always family around."

Carollyn noticed the purity of aura encompassing Marissa. It was obvious why her grandfather loved her so much.

"Are you enjoying your visit?" Marissa cut into her thoughts.

"Yes, very much. We feel so fortunate to have this opportunity to know Granddaddy."

"You finding him means the world to daddy," Marissa said with a sweet, tender smile. "Just looking at his face I can see the peace has settled in his soul. I can't tell you how long I've been praying for this."

"You have been very kind to him," Carollyn said as she brought the cup of coffee to her lips.

"How could I not? The karmic values of the universe would have it no other way."

"Still, I appreciate all you are doing," Carollyn said, the tone of her voice expressing sincerity.

Marissa thought for a second before opening her pain. "In 1992 I met this man, Danny, when I was in school in Seattle. He was a bit older than I and totally won me over with his worldliness. He turned me onto LSD and psychedelic mushrooms. I was taking trips, unbelievable trips, without ever leaving our pad. Danny said he would always be there for me." Marissa stopped as if the pain was suddenly new.

Carollyn held her trembling hand.

"When I became pregnant, he asked me who the father was. I became infuriated; I threw a lamp at him, gashing his forehead." She paused to capture her breath, wondering what evoked her to reveal this wound. "Danny fell to the floor, grasping his head, blood squirting all over the room. My first thought was to run. But I gained my courage and ran to his side to help him. I really did love him. His every word was heaven sent. He looked up at me and said 'I hope your child isn't going to be black.'" A small tear formed in her eye. "Please, don't take offense at this, but I have never been with a black man. Danny was just trying to hurt me."

Carollyn gently patted Marissa's hand.

"He stood up and then told me he couldn't handle being a father, and then he walked out of our trailer. As he was leaving he took the time to take all of the money from the desk, most of which I had earned."

"What did you do?" a compassionate Carollyn asked.

"Foolishly, I waited around for a few weeks, hoping that he would change his mind and return. I'm not sure why I wanted him back; probably I just was afraid of being alone."

"What about your parents?"

Marissa laughed sarcastically. "I've been on my own since I was sixteen. My real father took off before I was born, if my mother even knew who he was. I was raised by a series of 'uncles' who really didn't care if I was there or not. When I was sixteen, my mother brought a man home who found me more attractive than her. One night while she was passed out in a drunken stupor, he tried to rape me. I managed to escape. That night I left home and never turned back. My mother probably used the agony of me leaving as an excuse to continue to get high and drunk. This I do know; she never made a strong effort to locate me. I lived a few blocks from her and worked at a grocery store where she shopped. Part of me wanted her to find me; another part never wanted to see her again."

She paused for a second; her eyes seemed to glass over. "After a few months the part that didn't want to see my mother won the battle. I left Southern California and moved to Seattle."

"Why Seattle?"

Marissa laughed nervously. "On my limited budget, it was as far as I could get on the Greyhound."

"Have you ever had an opportunity to reconcile with your mother?" Carollyn asked in reflection of the reunion she was now experiencing.

Marissa shook her head sadly. "I know this is going to sound shallow, but some things are best to remain untouched."

Carollyn patted Marissa's hand knowingly. Carollyn's mind went back to the pain her mother lived with because of the alienation with her parents and then the pain she felt now from missing her mother. She could not help feel that Marissa was suffering more than she was willing to admit.

They sat in silence for a few minutes as they watched a grey and brown rabbit slowly hop around the parameter of the house. A long ear popped in and out of the shrubbery. When in full view they could tell that one of the ears was badly mangled, probably as a result of an attack from a dog or a cat.

"Anyway," Marissa continued, "I had done fairly well on my own. I studied and got a GED. I enrolled in a community college, and then I met Danny."

"I'm sorry for your pain," Carollyn said softly.

"After I decided Danny wasn't coming home I became desperate." The story sounded as if it was recent. "I decided to get an abortion." Marissa broke down in tears.

Carollyn stood up, leaned over her new sister, and hugged her.

In a few minutes Marissa regained enough composure to continue. "Still, not knowing what to do with my life, I decided to leave Seattle. I sold my car and bought a bus ticket to Tampa."

"Why Tampa?"

Marissa laughed. "Danny was from there, so I foolishly rationalized that even though we were not together, I would feel closer to him." She stopped briefly to wipe a tear. "Also, his mother lived in Tampa, and I thought there might be a small chance he would return home."

"That makes sense," Carollyn reassured, not being sure if it really did.

"It is sad." The tears continued. "Even after all he did, I would have accepted him back."

"Unfortunately," Carollyn reassured, "many women in your situation would have done the same thing."

"I got a job at a Village Inn on Dale Mabry Highway, as a waitress. For the next six months I circled Danny's mother's house looking for just a glimpse of him. One day, I rang the doorbell, pretending I was the Avon lady." She laughed. "His mother became real curious when I didn't have any products to sell her."

Carollyn smiled, understanding that this was not uncommon behavior for a person that felt betrayed.

"One morning I came to the realization that my life was going nowhere. There was no Danny, and even if there was, I did not want or need him. It was time to leave Tampa and the memory of the bum. The only problem was that I really had no clue as to where to go. One of the cooks offered to give me money if I drove him to Daytona, so I said why not."

Carollyn nodded that she was listening.

"I should have taken the money before we left Tampa, because when we arrived he stiffed me."

"Oh no," Carollyn whispered, putting her fingers to her lips.

"Anyway, I decided to head north, maybe to Atlanta or wasn't sure where. My gas gauge was broken, so I didn't know how much fuel I had left. My calculation was that I could get to Jacksonville and probably find someone to bum a bit of cash from or possibly do day labor to take me further. If I had to, I could waitress a couple days for tips."

"That must have been dreadful."

"I ran out of gas as I was passing Charkey's, so I allowed the car to coast in. I remembered getting out of the car and kicking the tire in disgust. Looking up toward the window, Vanessa was looking out at me. Having no pride left, I decided to give them a sob story and hopefully get a meal and a couple gallons of gas. I definitely had no plans of staying in Daytona."

"But you stayed," Carollyn commented.

"When I reached the door, I noticed a 'help wanted' sign. I asked to see the manager. When I met your grandfather and Vanessa, I looked your grandfather straight in the eye and said, God has sent me here to liberate you from your labor deficiencies."

Carollyn burst into laughter.

"That's precisely the reaction your grandfather had. However, Vanessa had pity on me. She and Daddy interviewed me for about an hour. For the first time probably in my life, I came totally clean with who I was and where I'd been." She paused for a few seconds. "Daddy just has a strange power that prevents me from lying to him."

"That must have been difficult," Carollyn said softly.

"It was the best thing that ever happened to me. At the end of the interview, Vanessa turned to Daddy and said, 'There's an old Chinese proverb that says give a man a fish and you feed him for a day, give him a fishing pole and teach him how to fish and you feed him for a lifetime.'" Marissa stopped for a few seconds to notice the interest in Carollyn's face. "Daddy looked at me and said, 'You are hired. The only stipulation is that you need to take our good faith and return to it us. Not for the sake of paying us back, but rather for the sake of honoring your true self.'"

"Wow, that is a Zen concept," Carollyn mused.

"He put me to work right away, gave me an advance for my uniform, and put me up on a temporary basis at Uncle Gus's apartment building, while I was getting on my feet. Of course," she laughed, "he made me do a few alterations of my personal appearance."

"That is a lovely tribute; it is no wonder you love him so much."

"He restored my soul and undoubtedly saved my life," Marissa beamed. "After working at Charkey's for a few months, Daddy called me into his office." The lady hesitated momentarily. "I thought I was going to be chewed out about spilling lemonade on a customer." Marissa giggled as her face blushed slightly. "The boy was getting fresh and I thought it was my only recourse."

"Oh no," Carollyn laughed.

"Daddy actually had called me in to talk about my drug addiction. He said that my dilated pupils were a dead giveaway—that early in each shift my language was a bit slurred, progressively getting better the further I was into a shift."

"What did you say?"

"Being a bit nervous, I answered with my usual sarcasm. I asked him when he became Colombo." She paused for a moment. "He just stared lovingly at me and said nothing. The silence was more than I could stand. I immediately burst into tears, confessing my entire ordeal with drugs."

"That must have been difficult," Carollyn said as she patted Marissa's hand.

"Daddy made it easy," Marissa sighed. "He had a list of agencies that offered assistance as well as a name of a person connected with AA and NA." A tear formed in her eye with the memories. "He said that he would arrange for someone to cover my shifts while I got the help I needed."

"Wow, he really understood," Carollyn said.

"The words he used to convince me to go were simple but are forever etched in my memory. 'Marissa, you have two choices. You can run away from Charkey's and the problem. Or you can stand firm and beat this demon and other demons that have been torturing you for years. My bet is that you will be much happier conquering the demons.' He then gave me a big hug and said, 'Let's go find some help.'"

"What a wonderfully compassionate man."

"There's more. After I had worked at Charkey's for a year, he dictated I return to college. He said that I was too bright not to have an education. Please understand, he did not give me an option; he insisted that I enroll. As Daddies will do, he paid the entire tuition. The original deal was for me to pay him back after graduation. I've been trying to pay him back for seven or eight years; he keeps ripping the checks up or conveniently forgetting to cash them. If I give him cash, mysteriously it turns up in my desk drawer or pocketbook. So I got even. Mark, who is helping to remodel the restaurant, refuses to take any money for his labor." They both laughed. "It's my way of honoring my true self."

Carollyn stared at the redhead sitting across from her, totally in awe of how her grandfather helped restore her life. The true love he had for humanity was a testament to the man he truly is. He displayed proof that good could evolve from of all people.

"So, why did you decide to seek your grandfather out?" Marissa asked hesitantly, "Not that it is any of my business."

Carollyn smiled broadly. "Ever since I was a young girl there was a yearning in my heart to know him. It may have been because my mother constantly quoted his wisdom, or because he was a mystery. Daddy and Momma rarely spoke of him, other than the quotes. Once in awhile, when they thought I was asleep, they would discuss Daytona and the bitterness that transpired here. Daddy would viciously refer to it as Charkey's Little House of Horrors. I think my momma was conflicted between reconciling with her father and remaining at peace with Daddy.

Also, she was somewhat reluctant to try, because of the uncertainty of the type of reception she would receive. It is a shame Momma could not see the man that Granddaddy has become or probably always was. Finding him is my way of honoring my mother." She paused for a second. "And yes, it is your business. You are our family now."

Marissa did not reply verbally at first. She reached to Carollyn to give a warm welcoming embrace. "Welcome home," she whispered in her ear.

"I'm glad I'm here." Carollyn wept.

"I am sure your mother is here with you," Marissa continued. "I can feel her presence. Actually, I have felt it for some time now, maybe a year or two. Before you arrived, I was not able to identify whom the energy was coming from. I am sure that your mother is aware of who her father has become." Marissa smiled warmly at Carollyn and then gave her a reassuring hug that became a warm embrace.

The ladies chatted for the next thirty minutes, getting to know each other. Together they embraced the freshness of a new day and reveled in the beginning of a new sisterhood. The bond of love and respect was taking root. It promised to grow into a strong-stemmed, beautiful flower.

After Marissa continued on her walk, Carollyn sat on the porch feeling relaxed and freer than she had ever felt before. It wasn't long before her grandfather, cup of coffee in hand, joined her. They both sat in silence for a few minutes meditating on the waves.

"Momma never spoke about Uncle Gus," Carollyn said, sounding puzzled. "Did she know him?"

The old man stared longingly as the high tide made its presence known. In some ways time had been good to him, yet in others it had laughed in his face. Not only had he lost his daughter, then his wife, but a dreaded curse had a death grip on his best friend.

"Gus and I grew up together," the man recalled. "Gus, Denny O'Reilly, and I were glued together at the hip since we were toddlers. The townfolk always referred to us as the three musketeers. As we became older and began playing baseball together, our opponents started to calling us the terrifying threesome." The man stopped to sip the coffee, and perhaps to end the story without further explanation.

After a momentary silence, Carollyn became antsy for the remainder of the story. "So, are you going to finish the story? Or are you going to let me sit here guessing?"

"Uncle Gus was your momma's godfather," the old man added, reopening the saga.

"Then why didn't Momma mention him?" Carollyn asked, wanting to know the rest of the story.

"His father was the minister of the Baptist church. He wasn't really fond of Gus hanging out with Denny and I. He always complained that being non-churchgoers, we were a bad influence. By that time Grandma Ruth had quit forcing me to go to church. If the entire truth were to be known we were probably all bad influences on each other."

Carollyn laughed, picturing tales from *The Adventures of Tom Sawyer*.

"In order to preserve the comradeship Denny and I elected to become protectors of the faith. This probably caused Gus's father even more anguish. Now the predicament was how to keep us apart." The man coughed. "When Gus turned eighteen, his father convinced him to serve his country in the military. I remember him preaching to Gus, 'It will make a God-fearing man out of you.' To his father's dismay, Denny decided to enlist with him. They tried to convince me to follow; but I had just been signed by the Red Sox. If I had known that I would be drafted a year later, I would have put Boston on hold."

The man paused as a seagull stopped on the porch to eat a piece of stale bread left from the night before. "I always wondered why Gus and Denny did not join me in the ranks of professional ballplayers; they were both better players. I didn't find out until years later that Gus's father never gave him the telegram invitation to tryout for the St. Louis Cardinals. Denny was invited to tryout for the Brooklyn Dodgers, but felt that it was patriotic to follow Gus into the army." He paused for a few seconds. "It made me feel a bit disloyal to my buddies not following them."

"You were just living your dream; there is nothing wrong with that," Carollyn reassured the old man. "What did you do that caused the ire of Gus' father?"

"Kid stuff," the man laughed. "In the spring we would play hooky from school to go to baseball games or surfing. We encouraged Gus

121

to exchange Bible study for fishing. On Halloween we would soap car windows." The man shook his head. "There was one Halloween that the local police picked us up for throwing eggs at a side of a building. None of us were able to sit down for a week."

"Ouch." Carollyn laughed.

"The problem was we were innocent, at least that time. Even though we pleaded with our parents, they took the word of the law over ours."

"That must have been humiliating," Carollyn said as she continued to laugh.

"We all figured that we deserved the punishment to make up for all the times we failed to get caught."

"The type of kid stuff my boys better never try," Carollyn said, laughing. "Hardly enough to have you branded a delinquent."

"After I received my notice from the draft board, I returned to Daytona to wait my scheduled time. Partly because I had nothing to do, partly to irritate Gus's father, I returned to church. That fall I met Emma at the church picnic. Indirectly, I guess, Gus was responsible for us meeting."

"What happened to Denny?" Carollyn asked, not being ready to give up the story.

The man grew quiet, his skin turned ashen. A lump in his throat prevented him from speaking immediately; a tear welled in his eye.

"Denny and Gus were deployed to Germany to help defeat the Nazis." The man stopped, resisting continuing the story, but forged on for his own liberation. "May 6, 1945, one day prior to the German's surrender, their platoon was attacked by one of the final Nazi campaigns. Thinking the war was all but over, the troop had been at ease and was unprepared for the offensive. Gus and Denny made it safely to a foxhole, where they endured relentless bombing for over six hours. They were low on ammunition and supplies. Their commander felt that the only hope was to last to nightfall, as he didn't think the enemy would try to advance during the dark. The captain had already radioed for reinforcements and was assured that help would arrive before daybreak. Just before sunset one of the Germans was able to sneak close enough to the foxhole to hurl a grenade into it. In order to save his buddies, Denny dove onto the explosive and sucked it into his abdomen."

"That's a tragic story," Carollyn said, tears in her eyes.

"I was at a hospital in England at the time, recovering from my own afflictions," the old man groaned. "I didn't even learn of Denny's death until long after his burial. The sad part is Gus' self-righteous father refused to perform the funeral because Denny was Catholic, even though his family never attended Mass."

"Denny saved his son's life," Carollyn protested.

"Gus decided to remain in the army until retirement. He vowed to never step in his father's house again." The old man took a break to capture his thoughts. "When Emma and I were married, we chose to do it in the Methodist Church."

"I understand your anger." The tone of disgust was present in Carollyn's voice.

"Please, don't misunderstand me; I wasn't disenchanted with the Baptist Church or anyone in their congregation. My hatred was directed toward the devil in the pulpit."

"As it should have been," Carollyn agreed.

"Gus spent the next twenty-two years proudly serving our country. He had the good fortune to travel to many different countries, experience many cultures. Every year he would return faithfully to Daytona on leave." The old man laughed. "On three of those occasions he brought a woman with him to give me the honor of being best man."

"Did he ever reconcile with his father?" Carollyn asked.

"Not really. His father was asked to leave the church a short time after Denny's death. From what I understand he moved to Jacksonville, where he led a flock foolish enough to hire him." The man rubbed his nose. "Gus would drive to Jacksonville one day during his leave to visit his mother and brothers and sister, but said very little to his father."

"What about Denny's family?" an intrigued Carollyn asked.

The captain was still debating whether to reveal more. "His folks took the tragedy really hard, especially with him being an only child. The distress caused his mother to lose her mind; she spent the remainder of her life in an asylum. After putting the mother away, his father pulled up stakes and wandered aimlessly around the country, surviving by panhandling or doing odd jobs. Rumor has it that he occasionally would visit Denny's tomb and then go to see his wife; however, I never saw him around town." There was more hesitation. "Denny's daughter continues to make her home in Daytona."

"Daughter?" a confused Carollyn asked.

"Prior to going to war, Denny had a premonition of his own demise. At least that is what he told those he was close to. One of these people was Lisa Gallery. She was the only person that could make Denny's head turn. We all met Lisa when her family moved to town while we were in seventh grade. Immediately, we all fell deep into puppy love."

"Denny was hit the hardest, and much to my and Gus' chagrin she felt the same about him. They never dated anyone else. If Denny wasn't with us, he was with her. At times it became a little annoying," the man said, laughing. "Once he skipped an important baseball tournament to be at her bedside after she had her tonsils removed." The man paused to collect his thoughts before continuing. "To my knowledge, and I think I would know, Denny did not touch her until after he enlisted. Though it was something 'good girls' didn't do, Lisa and Denny decided to consummate their love."

"Oh my," Carollyn exclaimed. "Why didn't they just get married?"

"Probably the same reason Emma and I didn't. I was afraid of leaving someone I loved a widow." The man paused. "I couldn't take that burden into battle with me."

"I understand," a solemn Carollyn said.

The preacher from the church, Gus' father, attempted to convince Mr. and Mrs. Gallery to send Lisa to a home for unwed mothers until the baby was born, after which she should give the child up for adoption." A stern look covered the old man's face. "He had no right to interfere."

Realizing the 1940s was a totally different time, Carollyn wondered if the parents considered it.

Reading his granddaughter's mind, the man continued, "The Gallerys were enraged that the minister would be so bold to offer the unsolicited advice." The old man cleared his throat. "They refused to even consider it. They were so insulted that they switched to a church with a much less judgmental minister."

"Good for them," Carollyn cheered. "Did they hold the fiasco against Gus?"

"Not for a second. We all thought Gus was adopted anyway, because he wasn't a thing like his old man." The man stared at the ground. "Gus was probably the most accepting person I have ever known; except maybe Emma. Luckily, Lisa's parents were supportive of their daughter. With the help of friends and siblings she raised a very fine young lady, Renda. Now she has seven grandchildren and twenty-one great-grandchildren."

"And you were one of the friends that helped her?" Carollyn asked, already knowing the answer.

"In the memory of Denny," the old man whispered. "Gus sent part of every paycheck to Lisa. We both played the role of uncle."

"Did Lisa ever marry?"

"Lisa told me once that Denny was the kindest and gentlest man she had ever met. She felt if she were to marry she would be doing the man a disservice by constantly comparing him to her first love. Lisa was also of strong opinion that Renda would adopt a new man as her father, and that would tarnish the image of Denny."

"Renda is an unusual name; what nationality is it?"

"American Indian, I think Cherokee," the man replied. "Lisa's grand-mother was full-blooded Indian." The captain scratched his right ear. "Don't quote me, but I believe that it means 'enchantress.'"

"What a beautifully sad love story," Carollyn smiled, patting her grandfather's hand. "It sounds like it was an enchanting relationship; the name fits."

For the next half hour they watched the boys play on the beach. Marissa, at the captain's request, had bought them boogie boards. Carollyn and the captain found great delight in watching the old sea show her mastery over the young boys.

"Being here is like being in heaven," she smiled.

"Paradise," the man mused.

"Tell me more about Grandma Ruth," Carollyn inquired.

The man smiled.

A gray cat slowly walked up on the porch. Seductively he purred, asking for food. When it was understood the pleas would go unanswered he slowly hopped down the steps.

"You feed one and a hundred will scramble to your doorsteps at all kind of ungodly hours, all begging for handouts," the man huffed.

Carollyn laughed and shook her head.

"Grandma Ruth was the mortar that held our family together," the captain remembered. "She was a strong, saintly woman. I think the best description would be austere. My recollection is that she always had a Bible in one hand and a strap in another." There was a brief pause. "She took great pride in being self sufficient. I guess she had to, with Grandpappy spending most of his time at sea."

"That must have been difficult," Carollyn commented.

"According to Daddy, it was probably the only thing that prevented them from killing each other. It seems as if she was always preaching to Grandpappy about his sinful ways. And he was constantly providing inspiration for the sermon." The man sneezed. "She and Grandpappy met soon after he moved to Daytona. If I have my history straight, Grandpappy went to work for her father, my great-grandfather. Of course she was just a toddler at the time, so they had a long courtship."

Carollyn laughed.

"Grandma Ruth was used to her father being gone for extended periods, so having a husband doing the same wasn't out of the ordinary."

Carollyn smiled, realizing how nice it was to have a husband that was constantly underfoot.

"Anyway, after Momma died she helped with us kids. I can still remember every Sunday morning before church was ear inspection day. One by one, she grabbed our ears and lectured how it would be embarrassing to go in public with kids who had dirty ears. She would take a rag dipped in kerosene and scrub each ear."

"Kerosene?" Carollyn said, the expression on her face turning to a frown.

"I know it wasn't the best smelling cologne, but it did keep them clean," the man laughed.

"Kerosene," Carollyn said again, shaking her head in disgust.

"Even though Daddy quit going to church, Grandma Ruth continued to force Rufus and me to attend. Every night before we went to bed, she read Bible stories to us and made sure we said our prayers."

"Was she a good cook?" Carollyn asked, attempting to vanquish the kerosene from her mind.

The old man's face lit up. "The best! I can still smell her chicken and dumplings. The cookies and pies she made melted in my mouth." The man stopped to think for a second. "Sunday dinner was always the biggest meal of the week. We all had to dress in our best clothes. Grandma always invited friends and neighbors. After all the food was put on the table, we prayed our blessings. Even Daddy would bow his head. Of course the restaurant was closed on Sunday, a tradition we continue today. After dinner we would sit on the porch for hours listening to Grandma's stories."

"Sounds nice," Carollyn commented.

"While we sat, she sewed or knitted. Her hands were always busy. 'Idle hands are the devil's helper,' she would always say."

"I bet she was a talented seamstress."

The man nodded in acknowledgment. "She sewed Momma's wedding gown. It was the same one that Emma wore." The old man paused for a second, his voice saddened. "Your mother would have worn it, if not for me." The captain lowered his head for a second. "Vanessa wore it when she married David. So did her eldest daughter."

"She was a wonderful matriarch," Carollyn remarked.

"She was," the man mused. "Grandma Ruth was a big part of my upbringing. I think I grieved her passing even more than my daddy's."

"It must have been nice for your father to have the help of his mother."

The captain smiled and said, "She was a blessing to everyone that met her."

The rest of the afternoon was spent with idle talk and watching the boys try to outsmart the tide. Just as they felt they had mastered the waves, the rain came.

The early afternoon shower vanished as fast as it arrived, leaving the air a bit more crisp, though the Florida humidity would soon take over. The sun escaped from the spell of the clouds reflecting brightly off the white sand below. At four o'clock it was time to head for Charkey's to the family reunion, or union as Nathaniel referred to it. The boys ran ahead of the grownups so they could visit with Charkey, who had returned to his throne earlier in the day.

The first thing the captain noticed, upon entering the restaurant, were the new pictures on display. Immediately to the right was a picture of Jason and his big catch. Inscribed on a brass tag was "Jason Out-Duels Mako." Beside that there was a picture of Carollyn, the captain, and the boys talking in the restaurant, evidently taken by Trudy on their first night in Daytona. There was also a picture of both boys talking to Charkey on the old man's porch. On one of the support poles the picture of Terisita and Dominick hung with a marker above that read "Ghost Legends." Obviously this plaque was placed to incite lively conversations.

Carollyn and her grandfather walked around looking closely at each picture on the wall. When they arrived at Grandpappy's photo, Carollyn winced again, then lovingly accepted him as part of her history and herself as a part of his legacy. The fierceness in his eyes vanished; she no longer felt the hate lingering behind. Then, she thought, maybe it was her hate she was feeling, not his. On another support beam there was a portrait of a regal bald eagle sitting in a nest atop a giant tree overlooking a lake. Carollyn thought about how noble the bird looked and wondered if mankind would ever reach such nobility.

"Momma, come quickly," Nathaniel screamed with delight, standing in the doorway of the Sand Castle Room.

She hurried to his side while motioning for him to keep his voice down so as not to disturb the patrons.

Pointing toward a painting in the middle of the room, he continued, "Momma, that's Grandpa's and my sand castle."

In the middle of the far wall was a large painting of a five-towered sand castle, exactly like the one destroyed by the rain the day before. Purple haze and charcoal gray blended to create a mysterious skyline. White-capped teal waves gently met the shoreline. The castle was constructed of golden sand on a white beach. Detail by detail, this was the architectural design the captain had been creating for decades.

Carollyn gasped in horror, placing both hands to her cheeks as her jaw dropped in agony. This was the castle that she made with her parents on Tybee Island. The one destroyed by men wielding hatred.

"Momma, isn't it great?" Nathaniel shrieked in delight as the two moved toward the painting.

The old man grabbed the boy's shoulder from behind. "I've asked Marissa to pack this painting to ship to you in Chicago on Monday morning. It was painted by your Grandmother Melissa." Motioning to all the paintings in the room, he continued, "All these paintings were Melissa's. This one, though, is my favorite because I have made this with so many different people. When Emma and I first started dating, before I went to war, we created this design."

"Momma, did you hear? Grandpa is going to send this to us!" Nathaniel's excitement echoed hauntingly into Carollyn's ears.

Carollyn's mind drifted back to the horrible fifth birthday. The Klansman's voice ringing above the words of her grandfather, "Boy, don't you know the likes of you don't belong here." A vision of the ringleader, a young man of about twenty-five who already had a receding hairline, ran through her mind. "If you ain't gone by the time my boys and I get our hoods, your pretty little daughter will be missing her daddy." The girl's legs started to tremble just as they did on that night.

"Momma," Nathaniel broke the spell, "Can we hang it in my room?"

"Let's talk about it later," she cautioned. "We need to see if we have enough room."

"Sure we do," the young boy insisted.

"Would you mind helping Marissa get the buffet table set up?" the old man asked Nathaniel, recognizing that his granddaughter was troubled by the picture. As the young boy scurried off, he turned his attention to the still trembling girl. "I'm sorry," he said softly, putting his own trembling hand on her shoulder, "I didn't mean to upset you."

She reached up to hold his hand tightly. "It's all right," she sighed.

"Is there something we need to talk about?" the concerned grandfather asked.

"No, I'm really alright." She tried to sound reassuring. "The picture just reminds me of another time in my life."

"If it would be better, I can find an excuse not to send the painting."

Carollyn smiled, peering over her shoulder. "Let's discuss it later; tonight is a night for family, friends, fellowship, and laughter. I'll be okay. Why don't you go find me a bottle of Charkey's while I study my mother's masterpiece a bit longer?"

"If you're sure you're going be okay," her grandfather said.

She nodded as he walked away. As a mother she could not allow the memory of hatred to deprive her son of the painting he idolized. As a daughter she could not expose this painting to her father and risk dredging up humiliating memories. Carollyn was truly conflicted. She thought about the dilemma, not knowing what to do.

"That's my favorite painting in the entire restaurant." A soft, gentle voice came from behind.

Carollyn turned to see a middle-aged man with a goatee and a long, sandy blond ponytail to her left. He looked as if he were frozen in a generation lost, with his tie-dye shirt, khaki shorts, and rubber flip flops. Without an introduction she knew this was Mark.

"Sometimes to really live what the artist was saying; it is necessary to shut your mind to all things and just breathe in the picture."

Carollyn frowned, "How do you that?"

Mark smiled shyly. "I close my eyes and put my hands over a section of the painting. I don't touch it; I just get close enough to feel it. Then I concentrate on the vibrations that the painting sends out. All things have vibrations because all items are composed of energy."

And they refer to Marissa as moonbeam, Carollyn thought.

"If you allow it, the artist will speak to you through universal energy left behind," Mark said with unbridled confidence in his voice.

"Okay," Carollyn mumbled, "and if I feel that a painting represents a bad experience, how do I conquer that?"

The man stared at the painting. "A piece of canvas with colors splashed on it can not be evil. Only the artist creating the work can leave foul residue behind. If the artist is pure of heart, as the one who painted this, then only good vibrations remain."

"What makes you think the artist that painted this was pure of heart?"

"The vibrations from the castle," Mark responded quickly. "Of course, you already know the heart of your mother."

Carollyn smiled at the man. "Yes, I do."

"Please, do as I suggested. When you open your eyes, see if the painting has transformed into a piece of you," Mark said with conviction.

Carefully, she looked at the painting, marveling at her mother's artistic eye. The contrast and meshing of the colors was surreal. The background created a three-dimensional appearance as the castle appeared to be protruding from the page. One of Melissa's artistic talents was to make each painting somewhat flawed so it appeared more realistic. In the sand castle the walls were slightly uneven, just like they would be in real life. "Imperfection in a work of art gives the piece character, just as imperfection in humanity does," was her mantra.

Carollyn held her hands close to the painting as instructed to experience all of its energy. Reluctantly, she closed her eyes, then quickly opened them, then closed them again. Starting with the first tower, she felt the texture of the painting, letting her soul understand what her mother was experiencing as the brush touched the canvas.

Immediately a sense of warm innocence trickled through her veins. At the second tower the thought of a mysterious and open universe was at the forefront of her consciousness. Briefly she opened her eyes to contemplate the painting. She came to the tower with the sculpture of the head. Lightly, she placed her hands over the face. Shutting her eyes, she allowed her mind to go totally blank; when her consciousness was totally still, she removed her hand and opened her eyes. Carollyn was stunned by the face on the castle. It was that of her father, the king of her mother's life. Her heart sang of reconciliation with the past. Beyond the grave her mother had taught yet another lesson. "All things in God's universe have some good in them. It is your responsibility to find it."

She turned toward Mark, astonishment written on her face.

"I will help Marissa wrap it on Monday to ship to Chicago," he said with a beaming smile.

"Thank you," she gasped, "for teaching me to see." Carollyn turned back toward the sand castle. Without another word Mark retreated.

"Carollyn," the old man interrupted.

"This painting speaks to me," she said without turning. "It captures the very essence of Momma's truth."

The man smiled and rubbed her shoulder, unsure as to what had changed her mind. "Carollyn, there is someone I would like for you to meet."

She turned to face the man. Standing at his side was a gorgeous lady who had the appearance of a model.

"I'd like for you to meet Vanessa," the old man said, obviously happy that they were meeting.

The two ladies smiled at each other. Carollyn extended her hand; Vanessa ignored the gesture and hugged her.

"It is nice to get this opportunity to meet you," Vanessa whispered. "Daddy has been talking my head off about you every day."

"I'm happy too," Carollyn smiled. "I have heard some pretty nice things about you too."

"I'll get both of you a beer," the old man volunteered. "Why don't you find a seat and get acquainted with one another."

Vanessa turned toward a table and spotted Gus walking into the room. "Uncle Gus," she called out. Gus' escort waved hello as the two walked toward the ladies.

"This is my Uncle Gus," Vanessa said excitably, "and his granddaughter, Sheila." Turning to them she continued, "This is Carollyn."

Gus studied Vanessa's face carefully and said, "I don't know you. Who are you calling uncle?"

"Grandpa," Sheila countered, "you remember Vanessa. She used to live in your apartment building."

"I don't have an apartment building," he stammered.

"That's okay, Uncle Gus," Vanessa continued. "We will get to know each other over dinner."

Sheila turned to Carollyn and said, "I'm so sorry about my grandfather."

Carollyn gave her a knowing smile. "That's all right; I really understand. It is so nice to have the opportunity to meet you."

The captain returned with their beer. Gus stared at him blankly, having enough cognition to recognize the face of his oldest friend but lacking the ability to weave all the thoughts together.

"Gus, it's great to see you," the captain said. He reached to Sheila and pecked her on the cheek. "Thanks for coming, dear."

"We wouldn't miss it," she said sincerely. Dark circles colored the skin under her eyes. Her high Scandinavian cheekbones were tense. The nightly visits to her grandfather's nursing home were catching up with her. The pressure of not knowing what type of reception she would receive was wearing down her psyche. The doctor and staff had advised her to cut the visits to only a few times of week, especially since the incidents of him recognizing her were decreasing. She wasn't willing to take a chance of missing one glimpse of her grandfather before he slipped into a permanent fog.

Gus looked at the old man, a crooked smile covering his face, "Buddy," he managed to say but for the moment was unable to find more words.

"Yes, we've been friends for a long time, ever since childhood," the old man acknowledged him.

The two stared at each other affectionately as the rest of the guests slowly gathered in the room.

Trudy and one of the cook's assistants started to fill the buffet table with the mélange of lobster, crabs (in shells already cut down the center), grouper, swordfish, and for the land-lovers, prime rib with the captain's secret horseradish sauce. Side items included fried green tomatoes, baked potatoes, sweet potatoes, fresh green beans, corn fritters, and hush puppies.

"I don't have my ..." Gus stuttered, "my ... ah, stick thing."

"Stick thing?" Sheila asked patiently.

"You know," he raised his voice in frustration, "to fish with."

"Don't worry about the fishing pole," the old man jumped in. "You can use one of mine." The man coughed. "Why don't we eat before we go fishing?"

Gus looked at him perplexed; but appeared to be in agreement with the old man.

"Thank you," Sheila mouthed.

The captain turned to the rest of the room. "Excuse me, please," he said in a loud, commanding voice, as though barking orders from the deck of a ship. Silence fell over the room. "First I would like to thank everyone for coming to our family reunion. I know this was short notice, so that makes it even more special. A special thanks to Marissa for making all the arrangements. And to the staff of Charkey's for all the extra work they put into preparation of the feast. It all looks succulent, as I would expect from the finest restaurant on the east coast of Florida. I would like to introduce the guests of honor, my granddaughter, Carollyn, and her two fine sons, Jason and Nathaniel."

Everyone clapped.

"Before we partake of this celebration, I would like for us all join hands in prayer," the man said as a mischievous grin covered his face.

The group formed a circle with everyone clasping hands.

"As is tradition," the old man continued, "the newest member of the family has the honor of saying grace." He looked at Carollyn and winked.

She gave him a dirty look; but went with the flow. "Before we pray," she began, "I want to extend my thanks to my grandfather for accepting my boys and me into his family. It is also very exciting for me to have an opportunity to meet Granddaddy's extended family."

She smiled broadly at the old man. "In the short few days we have been here, I have discovered a bright, articulate, amazing man. It is obvious why he is so loved." Carollyn squeezed his hand tight. "Our Lord has bestowed many blessings on me; however, this week is one of the most special." She paused, letting go of Vanessa's hand briefly to wipe a tear from her eye. "I believe strongly in God and give him credit for all he has provided."

All eyes, even Gus,' were fixated on Carollyn.

"However, I also respect that some of us have may have different spiritual beliefs," Carollyn continued. "We should embrace that diversity. For this reason I do not particularly like public prayers. I believe that prayer is personal between a person and God. What I say to God, may not be what you have in your heart. It is a tradition among my friends and colleagues when we gather to hold hands as we are doing here and share a moment of silence in unity. This gives everyone the opportunity to meditate on what is in their heart and soul. It provides God with the opportunity to hear all our prayers and not just the speaker's."

There was a pause as all tension evaporated from the room.

"Join me, please, in a brief period of silence. Pray, meditate, reflect, or do as you wish." Carollyn bowed her head in silent prayer.

Most of the guests bowed their heads; some kept their eyes open and stared at the person across from them, the floor, or the sea. A few reflected on their blessings, some on their grief. All felt serene. Finally, Carollyn announced in a barely audible tone, "Amen."

"Amen," the group chanted in unison.

Carollyn squeezed the old man's hand tightly whispering, "I will get even."

"I'm sorry," Vanessa said. "I should have warned you that Daddy would try to stick you with the prayer." She giggled. "But you handled it well."

They both laughed.

"Jason and Nathaniel, if you could start the line, and we will all fall in after you," the captain barked.

"Nice prayer," David said as he stretched his hand out to introduce himself. "I'm David, Vanessa's husband."

"It's a pleasure to meet you; Granddaddy has told me wonderful things about you."

"I'm sure they're all fabricated," he laughed. He turned toward his wife. "I'm going to do kids table duty so Cynthia and Bill can have a relaxing dinner."

"Thank you," Vanessa said with a tender kiss. Turning to Carollyn she said, "Cynthia is our oldest; she and Bill have a set of three-year-old twins and seldom have a moment's peace."

They all went through the service line and sat at their table to get to know each other. Gradually, different people from the community stopped by to say hello. The captain had invited many friends from the area to share in the festivities.

"These get-togethers are always so much fun," Vanessa remarked. "We never know who might show. Some of these people I haven't seen in years."

"Carollyn," Marissa interrupted, "Dr. Richter has just arrived. I thought you might want to meet her."

"Now, why you would do that," the old man whined as Carollyn put on her physician face and went to meet his physician.

"Dr. Richter," Carollyn said, extending her hand. "I'm Dr. Carollyn Morris-Bower." Carollyn stared at the young lady. She had expected a much older doctor, and not to be sexist, a male.

Dr. Richter could see the momentary surprise in Carollyn's face. "Nice to meet you; please call me Sue." She smiled as she extended her hand. "It is so nice that you came to find your grandfather. I hear it has done him a world of good." Sue paused for a second to study Carollyn, who was busy sizing her up. "My family has been treating your family for three generations."

"Oh," Carollyn sighed, realizing that she had unintentionally put Dr. Richter on the defensive.

"My grandfather actually delivered your mother," she said smugly. "From what I've been told he removed her tonsils, too."

Carollyn felt somewhat embarrassed for her own prejudices. It didn't help that Sue's long, platinum blonde hair and blue eyes gave an appearance that she should be going to sorority parties as opposed to practicing medicine.

"I'm sorry for staring," she sighed. "I was expecting someone a bit older."

Sue laughed. "That's not the first time I evoked that reaction. In time I will find the appearance of youth a blessing, but at times now it is a professional curse."

"Again, I'm sorry; I had no right to make you feel uneasy."

"My father asked me to convey his condolences for the loss of your mother," Sue continued. "He would be here, but he is vacationing in Europe with his new wife." Her tone did not hide the resentment of the intruder in the family.

"Did your father know my mother well?" Carollyn asked.

"As I've been told, as preteens they were inseparable. As teenagers they were 'madly in love' with each other. Daddy said the first girl he kissed was your mother. As their teenage interests varied, the gap of the romance widened. One day they mutually decided that they would be better off as just friends."

"Okay," Carollyn started. "I think I remember Momma telling me about the puppy love," she lied, having no recollection of any such story. "She did seem to be rather fond of your father."

A young couple stopped to pay their respects to Dr. Richter prior to moving on to talk with the captain.

"I know this is a party," Carollyn started slowly, trying not to trudge on professional boundaries, "but can we talk for a second about my grandfather's oxygen?"

"Sure, what would you like to know?" Sue replied in a nonthreatening tone.

"Don't you feel that it would be beneficial if he wore it all the time?" Carollyn asked.

Sue asked the waiter for a glass of white wine. "I've spoken to your grandfather several times about portable oxygen. He wants nothing to do with it. There is always a reason it won't work."

"Such as?" Carollyn asked, sounding a bit confused.

"The first time I asked him, he told me that it wouldn't be proper for Santa Claus to wear oxygen," Sue laughed, thinking about his numerous excuses.

"Santa Claus?" Carollyn responded, not certain she understood the humor.

The physician smiled and said, "Every year since I can remember your grandfather dresses up as St. Nicholas to visit the sick children in the hospital. He gives them presents and encouragement. After all the presents are given out, he returns to their rooms to sit with the patients and tells them stories. He doesn't read to them; all his stories are from his mind and heart. It is an all-day affair."

"That's sweet," Carollyn whispered with tears in her eyes. "The kids probably wouldn't understand why Santa was attached to oxygen."

"After the Santa Claus excuse, he tells me he may have a date for Valentine's Day, and a tank strapped on his shoulder would detract from his sex appeal."

Both ladies laughed.

"Sometimes as healers we need to realize that what is medically prudent may take away from some of the quality. Yes, there are lightweight portable tanks that your grandfather can wear to do almost anything. But if he finds that they are inconvenient and prevent him from walking on the beach or going fishing, or having a good cigar, is it really worth it? At his age he has a right to choose his quality, regardless of our personal or professional opinions. A portable tank may increase his life span a few months or even a few years, but at what cost?"

"He would probably feel better," Carollyn countered.

"Does he complain about feeling poorly now?" Sue asked.

"Well, no ..."

"Precisely. Medically daytime oxygen is indicated, but emotionally I believe it would be a death sentence."

"Well spoken, and your point is agreed upon," Carollyn said. "However ..."

Sue could hear hesitation in her voice.

"I don't know, I'm just listening to my clinical training, but maybe I'm just a bit too close to the situation to be objective," Carollyn admitted.

The two women changed the subject, moving to other areas, continuing to have light conversation for several minutes.

"Excuse me, Carollyn, there are a couple of people I want you to meet," the captain interrupted.

Carollyn excused herself from Sue and turned to her grandfather.

"This is John and Lori," he said excitedly. "They're the two people who sent me the ghost pictures."

"Nice to meet you," a reserved scientist greeted.

"Nice to meet you," they both said in unison.

"They just came from another hunt in St. Augustine and decided to drop by on their way home." The man coughed. "I asked them to join the party."

"He's trying to give us another free meal," John mumbled, embarrassed.

"Seems as he does that with a lot of folks," Carollyn reassured. "I don't think I would worry about it."

The old man turned his attention elsewhere and shuffled away, leaving Carollyn to entertain the visitors. In his hand was a folder of pictures of new discoveries the ghost hunters had brought him.

"So just how do you hunt for ghosts?" she asked, not quite sure how or why she was in the predicament.

"We walk around locations where there have been reported hauntings," John started. "In areas that we feel some type of internal vibrations we take pictures with our digital camera. We never see the images that our camera captures as we are taking them. Sometimes we will see them on the camera screen right after we snap the shot. At times we don't see the picture until we download them to the computer."

"Really?" questioned the skeptic.

"We also have a laser thermometer," Lori said. "It enables us to discover variable temperature in any location. It appears that many of the spirits emit a lower than normal temperature."

Carollyn's interest was slightly aroused. "Can you give me an example?"

"Certainly," Lori continued. "Last night we were standing outside the old Catholic cemetery in St. Augustine. I located a spot on a tombstone that registered eighteen degrees. John took several pictures. When we returned to our room and enlarged them on the laptop we saw a lady's face on the tombstone."

"That sounds interesting, but could it be a reflection of light?" Carollyn said.

"Possibly," John countered. "But doubtful. We're not saying these are necessarily ghosts. We are just saying they are unexplainable phenomenon." The man cleared his throat. "One theory is that our energy molecules leave residue that can be picked up long after our demise."

"Another item we use is a digital tape recorder," Lori said. "The recorder picks up higher frequencies where the spirit world may be communicating. We have managed to pick up footsteps and even leaves rustling when there is nothing around."

"But no voices?" Carollyn asked with a frown on her face.

"Nothing that we can verify," John responded. "However, we do have suspicious whispering sounds. Granted, these noises may be secondary sounds to the recorder, but they could also be spirits."

"Excuse me if I remain skeptical," Carollyn said in a more curious than judgmental tone.

"Recently we have started a Ghost Safari," Lori stated. "It's like a ghost tour, offered in the historic district of most old cities with the exception that they are later at night and last several hours."

"After each safari we place our digital pictures on the computer and discuss them," John cut in. "Areas of highest concentration we revisit and take more pictures. As amateurs go, we attempt a scientific approach." John paused for a second. "It's an interesting hobby. Recently, we created our own website, if you would like to follow our journey. Our website is ghozhunter.com," the man stopped talking for a second, pondering whether he was being too zealous. "It may be possible, as I mentioned before, that just as when a rock is thrown in the middle of a lake it creates a ripple, that our bodies do the same."

"I'll have to log on to your website. Your theories intrigue the scientist in me," Carollyn replied, sincerely interested. "So what do you do when you're not chasing spirits?"

"I'm a psychiatric nurse," John answered.

"I manage a durable medical equipment company," Lori added.

Instinctively Carollyn wanted to talk to Lori about portable oxygen for her grandfather; however, knew it would be of little use.

"More accurately," Lori continued, "I've taken an early retirement."

"I wish I could to do that," Carollyn chuckled.

"Well," Lori whispered, "No, you don't; it is a medical retirement."

Carollyn gasped. "Oh, I am sorry about my comment." The physician resurfaced. "What type of medical problems do you have?"

Tears formed in Lori's eyes. "Stage four colon cancer with metastasis to the liver."

Carollyn was stunned. "How old are you?"

"Forty-three," Lori replied, John putting his right arm around her shoulders for support.

"The doctors feel she had the tumor in her colon for over seven years," John said.

Carollyn waved John away. "Why don't you go through the buffet and get some food while Lori and I talk for a few minutes." She motioned for Lori to sit down.

The ghost hunter did as directed and started to the buffet line.

Carollyn sat next to the tearful girl. "I am an oncologist," she began. "I understand personally and professionally that you are going through a very difficult time. Would you like to talk about it?"

"About six months ago, I started hemorrhaging from my rectum. Though I was reluctant, John insisted that we go to the emergency room. Once there the doctor ordered a stat colonoscopy. Even before the procedure I knew the answer." Lori paused to wipe tears from her eyes.

Carollyn held her hand gently, tears forming in her own eyes.

"The doctor looked at the pictures, dropped them on my stomach, and said 'you have cancer.'" She paused to regain her composure. "He then turned and left the room, just as if it was a routine occurrence."

Carollyn was embarrassed by her colleague's lack of empathy.

"The statement I was just told screamed deeply in my soul. Literally within seconds, the person I knew myself to be was shattered. After surgery, I met my oncologist. His words echo in my ears, 'It is Stage four, biggest tumor I have ever seen. We caught it too late.'"

There was a momentary pause. "I'm sorry," Carollyn whispered.

"That is when Satan started showing up," Lori continued, anger resonating from her voice. "My faith is so deep, it is not right that he just showed up. But Satan did; he started showing up at my dinner table. He talked to me at night so I couldn't sleep. He embraced me, his essence started to envelop me. Finally, I stared him down declaring my faith in God. It did not make him totally disappear, but when he arrives, I am able to keep from giving him power."

Carollyn smiled. "God will give you the power to conquer Satan's dark shadow."

"Still," Lori continued, "fear has become part of my life. My dreams have been replaced with sorrows, remorse, and regret. I have so many, 'what ifs?' I have cancer. I am terminally ill. The statistics claim that my life expectancy is less than eighteen months, six of which have already been spent."

Carollyn peered into Lori's deep, lustrous hazel eyes. "Please, remember that statistics are only numbers. They do not have the ability to factor in the human spirit. It would be highly unethical of me to give you false hope, but miracles do happen. In my practice, I have encountered numerous patients that defy the odds and are still living. There are miracles that medical science cannot explain. I understand that you are terrified. You have every right to be. But if you allow the fear to overpower the hope; you are giving into the disease."

"I know," Lori admitted, between sobs.

Carollyn reached into her purse and pulled out a business card. "If you would like I can look at your records and see if there is anything that I would recommend. Sometimes an extra opinion isn't a bad idea."

Lori reached for the card saying, "Thank you. I have good ins—"

Carollyn stopped her before she could complete the sentence. "Nonsense, there will be no charge for my services. All I'm doing is reviewing records."

"That's kind," Lori whispered, tears still in her eyes.

John rejoined them with two plates of food.

"The most important thing," Carollyn continued, "is to take Tim McGraw's advice and live like you are dying." She paused to reflect on her mother's battle with cancer. "There is only one appointed day that you must die; spend the rest of your time enjoying life."

Carollyn and Lori talked for several more minutes about alternative treatments and faith. Lori promised that she would send her records. Carollyn then excused herself and returned to her seat beside Vanessa.

"Hey pretty girl," Gus flirted, instantaneously forgetting what he was talking about. His stare at Carollyn lasted a bit longer because she took the time to give him a warm smile. Soon his attention was focused elsewhere in the room.

"Did you have a nice talk with Sue?" Vanessa asked.

"Yes, and I believe she might have set me straight," Carollyn sighed.

"Daddy is going to do what Daddy's going to do; reasoning with him is futile," Vanessa said.

Carollyn laughed. "In the short time we've been here, that is quite evident."

"You do know he is a good person," Vanessa said.

"Yes, beyond a doubt."

"My daddy died during the Korean War. I never had an opportunity to know him. Mother raised my three sisters and me alone. When it was time for college there wasn't any money in the piggybank." She paused for a second, wondering if she was saying too much, but decided to continue. "Determined to go to school, I enrolled in Bethune Cookman, here in Daytona. With student loans I set out to get my degree."

"Unfortunately student loans don't pay to put bread on the table. I searched all over Daytona for work. The African-Americans warned me to avoid Charkey's because the owner was a bigot. After being turned down by all other businesses, some even owned by African-Americans, I had no choice but to try Charkey's."

"And he hired you," Carollyn said as she smiled.

"More than that," Vanessa continued. "He called Uncle Gus and asked him to give me a discount rate on an apartment."

"You stayed at my apartment," Gus interrupted with a moment of lucidity.

"Yes, I did," Vanessa said with a smile as she held onto his soiled hand. "I love you, Uncle Gus." A sad expression crossed her face as she remembered the good times. It was unfair that time had robbed Gus of his memory.

"It is going to be okay," Uncle Gus reassured her. "I will make sure everything is okay." For a brief moment a twinkle reappeared in his eyes.

Vanessa smiled. "I love you, Uncle Gus."

"I love you too," Gus replied, and then he was gone.

Returning her attention to Carollyn she said, "When David and I got married, Daddy and Momma Emma sent us to Hawaii on our honeymoon. I'm not sure what your grandfather was before I met him; but he has become my daddy."

Carollyn smiled.

"Shortly after David and I were married, my mother died of a heart attack. He is the only parent I have left. He has been a wonderful grandfather to my kids."

"Not only that," Sheila broke in, "The captain has paid for my grandfather to have a private room at the nursing home and a part-time sitter. There are many other tales of lives he has changed, just for the sake of being a Good Samaritan."

Carollyn stared across the room at her grandfather, who was engaged in a conversation with a man in a safari hat and a woman who looked as though she was from India. "He is an amazing man," Carollyn echoed.

Vanessa looked at Marissa, who had just rejoined them at their table. "Are you and Mark going to church with us in the morning?"

"Well, I'm not sure," she stumbled. "We'll be getting to bed late after the clean-up."

"Sounds like a no to me," Carollyn chimed in.

"I seem to remember that we made this deal if David and I would go to Cassadaga with you, you would attend church with us."

Carollyn looked at Marissa and said, "Sounds like a promise to me."

"Well, yes but …"Marissa said, trying to find a good excuse.

"A promise is a promise," Vanessa teased.

"All right, what time is church?" Marissa relented.

"Eleven AM until about noon," Vanessa replied.

"Eleven," Marissa crowed. "The chickens don't get up that early."

"Excuse me," the old man interrupted. "Carollyn, I have a friend that I would like for you to meet."

Carollyn looked up at her grandfather with the eyes of a child. "Gladly," she whispered.

Marissa and Vanessa continued to banter about the virtue of church attendance as Carollyn walked away. Even though she had no experience with siblings, she was sure this was how siblings would interact. She followed the captain to a table near the buffet where the man with the safari hat, now removed, was eating with his wife.

"This is Jeremy Feldstein and his wife Rhami," he said politely. Turning to them, he said, "This is my granddaughter, Carollyn, from Chicago."

Jeremy held out a hand as the three exchanged pleasantries. Carollyn sat in a chair directly across from both of them.

"Jeremy and his wife are both family law attorneys," the captain mentioned.

"Actually, practicing law is more of a hobby," Jeremy cut in. "It gives us the financial ability to pursue our real passion."

"And your passion?" Carollyn asked curiously.

"We operate a wild animal refuge," Jeremy said humbly.

The captain laughed. "It is just down the street from Cassadaga," he volunteered, unsure as to why he found humor in that.

"What type of animals?" Carollyn asked.

"Any animal needing protection from a predator known as man," the curator boasted. "We have several tigers, quite a few deer. Of course, they are segregated. There are also some Florida panthers, an aviary, and numerous others animals."

"Where do get all these animals?" Carollyn asked.

"Different places. Some are retired from circuses or zoos that have closed; others were found injured on the road. A couple of our panthers are cubs that were orphaned when their mother was killed by a poacher." The man stopped to take a sip of beer. "We are fortunate to have seventeen hundred and fifty acres to house these varying breeds. Some of the injured ones get well enough to return to the wild. Officials from the game and wildlife department assist in reintroducing them to their natural habitat. Others are permanent borders."

"That sounds rewarding," Carollyn interjected.

"My culture," Rhami stated, "instructs us to honor all living creatures. To me this is our way to pay tribute to the words of our ancestors."

"With your love for animals why didn't you study veterinary medicine?" Carollyn asked.

Jeremy replied smiling, "My father was an attorney and strongly felt that his only son should become one also. It wasn't that I didn't want to disappoint my father; he wouldn't allow me to. My first semester of undergraduate he selected all my classes." The man paused. "Dad died my last semester at Stetson Law School, so he never even had the opportunity to see his dream realized."

"I will have to remember to allow my children to chart their own course," Carollyn responded. "How did you come about fulfilling your dream?"

"My grandfather died twenty years ago. I was his only heir. Among other things he left me was seventeen hundred and fifty acres of farmland and forest. A few weeks later Rhami found an injured black cub that was hit by a car on highway forty, and our odyssey began."

"How do you manage to run a law office and take care of the refuge?" Carollyn asked.

"Jeremy and I split the time at the office," Rhami offered. "One of us is always at the refuge. We also have three teenage boys that diligently assist us." She pointed toward a teenager sitting with Jason watching Mark perform magic tricks. "That is our youngest, Cody; the other two stayed home tonight."

Nathaniel came to his mother and crawled into her lap.

"Tell them about Pete," the old man coaxed.

"Who's Pete?" Nathaniel asked.

"Our property is divided by three creeks," Jeremy started. "All three creeks flow into a small lake near the center of the property. A very old cypress tree stretches toward the heavens at the edge of the lake. At the top of the cypress tree is the guardian of our land, a bald eagle we call Pete."

"Pete's been there for seven or eight years," Rhami interjected.

"Sounds wonderfully peaceful," Carollyn whispered.

"I want to see it," Nathaniel begged.

"Tell them about Pete saving your life," the captain continued, coaxing the humble attorney.

"About two years ago I was taking a weekend hike to the lake. It had been several months since I had been there, so there was an abundance of underbrush growing. I was using a machete to cut it back. Evidently I disturbed a bee, which in turn stung my left hand. As the stinger went in, I dropped, ah ... rather, flung the machete. When I went to pick it up, the jangle of a three-foot rattlesnake stopped me in my tracks." The man paused for a sip of beer. "The snake was coiled by my knife, ready to strike."

"The fool wasn't wearing his hiking boots either," Rhami reported.

"I froze stiff so as to not startle it further. For some reason the viper was set on guarding the knife. Common sense would have begged me to leave the knife and return for it later. However, no one has ever accused me of having common sense. I picked up some stones and started throwing them at the rattler to entice it to leave. The agitation didn't work quite the way I had anticipated. The killer sprung from its coil faster than lightning toward my hand. Pete swooped down from nowhere, latching on to the rascal's neck with his beak, and faster than the speed of light was soaring through the air again."

"That is an incredible story," Carollyn gushed.

"That is why we call him the guardian of our land," Rhami added.

Nathaniel scooted out of his mother's lap and raced off to tell his brother the story.

"About ten years ago," the old man said, "Charkey became really ill. I thought he was going to die. The veterinarian told me that it was just his time, that prolonging his life would only increase his suffering." The man paused. "One night Jeremy and Rhami came into the restaurant. I told them about Charkey, and they talked me into delaying putting him to sleep for about a month. The next day Jeremy came back with a special feed that had been mixed with natural herbs. A few weeks later Charkey was back to his old cocky self."

"We believe," Jeremy said diplomatically, "that medicine is toxic and where it may kill the targeted pathogen, it also will attack healthy tissues. Sometimes the healthy tissues cannot resist the attack."

"Yes," Carollyn said sarcastically, "Doctor, I have good news: I cured the fever but I killed the patient."

They all laughed.

"I agree with many herbal remedies and other homeopathic cures," Carollyn said in lecture mode. "However, I believe that they need to be used in conjunction with modern medicine to maximize their usefulness. I understand many of these potions have been around for centuries. But it wasn't until the advancement in modern medicine that life expectancy and quality in humans have increased."

"Point well taken," Jeremy agreed. "I do believe modern medicine has improved longevity and quality of life in both animals and humans. However, I do not believe that it should be viewed as an exclusive medicine."

"Again, I will partially agree with you. As an oncologist I see cancers caught at such an advanced stage that the only thing that will eradicate it is radiation and chemotherapy. Yet both those treatments attack healthy cells."

"Many times even with the radiation and chemo the patients die due to complications with treatment," Jeremy countered. "Why not try alternative medicine?"

Painfully aware of her mother's painful battle with cancer, Carollyn continued. "I believe alternative treatments should be used in conjunction with modern medicine. Even Andrew Weil, the leading advocate of alternative medicine, suggests that homeopathic and traditional medicine work to complement each other." Carollyn remembered that after her mother's terminal diagnosis, along with palliative treatment she also experimented with homeopathic therapy. The homeopathic was not effective, though she realized that could have been due to the late stage in which it was started. Although, there was some evidence that suggested that some of the natural treatment helped lessen the side effects of the chemo.

"Before we continue the debate," the old man cut in, "can we get to the topic of your newest orphan?"

Sheila and Gus walked past the table to say good-bye. The captain and Carollyn excused themselves temporarily from the Feldsteins so they could walk Sheila and Gus to the door.

"I'm going home," Gus said to the captain. Looking toward Carollyn he said, "I really do like your new wife. She sure is a looker. Congratulations, this has been a great reception. Call me when you get back from your honeymoon."

"Thanks for coming," the captain offered, patting him on the shoulder. The old man and Carollyn hugged Sheila. Gus and his escort strolled out into the dark.

As they turned back towards the Sand Castle room, Carollyn saw a picture of the captain and Gus standing on a beach, each with a fruity drink.

"That was taken in Jamaica in 1977." Her grandfather smiled at the memory. "We were celebrating Gus' fourth divorce and mourning Emma's death. Having a desire or maybe a need to get away from Daytona, we decided to go the islands. It was meant to be a week of fishing and remembering old times. It turned out to be a week of fishing my head out of the toilet. I never drank so much in my life. Most of the week was forgotten before it was even over."

The man paused. "The last night I was there I met this island girl, and we started to dance. One thing led to another, and before I knew it she was in my hotel room." The man stopped to wipe a tear. "I took one look at the picture of Emma on the nightstand and instantly I sobered up. I politely asked the girl to leave, or maybe not as politely as I would like to remember. Then I curled up in a corner and cried like a baby until I went to sleep. I haven't touched a drop since. If alcohol can relieve me of my senses, I have no business drinking it."

Carollyn hugged him. "You were going through a really tough time; these things happen. Don't be so hard on yourself."

"To other people, but not to me," the old man said stoically.

"What about Gus?"

The captain shook his head. "He should have given up the booze too. The fool met and married his fifth wife that week, Penny."

"How long did that marriage last?"

"Until she took Gus for every last penny he had," the captain snickered sarcastically. "That is why I called her Penny—because that is all she was interested in."

"So if the picture brings so much grief, why is it hanging here?" Carollyn asked, somewhat puzzled.

"Sometimes, you have to look where you have been to appreciate where you are, and use that knowledge to guide you where you need to go. Gus and I are thankful for that week; it defined who we were. It, also, provided us with the direction we needed to go."

Carollyn was speechless. She realized she was in the presence of a sage, and a smile broke out across her face.

Trudy interrupted the two to introduce the captain to an artist who was admiring the pictures and numerous other items that helped create the ambiance of the restaurant.

"Captain, I really hate to disturb you, but I have a patron that really wants to meet you."

"Pretty lady," Charkey called from his cage.

"Hi." The lady offered a hand and said, "My name is Betty; I really hate to disturb you."

"That's what we are here for," the man said, revealing a toothy grin. Putting his hand on Carollyn's shoulder he continued, "This is my granddaughter, Carollyn. He paused for a second and then said, "And just call me captain."

"This is my first time here," she confessed with a cheerful smile. "I am just so enthralled with the rustic, aged edifice with a majestic sea serving as its humble backdrop."

"You are a definite artist," the captain commented, "and a poet too."

"I would consider it an honor and a privilege to capture Charkey's on canvas. If you permit me, tomorrow morning I will come by and take a snapshot as my model. I promise I won't disturb you."

Carollyn looked into the room and saw Jason and Nathaniel politely sitting with Jeremy and Rhami, bombarding them with questions.

"If you want to capture the real beauty, be here at sunrise. If you are lucky, the sun will put on a dazzling potpourri of colors."

"Then I have your permission?" Betty said, showing an enchanting smile.

"How could I deny such a lovely lady of such a small pleasure," the man flirted innocently. "My only request is that you give me the privilege of viewing your masterpiece upon completion."

"You have my word," the woman vowed with a handshake. "If you like it," she continued, "I will gladly do another for you."

"Pretty lady," Charkey shrieked again.

The man thought for a second, "If you do a second, I would greatly appreciate you including my big mouthed friend in the painting." He looked at the bird.

"With delight!" Betty exclaimed.

The two stared at each other for a few seconds, not in a romantic sense, but rather with a sense of understanding of the depth of their souls.

"I do admire the paintings that adorn your walls," Betty continued. "Are they all done by the same artist?"

"They are all painted by my mother," Carollyn proudly interjected.

"My daughter," the captain added.

"There is a sense of serenity in them. They are as if she was capturing the quintessence of the inner aspect of the subject, not just the surface."

"She had a magnificent gift," the old men acknowledged. "Would you care to look at the ones in the Sand Castle room?"

"No thank you, not tonight," the lady replied. "My party is waiting for me." She stood still for a second, thinking, "On second thought my friend can wait!" She turned to the old man, saying, "Would it be overly rude if I took a quick self-guided tour?"

"Absolutely not," the captain replied.

Betty hurried into the room, as if not wanting to be seen by her dinner partner. Carefully, she examined the texture and depth of each painting.

As Carollyn and the captain walked back into the room, the old man whispered in granddaughter's ear, "Trudy is always trying to fix me up with someone."

"She was attractive," Carollyn teased.

"Way too young," the man bantered, "I doubt that we would have anything in common."

Marissa and Mark met them at the entrance to the room. "If we are going to be forced into institutional theology," Marissa said in a teasingly sardonic tone, "we need to be calling it a night."

The old man looked at Carollyn quizzically.

"So this means you are going to join us for church in the morning?" Carollyn asked.

"Why can't you just say church instead of all your mumbo jumbo?" the man said with a well-meaning chuckle.

"We're going to ch—church tomorrow," Marissa said, mockingly.

"You can change the hippie's clothes and their hair. You can give them a good job; but still deep inside they are still a hippie," the old man quipped to Carollyn.

"We all have our egocentricity," Carollyn said defending them.

They all smiled, enjoying the good natured bantering.

"I thought you were staying to clean up," Carollyn teased Marissa.

"Okay, you are onto my fabrication. It was a futile attempt to skip out on my obligation."

Patting Mark on the shoulder, the captain switched the subject. "This is the maestro that is orchestrating the renaissance of Charkey's," he announced.

Carollyn smiled. "We talked earlier in the evening," she said to the old man before turning her attention to Mark. "This is an impressive job."

"Thank you," Mark said with his head humbly lowered.

Marissa and Carollyn exchanged hugs, and then Marissa kissed the old man on the cheek.

Before returning to Jeremy's table they stopped by to talk to an elderly lady wearing a canary yellow dress offset with a string of pearls. "Lisa, I'm not sure if you had a chance to meet my granddaughter," the old man said. "I regret that I have been such a poor host."

She was much shorter than Carollyn envisioned her to be. Though her skin looked as if it were aged leather, her braided hair remained jet black as a tribute to her ancestors.

"What's new?" Lisa teased. "I see you chasing all these young women around."

She looked at Carollyn. "You have your mother's cheeks," she said in a rather loud voice. "Melissa was a wonderful lady." Lisa looked toward the old man. "She must have taken after Emma's side of the family." Returning her focus to Carollyn, she said, "This old man has always been too ornery to be any count."

Carollyn laughed while hugging her grandfather. "I don't know, I think he's pretty special."

"Each to her own," Lisa shouted back.

"Where's Renda?" the man asked.

The woman looked around slightly bewildered. "I don't know; she was just here a minute ago. Lisa half stood out of her chair, using a cane to support herself, and peered around the room. "I guess Renda decided to get some fresh air. I'm sure she will return shortly."

"If we don't see her, tell her we were asking after her," the old man requested.

"Don't be rude," the woman chided. "When she returns you best come over here and pay your regards."

The captain smiled, bending over to kiss her, and whispered, "It is great to see you."

Lisa returned the smile. "I'll never miss a chance for some free food." She glanced at Carollyn. "It was a pleasure meeting you. Despite what I say, your grandfather has been a marvelous friend."

As the two walked away, Carollyn said softly to the old man, "She sure has spunk."

Carollyn returned to talk with Jeremy and Rhami, who were now deserted by the boys, curious to hear about their orphaned animal. The old man decided to allow Carollyn to talk to the Feldsteins alone and ambled out to the main dining room to sit with his old friend Charkey and discuss the events of the evening. As he sat, he saw Betty elegantly leaving the restaurant in grand fashion with her gentleman companion tagging behind.

"Charkey," he said shaking his head, "she's still too young for me."

"Too young," Charkey echoed.

As the old man sat with his friend, Renda returned from her walk. She joined him for a few minutes, sipping lemonade while reminiscing about days gone by. They sadly talked about Melissa's death. Renda fondly remembered that babysitting Melissa was her first job.

Peering into the Sand Castle room, they recounted the days of her youth when the captain would spend hours sitting in the sand with them constructing majestic structures of sand.

"Melissa's passing brings to light that we are all mortal," Renda whispered. "I was just walking along the beach trying to make sense of life."

"A person's life is but a mere pebble of sand in the annual of time," the captain quipped.

"Will it ever make sense?" Renda asked rather rhetorically.

"Maybe it will when we arrive in heaven," the man said in a questioning tone.

"What was my father really like?" the lady asked.

This is the first time he remembered Renda asking this question. When she was a young girl he tried to keep Denny's memory alive with exaggerated tales of adventures.

"Your daddy was a kind, gentle soul," the man said as he started his testimonial. "As a friend he was loyal, trustworthy, and always considerate. I understand why Gus was proud to go to battle with him. He was the type of guy that would always look out for his buddy's back. To this day I miss his companionship, his wit, and his opinions. It was an honor for him to consider me a friend."

"If the war wouldn't have arrived, do you think he and my mother would have married?" Renda asked.

The old man laughed and patted her on the knee. "War or no war, wild stallions would not have been able to keep them apart. You're Daddy and Momma was as much a perfect match as Emma and I."

"Do you think that is why Mother never entertained the thought of being with another man?"

The man thought on this for a few seconds. This line of questioning was peculiar after so many years. He wondered if Melissa's death brought on these long-awaited questions. "If you feel that you are a perfect match for someone, and then death occurs, it is hard to move on. I know after Emma died I could not see myself being with another person. It is kind of like I am saving myself to be reunited with Emma in heaven." There was a brief pause. "I'm not saying that is right or wrong; it just is. Your mother filled her life with so many things of interest a relationship with another man never appealed to her. Please, if you are feeling sad for her, don't. I have never seen a more fulfilled and satisfied woman as she."

Renda smiled at the man as they sat in silence for a few minutes.

After some lighter conversation, Renda rejoined her mother. The man and Charkey were alone again. The man stared behind the bar at a painting of a rowboat, the only painting in the restaurant not painted by Melissa. It was of a man with a white shirt, and thick, blond hair. His biceps were bulging as he sat backwards, rowing down the Halifax river.

Facing him was a young lady, her wavy, long brown hair blowing in the gentle breeze. Her innocence was highlighted by a light blue sundress with white polka dots. A navy blue scarf with red and green accents streaked through it concealed a long slender neck. There were no buildings in sight, just the boat, tall green trees, himself and Emma under a cloudless sky.

The man reflected about that trip down the Halifax, which had become their love canal. It was the morning he boarded the train to Charleston, where he would await deployment to Europe. Standing on the steps of the train Emma whispered in his ear, "Remember this wonderfully romantic trip we took this morning. May the thought of it keep your heart warm for me until we meet again. Be safe, I love you." Emma untied the scarf around her neck, and draped it around his brawny neck. "Bring this back to me," she said as the final whistle blew.

On D-Day the scarf was used as a tourniquet, tied around his wounded leg, to save his life. The rag of love was the instrument that allowed him to return to the woman that promised herself to him.

While he was gone, Emma re-created the Sunday in the park with watercolors, to keep their love alive in her heart. Years later she confessed to him, "I felt that if I could relive that moment over and over, a merciful God would send you home to me." Of all the paintings in the gallery this was the one that held the most meaning.

It was strange; Emma had such a great talent for painting, yet this was the last one she ever did. It was this painting that inspired the old man to encourage Melissa to paint. Unknown to the captain, Emma had made a secret pact with God that if he would return her true love home, she would give up her talent as a sacrifice.

The night turned out better than expected. There was an abundance of laughter and lively conversations. Old friends were given the opportunity to rekindled their bonds while meeting new friends and generating new memories. The captain, as he always did, floated from table to table, from guest to guest, recanting tales of days gone by. It was more nourishing to him to see the guests have a good time than the banquet set before him.

As all of his parties, there was plenty of food to eat and plenty to be sent home in doggy bags. At the end of the night, as everyone retired to their homes, the captain lay his head down grateful for the bonds he had formed and the life he had the opportunity to live.

The rays of the moon glistened off the soothing sea. Soft whisking sounds of the water gently rolling to the sand and the intermittent hoots of the front yard owl were the only sounds of the night. Jason was sitting on the porch, both legs propped up on the railing, busily scribbling in a notebook. The flashing of an occasional shooting star amused him, as he was always sure to make a wish. Carollyn quietly walked up behind her son.

"Do you know what time it is?" she whispered in a hushed voice.

Totally oblivious to anything but his thoughts, Jason shrugged, "No, not really."

"It's almost two o'clock," Carollyn replied.

"Really, what are you doing up so late?" he asked, knowing that was the question that was forthcoming.

"Just thinking about a wonderful vacation this has been for all of us," she mused, "but I think that is the question you are supposed to answer."

Jason laughed, aware of his failure to sidestep the inquest. "I'm just writing in my journal; I'll be headed for bed soon."

"What are you writing?" a suspicious mother asked, thinking that it had to be something about missing a girlfriend.

The boy turned around to look at his mother. "It is strange that when we first talked about making this trip, I didn't want to come."

"Actually, I believe your statement was, 'I am not going no matter what.'" Carollyn smiled warmly at her son.

Jason smiled. "I remember saying something like that," he confessed. "Part of my reluctance was because of things that Grandpa Laurence said. He convinced me Grandpa is an old mean-spirited bigot that would have no interest in meeting an African-American grandson. That first night, part of me agreed with him. Part of me didn't want to agree."

"In your Grandpa Laurence's defense, when he and Momma left Daytona your great-grandfather, by his own admission, was like that. Sometime occurrences and time can transform old beliefs into new."

"My great-grandfather has proven that to me."

"So, why did you decide to come?" Carollyn asked, interested in his change of heart.

"Dad and I had a talk about it. He told me that it was possible that my great-grandfather had not changed. It was also possible that he had a revelation and had become more accepting." The boy paused at the sight of a double falling star shooting across the satin sky. "Regardless of the type of man he was, it was my duty to myself to give him an opportunity to meet me. Dad said that if I don't give him a chance, I would always wonder."

"Your dad said that?" Carollyn reflected back on the discussion she had with her husband prior to leaving. He was not nonsupportive; however, he did voice numerous apprehensions.

The two were silent for a moment, listening to the sounds of the waves gently swishing upon the shore.

"So are you glad you came?" Carollyn asked while massaging his shoulders.

"It has been a wonderful trip; it will be sad to see it end in a couple of days," Jason said.

"If you would like, you can always fly down for a longer visit," Carollyn offered.

Her son grinned, but said nothing.

"So, that was a nice diversion from the original question. What are you writing?" Carollyn asked returning to the initial topic.

"Granddaddy is always telling stories and expounding on his philosophies. He has had such a vastly fascinating life. I think he has influenced a lot of people, some that he probably doesn't even remember. I really want to be able to remember some of the things he said and did, so one day I can share them with my children," Jason said, a tear in his eyes.

Chapter VI

Sunday

Do something every day that you don't want to do;
this is the golden rule for acquiring the habit of doing
your duty without pain.

—Mark Twain

The early morning rays of the sun shot sporadically through the clouds that were trying to occlude them. The only reminder of the overnight rain was a slow breeze blowing the leaves of the palms. Carollyn stood on the porch sipping her coffee, patiently waiting for Vanessa to join her for an early morning power walk on the beach. The party the night before gave her a sense of belonging to the family. Everyone treated her as though she had lived in Daytona all her life.

"Good morning," a familiar voice shouted from the beach as Marissa stepped out of the glare of the sunlight.

"Good morning," Carollyn responded, obviously happy yet surprised to see her. "I thought you and Mark were sleeping in."

Marissa laughed. "That was just a ploy to escape the wrath of the First United Methodist Church. But as you, say a promise is a promise." She hugged Carollyn good morning. "I never sleep past five. The early morning is when the Universe is most sensitive to meditative vibrations."

"I always thought that you could pray anytime," Carollyn said in a serious voice backed by years of indoctrination.

"Of course you can pray at anytime," Marissa quickly responded. "I feel that the Universal power is more receptive early in the morning before all the confusion of the day." She looked into the house to see if Vanessa was ready. "It is just possible that my mind is clearer then so I can better feel the spirit of God."

Carollyn decided to switch the subject from spirituality. "Are you joining Vanessa and me for our little stroll?"

"Stroll? Vanessa's power walk has never been called a stroll," Marissa laughed. "I wouldn't miss it. Every time Van is over here, we do 'the walk of death.' It is going to be an invigorating experience for you. She takes no prisoners."

"Are you talking behind my back?" Vanessa teased as she stepped out the door.

Carollyn turned toward her. "Is this going to be as bad as it sounds?"

"Worse! First we will start with a slow pace to warm up, and then we will speed it up," Vanessa warned as she sat on the steps of the porch to lace her shoes.

"It is a shame your kids couldn't stay," Carollyn commented.

"Usually they do," Vanessa sighed in agreement. "But they all have tickets for the circus this afternoon."

"It is nice that they all do things together," Carollyn said, reflecting about being an only child.

"They have always been close," Vanessa smiled. "Enough of the idle chatter, it is time to get going."

"Nazi," Marissa growled.

"Quiet in the ranks," Vanessa commanded as the trio headed south.

The waves continued to splash against the white sand. Occasionally the girls would step over a dead fish washed to shore from the nighttime storm.

"Who is the most interesting person you met last night?" Marissa asked, trying to breathe as instructed by Vanessa.

Carollyn was already feeling the tortuous Florida humidity. "Mark," she panted.

"Mark?" Marissa asked, confusion in her voice.

"He is a unique man," Carollyn continued. "He is soft spoken and unassuming, yet highly in touch with his surroundings. He taught me a new technique of how to look at art, which created a different perspective for me." She paused to catch her breath. "At the same time he has the patience to sit with children and perform magic. Your man is really something."

"I agree," Vanessa chimed in. "Since you have been dating, or, ah … living with him, you have become so much more centered."

"What do you mean?" Marissa asked.

"Before you knew him you were grasping for straws with your New Age dogma. You had all the right sayings, but you couldn't stay in one direction. One week you would go tarot card hopping, then you were into the palm or tea leaves, next you would be studying horoscope charts. You wanted answers but you weren't really finding them."

"Really?" Marissa asked, knowing that she was right.

"Mark has a soothing soul that is connected to a level head," Vanessa continued. "He was able to calm your restless spirit down. When that happened, I believe that you were able to focus on listening to God. You used to spend a lot time professing to know the answer. Now you spend your time living the answer."

"Wow, that's heavy," Marissa whispered. "Thank you."

"Sounds like you have come a long way," Carollyn added.

"Yes," Marissa huffed, "I guess I have. Both of you are right. Mark is a special guy. I guess with all this growth I have experienced we can skip church this morning."

"A promise is a promise," her companions chanted in unison.

The pace picked up a notch. The clouds that were attempting to kidnap the sun had all dissipated. The sky above was a pristine light blue with the moon remaining faintly visible.

"What's your big objection to church?" Carollyn asked.

There was silence for a few minutes as Marissa contemplated the answer. "When I was a little girl," she started, "my mother would put me on the church bus every Sunday morning so strangers could be my babysitter." There was an uncomfortable pause for a second. "If there was a Seventh Day Adventist church in the area I was 'allowed' to go on Saturday too." She paused for a second before continuing.

"I would learn the Ten Commandments and the Golden Rule. I was taught that 'God so loved the world that he gave his only begotten son, so whosoever believed in him would not perish but have everlasting life.' At the end of the service the same bus would take me from an environment that taught of love and forgiveness to my own personal nightmare. I would get home and my mother and her flavor of the month would be drunk or stoned. Sometimes they would be sprawled out on the floor. The people from those churches had to know what was happening, but yet they continued to return me. It seems that if they believed the love they preached they would have tried to rescue me from a situation that I had no control over."

"I'm sorry," Carollyn whispered. "You are right; something should have been done." Carollyn recognized her pain.

"Not all churches are like that," Vanessa went on the defensive. "The church has always been my salvation. Singing in the choir kept me in line with what God wanted for my life. Various activities sponsored by the church kept me from running the streets. The elders of the church helped guide my decision-making process."

"Where was your mother while you were at church?" Carollyn asked.

"At my side," Vanessa said without hesitation.

Again there was silence. The three stopped for a momentary hug and then returned on their trek. When they reached the two-and-a-half-mile mark, the commander shouted the order to turn around and the journey home began.

"Granddaddy told me that you have a book that is about to be published," Carollyn said to Vanessa.

Vanessa smiled in acknowledgment. "The publisher tells me it should be on the shelves of bookstores within the next six weeks."

"That is wonderful," Carollyn exclaimed. "Would you mind giving us a preview?"

"Sure," Vanessa agreed. "It is a self-help book entitled, Rescript Your Life."

Vanessa paused to watch a surfer do an unintentional back flip. "Ouch, that hurts," she mumbled before getting back on track. "The book is based on the premise that through childhood and early adulthood, our lives have been scripted for us. I strongly believe that parents, teachers, and other people of influence have helped develop who we are. For some people that is acceptable, but for others a change is desired."

"A reprogramming," Marissa cut in.

"I use a formula called PIM that allows a person to start to change some of their undesired behaviors."

"Excuse the ignorance," Carollyn asked, "But what is PIM?"

"PIM is an acronym for Positive Imagery Meditation. They are a series of short meditations performed each morning and evening used in conjunction with my revamped version of the AA twelve-step program."

"When you say meditation, are you referring to hypnosis?" Carollyn asked for clarification.

"Definitely it is a form of hypnosis. I try not to use that term. To a lot of people hypnosis creates a connotation of a weak-minded circus act. If the person has prejudices against the treatment it automatically decreases the likelihood of a positive outcome."

"So these meditations are meant to recondition the subconscious mind?" Carollyn asked.

"There is a bit more to it than that," Vanessa said, continuing her explanation. "After each meditation, a positive action should ensue. This action is in direct correlation to the desired change, so you have an immediate positive movement to reinforce the subconscious suggestion."

"Can you give me an example?" Carollyn asked.

"Sure," Vanessa said in between pants. "Let's say the reader is a chronic procrastinator. He does a short meditation on being a 'person of action.' Immediately following the meditation, the reader then completes a small task doing something that had been put off."

"I am assuming that you have outcome data to support your theory?" Carollyn asked, seeking analytical data to validate the book.

"I have been doing PIM in my private practice for over ten years. According to my tabulation approximately seventy-five percent of clients that have used it, have shown dramatic improvement," Vanessa said, bragging on her success. "A few of David's patients that he referred to me have utilized it to enhance their sports performance."

"How long does the program last?" Carollyn asked.

"I recommend that clients do it over a twelve-week period. Afterward, from time to time, they do a refresher to keep on track."

"I'm not trying to be picky, but how did you determine the time frame?" Carollyn inquired.

Vanessa laughed. "That is an excellent question. When developing it there were two factors that led me to such a short time period. The first is that most patients will not stay in therapy for an extended period of time. Secondly, insurance companies restrict the amount of care any one client can receive. I wanted to develop a program that could empower a client to continue positive growth after the sessions were finished. Ideally, the program would last a year. Again, with insurance restrictions and our need for instant gratification, there was a need to condense it."

"I am eager to read it," Carollyn said.

"One of my test readers was Marissa," There was a pause. "Ask her in private what she thinks."

"It is one of the best books I have ever read," Marissa volunteered. "It is in the same category of Shakti Gawain's *Creative Visualization*."

"Never heard of her, but it sounds like an endorsement," Carollyn replied.

"Actually, I believe Van is too modest when talking about her book," Marissa continued. "She has also utilized the program to assist high school and college students to improve their capacity to learn and retain new material."

The Florida humidity was becoming more of a challenge to the walkers.

"That is impressive," Carollyn panted.

"However," Vanessa countered, "that is not the scope of the book. When it comes to the welfare of a student's academic success I am not certain that a self-help book is the proper tool." She paused for a second to watch two seagulls fight over food. "I believe the struggling student would not utilize a self-study development program."

A small plane hovered over the ocean dragging a banner that read: *Cajun Jack's Sunday Seafood Brunch $18.95!*

"Rolaids only seventy-five cents!" Marissa shouted.

Vanessa and Carollyn laughed.

"Please don't tell Daddy, but I dedicated it to him and, of course, David."

"That's touching," Carollyn said.

Suddenly, Vanessa increased the pace.

"Do you do this every day?" Carollyn asked.

Marissa managed to laugh between gasps for air. "This is light compared to her usual day."

"I try to put in ten miles a day," Vanessa said.

"At this pace?" Carollyn gasped.

"This is the ideal pace for me," Vanessa replied.

"My ideal pace would be a tenth of this speed," Marissa complained.

The early morning breeze was dissipating.

"Speed walking is my form of meditation," Vanessa professed. "I can't quiet my mind like Marissa or Mark. So I speed walk. When I get about halfway finished, I become too tired to resist."

"Resist?" Carollyn asked.

"My mind becomes too tired to resist the words God is trying to tell me," Vanessa confessed. "I have no arguments left. I have to allow him to speak. And I have to listen."

"Talk about heavy," Marissa said.

"I envy Marissa's ability to commune with God by taking a slow deliberate stroll down the shore. When she hears the waves splashing against the sand it is God speaking to her. When I hear it, it's a voice telling me I have to balance the checkbook or go to the grocery store."

"We all communicate to God in our own way," Carollyn acknowledged.

"There are so many questions I want answers to; sometimes my mind races so much I don't listen."

"Answers to what questions?" Carollyn asked.

"Why there is war, why my father had to die? Why there are parents like Marissa's?" She paused. "I know that we are supposed to take all things on faith, but sometimes when I lie awake at night faith is not enough. Do you think I'm wrong?"

"Absolutely not," Marissa shot in, "The Lord of the Universe loves you for who you are. He wants you to find peace and happiness. I believe he rejoices that we have questions. It is through these questions that we are able to come closer to him."

"Wow," Carollyn said in agreement. "You are so different in your spiritual views, but yet at the same time so similar."

"The nice thing about us is that we have always been able to accept each other's path to God without passing judgment," Vanessa said.

"Aristotle said, 'It is the mark of an educated mind to be able to entertain a thought without accepting it.'" Marissa smiled and continued, "The very fact that Vanessa listens to my idea of spiritualism and does not sit in judgment of my nontraditional viewpoints proves we are sisters."

"The same can be said for you," Vanessa added, "in your acceptance of my more traditional spiritual truths. That's why you're going to church with us today."

"I am attending church because a promise is a promise," she teased. "Besides, I believe that going to church is showing my respect for Daddy. This is my way of honoring God, who is always with me."

"God is everywhere," Carollyn agreed.

The three hearts sung in unison to their spiritual master. Silence again overcame the sisters as they all listened for the voice of God.

On the porch David and Jason stooped over a chessboard, testing their wit against each other. Nathaniel sat watching, distracting their concentration while ignoring the code of silence. "Mr. David, how did you learn to play chess?" Nathaniel asked.

David smiled at the memory. "When I first started dating Vanessa, I had to come to meet the captain and Miss Emma. The captain brought me to the porch at Charkey's and sat me in front of a chessboard."

"Why did he do that?" Nathaniel interrupted.

"Let him finish the story," Jason demanded, as he moved the white queen-bishop to space F3. He was carefully trying to put his men in place for a quick checkmate.

David laughed. "He told me we could get to know each other over a friendly game of chess. I told him that I didn't know how to play. His only response was if I was planning on hanging around, that I had better learn." David moved the king-bishop away from the king to space D4 to threaten the opposing rook.

With a poker face Jason moved a knight toward the king to space F5.

"So how did you learn?" Jason asked without taking his eyes off the board.

"Your great-grandfather taught me." David smiled as he captured one of Jason's two rooks, using a bishop to slide to space A1.

Jason moved the white king- bishop pawn to space C3 to temporarily trap the bishop.

"How come the white men always move first?" Nathaniel asked.

David laughed. "That's a good question; I'm afraid I don't know the answer."

"Why not?" Nathaniel asked, being persistent.

"The game has been around for centuries," Jason said. "Usually chess is played in tournaments. To keep track of who moved first, they designated one color as the first to move. Then they dictated that each game, the colors had to switch." The young boy sounded convincing even though the answer was made up.

"Sounds good to me," David agreed. He moved the black king-knight to H6. Jason moved his other knight closer to the opposing king to space D5.

David smiled at his opponent. "You could have taken my bishop with your knight."

Jason shook his head in mock disgust.

"When I asked for Vanessa's hand in marriage, he told me I had to beat him in chess first." He moved the bishop out of danger to D4, directly adjacent to one of Jason's attacking bishops.

"Did you beat him?" Nathaniel asked innocently.

A black seagull landed clumsily on the rail of the porch. After peering at everyone, it quickly hopped to the ground to scrounge for leftover food. Nathaniel threw the crust of stale toast at it. The bird peered at the young boy, batted both eyes, grabbed the bread, and flew away.

Jason moved his remaining rook to space D6, appearing to carelessly placing it in line with David's bishop.

"I had played the captain thousands of games before and since. The game for Vanessa's hand was the only time I beat him." David laughed. "I believe the game was fixed. The captain told me that the game of chess showed him three things. He said by studying an opponent's skill he could determine their analytic ability, their determination, and patience. If I developed those three traits then I would be prepared for marriage." David looked at Jason and eagerly captured the second rook.

The old man walked out on the porch. Looking at board he laughed. "I see you are still falling for the rook giveaway!"

"Checkmate," Charkey shouted from inside the house.

Jason moved his second knight to space E7 saying, "Checkmate."

"The important thing to remember about chess," the old man coached, "is it is not a contest as to who captures the most men. Secondly, if it appears that your opponent is giving away men too easily, he's probably setting you up for a trap."

"I like this chess set," Nathaniel broke in.

"Thank you," the captain replied. "These pieces were carved from old cypress wood by my grandpappy. To fight boredom at sea, he would take chunks of cypress and carve them. After they were finished he sanded them and then polished them. Did the same with the board," he boasted.

"They still look new," Jason added.

"This set has seen a lot of action. The oil from different people's hands perpetually continues the polishing Grandpappy started back in the 1880s," the old man said.

"Are you ready for a rematch?" David asked Jason.

Jason readily agreed. They enjoyed three more games prior to leaving for church, each ending as the first. Though Jason had suspicions that David was throwing the games; the old man reassured him that he wasn't.

As Marissa had promised, she and Mark joined the others for the worship service. They sat in the pew, donated in the memory of Emma, near the front of the church. Though she was a bit fidgety Marissa managed to sit through the sermon. The preacher spoke eloquently about love, forgiveness, and acceptance. At the end of the service he announced the benedictional hymn would be sung by Renda McGee.

Renda stepped down from the choir loft to the podium. The old man smiled at her. Even though she had her mother's hair and complexion, today particularly he could see Denny in her. She had her father's rounded, turned up nose, his crooked smile, and lanky gait.

Briefly he reflected back to the first time she had walked. Gus was home on leave for the marriage with his first wife. The day before the wedding they had a picnic on the beach. They were all laughing and joking about the turns of life. They had taken their eyes off the toddler for just a minute. Simultaneously, they all looked toward her as she waddled toward the waves. After the first six or seven steps she toppled to the sand. She immediately sat up and stared at the crowd with a perplexing, bewildered look.

The old man's reflections were interrupted by Renda's sweet soprano voice. "Please rise," she asked. The music started to play.

Carollyn leaned into her grandfather. "I hope you didn't teach her to sing."

The man whispered back, "There's nothing wrong with my voice that earplugs wouldn't cure."

Our Lord is the guardian of truth and light
He is the guide through day and night
The protector during thunder and lightning
The healer of body and soul
Provider of meat and drink
Artist of sea and mountain
Author of life after death
All our thanks and praise we give thee
Aaaaaaammmmmmmmen

"Amen," the congregation joined in, in unison.

They all met for sandwiches at the house. After an hour David and Vanessa said their good-byes as they started home to Orlando. Mark and Marissa left to spend the afternoon in a meditation botanical garden south of the town. Carollyn started cleaning the kitchen.

"Leave that for later," the captain barked. "It's time we do some fishing."

"Fishing?" Carollyn muttered with the boys shouting in excitement in the background.

"You been here for almost a week, and you haven't put a pole in the water," the man quipped. "I thought you were my granddaughter."

"Fishing?" Carollyn moaned as she shut her eyes, made a face, and held her arms out in protest.

"Boys," the captain ordered, "put the gear in the boat. Be sure to put some ice and lemonade in the cooler. We will push off in exactly fifteen minutes."

"Isn't it too late to be going out in the boat?" the woman asked.

"Would you rather we go out at four AM?"

"No ..." her voice trailed as she was trying to think of a rebuttal.

"I expect you dressed and at the dock in fifteen minutes."

"Aye, aye," Carollyn relented as she slowly stood and started toward the bedroom.

At the appointed time the boat pushed off. The old man put the captain's hat on Nathaniel.

"Captain," he barked, "I want you to take us out about five hundred yards. Then we'll drop anchor."

"Yes sir," Nathaniel laughed as he gave a salute. He thought for a few seconds. "How far is five hundred yards?"

"Ask your brother," the man shot back. "I'm only along for the ride."

In a few minutes Jason turned the engine off and assisted his brother in lowering the anchor. Soon there were four lines in the water and a bottle of lemonade in everyone's hand. They sat intently listening to the waves meshing in with the faint sounds of laughter coming from the beach.

"Jason, what are your aspirations?" the old man asked.

"I would like to play professional baseball," Jason answered. "Or if that doesn't work out, I think I would like to go into politics."

"I want to play baseball too," Nathaniel interrupted. "I want to play for the Red Sox."

"The Red Sox?" his mother asked. "I thought your heart was set on the Cubs."

"I want to do both," he said, laughing.

"Wait," Jason broke in, "the other day you said you wanted to play for the Buffalos."

"I do," Nathaniel confessed, a bit confused. He covered his face with his hands.

Everyone laughed at his innocence.

The old man returned his attention to Jason. "Why are you interested in politics?"

"I would like to think I could make a difference," Jason said, sounding more mature than his age.

"So you want to change the world?" his great-grandfather asked.

A silver and black fish jumped in the air just a few feet from the boat.

"Just the things that need to be changed," the boy replied. "Senator Bobby Kennedy said: 'Some men see things as they are and say, why? I dream of things that never were and say, why not?'"

"What are the issues you are most interested in?" the man wanted to know.

"The main items I would focus on are health care, easy access to education, and retirement income for the elderly," the future politician quickly responded.

His mother sat in silence, marveling at the side of her son she was not acquainted with.

"That is quite an agenda," the man mused. "How did you arrive at those three issues?"

"Hey," Nathaniel cut in, "when are we going to start catching fish?"

The old man laughed. "We need to have a bit of patience. We just dropped our lines in." The captain paused for a moment. "Nathaniel, you probably should keep an eye on your mother's line too. I'm not sure she knows what she is doing."

Carollyn gave her grandfather a playful shove. "Hey, I do too know how to fish," she protested, while laughing. "I'm sure it is in my blood."

"I'll help you, Mom," Nathaniel eagerly volunteered as he inched closer to her.

The old man returned his attention to the eldest child. "So," he repeated his earlier question, "how did you arrive at that agenda?"

"Those are some of the issues we discussed in our government class at school. Other than national defense, they seem to be the most pertinent."

"What do you see wrong with our health care system?" his mother asked.

"The first thing is that there is an inequality in access," the boy started. "There are many Americans that cannot afford to see a doctor, yet they make too much money for public assistance." He paused thoughtfully. "Then there are those who do not work, yet have total access to the health care system. Another group are those who are insured but the insurance is not adequate. It does not seem fair."

Nathaniel tugged on his mother's line to check to see if a fish was trying to steal the bait. Carollyn looked at him and smiled before returning her attention the conversation.

"Shouldn't we take care of the poor?" the old man asked.

"Shouldn't we take care of the working class that is paying for the health care of the poor?" the child continued the debate. "Let's assume a man has a typical insurance policy that pays eighty percent of his bill. This man has a major heart attack and the hospital bill comes to fifty thousand dollars. After discharge from the hospital he will be responsible for ten thousand dollars, and that does not include the aftercare treatment." Jason paused as a fish pulled his line and escaped with the bait. "Then there is a man that is unable or chooses not to work that is on Medicaid. This man has a heart attack, is allowed to stay in the hospital for an extra week, and has no financial responsibility to the hospital upon discharge. Does this seem fair?"

"So how do you propose we rectify this situation?" Carollyn asked.

"Some type of socialized health care like they have in Europe," the boy was quick to respond.

"Who will pay for that?" the old man asked.

Nathaniel reeled in a small fish. Without the need to consult with his great-grandfather, he knowingly tossed it back in the water.

"We will pay for it through our taxes," was the thoughtful response from Jason.

"Not that I will be around long enough to worry about it," the man debated, "but do think that anyone wants to have their taxes increased?"

The boy thought for a few minutes. "We can evaluate what we are wasting money on and redistribute it to health care."

"Who determines what is wasteful spending and what is not?" the man asked. "For a person in their twenties, spending money to build a senior center may seem like a waste; but a person my age would think that it is a great idea."

"There will be always common ground that the majority of people can agree upon," Jason defended his view. "For instance in 2006 pork barrel funds were estimated to cost taxpayers twenty-nine billion dollars. That money could have been spent on more important issues, such as health care."

Carollyn did not have to reflect on his idea for long before she said, "The problem when the government becomes involved in the health care system is that they begin to dictate what type of treatment physicians can prescribe. Unfortunately, those treatment restrictions are not based on the need of the client; they are based on the cost of the treatment." She paused before continuing her platform, "Many times the decision of the legislature is based upon who in contributing to their reelection campaigns. I can guarantee that all pharmaceutical companies invest a great deal of money into the 'right candidate.'" Carollyn was getting angry just thinking about.

"Then maybe we should prevent pharmaceutical companies from contributing to any campaign," Jason suggested.

The man laughed and replied, "I believe that might be considered unconstitutional."

"Even if that was possible," Carollyn said, "although I believe your grandfather is right, there are many other problems with having the government in charge of health care."

"That is why when I become president, I will appoint you as secretary of health," Jason said, holding his right hand in the air as if taking a vow.

Nathaniel laughed at the proclamation.

"Thanks, but no thanks," Carollyn offered.

"So you want to be president?" the old man smiled at the revelation.

"Maybe," Jason offered thoughtfully.

Carollyn looked at her son in surprise.

The captain continued his counsel, "Don't aspire to be just a president. If you must aspire to be president, desire to be a good one."

The boy looked at him, contemplating what was being said. Slowly he reeled his line in, put new bait on it, and then dropped the line back into the water.

"If one day you are given the honor to serve as president, may the historians declare that you were a good and just leader."

Jason mused at the possibilities. "I hope so," he said.

"It is nice to live in a country where all our children can dream of becoming president," the old man finished.

"Thank you, Dr. King," Carollyn added with a smile.

After two hours of fishing, with no yield, it was time to head in. The old man gave Jason the honor of taking the boat to port.

The captain headed for his easy chair as soon as they arrived home. Carollyn and the boys were sitting on the porch watching the peaceful motion of the waves. The front doorbell rang, an unusual occurrence because most visitors would just walk around the back of the house. The captain shouted knowingly to Jason and Nathaniel to answer the door. They both raced to the front door.

"It's Mr. Jeremy and Cody," Jason shouted.

Carollyn stepped in from the porch. The captain slowly stood up from his chair. The visitors stood at the door with a large box covered with a sheet.

"Come in," Charkey screamed.

"Good afternoon, boys," Jeremy greeted them.

"We have a present for you," Cody added, excited enough to burst.

Nathaniel looked at the covered box. "Is it a baby tiger?"

Jason looked embarrassingly at his younger brother.

"Not this time," Jeremy replied. "I didn't know you were interested in one."

Jeremy and Cody placed the box on the table. Carollyn sat on the edge of the couch, while the old man stood by his chair.

"Well, boys," Jeremy directed, "Why don't you unveil it."

Both boys cautiously but eagerly removed the cover.

Charkey immediately screeched and flew rapidly from one corner of the room to the other and back again flapping wildly and squawking unintelligible words.

Under the cover, in a cage, was a young scarlet macaw. The boys' mouths dropped in shock. The young bird stared in silent fear, at the boys looking at him, totally oblivious to the older version making a commotion. Carollyn walked up behind them and put a hand on each of their shoulders.

"This is going to be a major responsibility," she cautioned.

"We're going to be able to keep him?" Jason asked.

Carollyn's smile of approval meant more than words as both kids hugged her waist.

The bird continued to stare around the room. He noticed Charkey, who was still flapping his wings, but ignored him.

"Where did you get him?" Jason asked Cody.

"About a little over a month ago we found him running around our backyard like a chicken with its head cut off," Cody laughed. "His right wing was broken, possibly from an attack by a predator, so he couldn't fly."

"We mended the wing; it seems to be healed," Jeremy added. "However I'm not sure if he will ever be able to fly again."

"How did he get in your yard?" Jason asked.

"We don't know," Jeremy responded. "He's less than a year old. He is definitely domesticated. It would be hard to believe that someone bought him as a pet, decided that they couldn't handle a parrot, and turned him loose. Macaws cost too much money to do that." The man looked at the bird. "For the past four weeks we have posted an ad in the paper, and no one has claimed him." There was a pause. "I guess it will always be a mystery."

"Maybe your eagle showed him where you lived," Nathaniel interjected.

"Maybe," "Jeremy agreed, trying not to laugh, "but now he is yours."

"What are you going to name him?" Carollyn asked the boys.

"Pete!" Nathaniel shouted.

"Charkey," the original bird shouted, flapping his wings wildly.

The boys looked at each other and then their mother before turning to the bird.

"Charkey," they said in unison. They looked towards their great-grandfather for approval.

"I think it is a splendid name," he smiled. "The real approval should come from Senior," he pointed toward his bird. "It seems as he has already endorsed the name."

"I have brought some of my special mix for Charkey Junior," Jeremy continued, "and am shipping some to Chicago tomorrow." The man paused. "Once you get home, Jason, you will need to find a vet who specializes in birds. This is not your mother's responsibility. I expect you to do it." He winked at Carollyn.

"Yes, sir," Jason answered.

"Thank you so much for continuing our family legacy," Carollyn said to Jeremy and Cody.

"Thanks for Charkey," both boys shouted.

Over the next thirty minutes, Jeremy and Cody gave instructions on how to care for the new family member, including tips on teaching him to talk. Gradually, Charkey inched closer to his namesake. Big Charkey was unsure how to react. This was the first time since he fell out of his nest that he had seen another scarlet macaw. The bird was somewhat mesmerized by his likeness. The old man invited the Feldsteins to stay for dinner; but they insisted that they needed to return to the refuge.

As the boys started to get acquainted with the new Charkey, the old man started to cook dinner. Carollyn sat on the counter top, as if she were a small child.

"So what are we cooking tonight?" Carollyn asked.

"We?" the man responded, raising his eyebrows.

The sounds of the children repeating words to the young bird could be heard in the background, with Charkey coaching from across the room.

"Well, I thought I could help," Carollyn begged in an almost girlish tone.

"Tonight it will be my famous Greek stew," the old man said with pride. "Tomorrow will be my famous chicken tetrazzini."

"So what makes these dishes famous?" Carollyn teased.

"The love and care I put into blending the ingredients to perfection," the man quipped. "This was a special recipe taught to me by Grandma Ruth. Although I think Daddy claimed he taught it to her."

"Then it will be an extra special treat," Carollyn said with a smile. "Of course, everything you cook is splendid."

The man smiled at the compliment.

"So what can I do to help?" Carollyn repeated.

"Get a beer from the refrigerator," he coached.

Carollyn hopped from the counter top, retrieved the beer and opened it. "Now what would you like me to do?"

"Sit on the countertop and relax; you're on vacation," the old man teased.

"How did you learn to cook?" Carollyn asked.

"In my family all the men learned to cook." The man placed raw steak into a frying pan and turned on the gas. Carefully he added the desired spices. "When I was about five years old Daddy had me in the kitchen peeling onions and peppers."

"Did your brother and sister like cooking?"

"My brother was probably the best cook I ever met. Rufus could take ordinary garden vegetables and a small slice of meat and turn it into a culinary delight fit for a king."

The man dropped chopped onions into the pan with the steak. "Growing up in the depression, unless it was fish, we had very little meat. The meat we did have was always entrusted to Rufus' skill." The old man was lost in thought for a few seconds. "I still miss him. We used to have a good time."

"And your sister?" Carollyn asked, as she nibbled on a slice of cheese.

"I was only three when she passed; I truly don't have any recollection of Allison, other than pictures. She had long dark pigtails and dimples in both cheeks. I think she had a likening to Shirley Temple." The old man spoke matter of fact with no sorrow in his voice.

Carollyn was slightly embarrassed that she had not remembered the captain was just a young child when Allison had died.

"So Grandma Ruth allowed the men to the run the kitchen?" Carollyn asked.

"I didn't say that," the man continued. "It was always her kitchen. We just participated."

Charkey, tiring of the boys, flew to the kitchen table. "Let's eat," he screamed.

The old man shook his head as Carollyn laughed at the bird.

"Did your father or Grandma Ruth help most with your culinary skills?"

"Grandma Ruth was a good old-fashioned, southern-style cook," the man chuckled. "Never anything overly fancy, but down-home good. She definitely taught me the basics." The old man smiled. "Some of my happiest moments were in the kitchen with her." There was a pause, as he tasted the sauce. "Needs more garlic," he said to himself. "Daddy was more into the sauces and fancy dishes. I guess I learned from both of them."

"They were obviously great teachers."

The captain smiled. "It's funny, though; outside of the restaurant Daddy never cooked. At home it was always Grandma Ruth or Rufus. Of course when I married, Emma inherited some of the cooking duties."

"How did you meet Gus?" Carollyn asked.

"I'm not really certain. I believe that we first met at a babysitter when we were too small to talk. Then we started first grade together and for some reason became inseparable. We probably took to each other because we both possessed a natural talent for mischief." The man peered out at the sea. "It was the same with Denny. It was like we always knew each other."

"It sounds like you guys always had a good time," Carollyn remarked.

"Before Gus and Denny went off to war and me to play baseball, we spent a weekend on the boat fishing." The man paused for reflection. "We caught plenty of fish, drank plenty of beer. Most importantly, we all spilled our souls to one another, our fears and hopes. It was that weekend that Denny revealed that he had a relationship with Lisa."

Again, there was a brief halt of words. "It was then that I could sense the fear of destiny in his voice. I begged him not to go. I encouraged him to stay behind and play baseball. Over the years I'm not sure if my intentions were necessarily all that noble. I may have wanted him to validate my own cowardliness."

"That may have been true," Carollyn agreed, "but you had good reason to worry, after losing your brother to the war."

"Anyway, my pleas were of no use; the ink had already dried on the paper. It's funny, Gus went to war confident that he would return; Denny was just as sure that he wouldn't."

"It sounds as if that weekend had a great impact on you," Carollyn said as she lifted the bottle of beer to her lips.

A couple of black and purple butterflies fluttered around the kitchen window. The man stared at them and smiled, thinking of Melissa's garden, before his mind returned to the weekend. "It had a major impact," he agreed. "That weekend we all realized that we were more than friends; we were brothers. As brothers it was our duty to be there for each other and our families. When I found out that Lisa was pregnant, the fact that her baby would be my niece or nephew was the foremost thought. Before leaving for my duty in the army, I asked Emma to watch after Lisa." The man reflected. "I carried a heavy heart into battle because of Denny's revelation, knowing that Lisa was carrying his baby."

"That must have been difficult."

"Actually," the man continued, "it made it easier. I felt that if our mission was successful, the war would end and my friends would return safely. I hit the beachhead with the confidence of ten men."

There was silence for a few minutes as the two watched the butterflies continue their follies outside the window.

"Watching the beauty of the butterflies reminds me of the frailties of life," the man mused. "Today we marvel at their splendor. This time a month from now, they will be dead."

"I never thought of it that way," Carollyn agreed.

"One day while I was recuperating in the hospital in England I became very sullen. I had a horrifying dread of immediate doom. The nurse tried to explain it as a natural reaction to my battle wounds." The man paused to sip a glass of water. "I insisted that it was something else; something terrible was about to happen."

"That was the day Denny died," Carollyn finished his thought knowingly.

"Yes," the old man whispered, reliving the day as if it had just happened.

Carollyn hopped down from the countertop and hugged him. For a few seconds the man wept in her arms.

"Let's eat," Charkey squawked, interrupting the train of thought.

"In a minute," the captain offered. Returning to the preparation, he poured some beer into the concoction. "Dear, can you boil some noodles for me?"

"Finally," Carollyn laughed, going to pantry. She looked on the shelf. "Do you want me to use the egg noodles or the spinach?"

"The spinach," the man answered after a brief hesitation.

Carollyn put the water on to boil.

"Don't burn the water," he joked.

"Well, I'm sure you can teach me how to do it, because I don't know the first thing about water," she mocked. "That wasn't one of the curriculum studies in medical school."

The man concentrated on the beef, adding additional spices.

"Boys," Carollyn called out, "time to wash your hands and set the table."

Jason and Nathaniel hastened to their mother's request.

"Have you ever thought about writing a cookbook?" Carollyn asked as she poured the noodles into the water.

The old man laughed. "We're due to get it from the printer next week. It is called *Charkey's Classic Recipes.*"

"And you weren't going to tell me?" Carollyn said, trying to sound insulted.

"Actually, I was going to surprise you and mail you a couple of copies. It has recipes from Charkey's that have been passed down from generation to generation as well as entries from Gus and a couple of Denny's."

"That is touching. Are you going to sell it at the restaurant?" Carollyn asked.

"We are donating half the proceeds to the Alzheimer's Association and the other half to the American Cancer Society."

"For Emma and Gus?"

"For Gus and for me in case I get the disease," the man laughed. There was a brief hesitation. "Yes for Emma, Daddy, and now my dear Melissa. Cancer has ravaged our family. I pray every night that another family doesn't have to suffer the way ours have."

"There are times," Carollyn confessed, "that I want to give up private practice and go into research."

"Then why don't you?" her grandfather asked.

"I'm not sure. The money isn't as good in research, but I think the real problem is I don't want to lose touch with the patient." She looked outside as rain began to trickle down. "The reassurance and hope I provide the patient gives me a lot of pleasure. I am just not sure that I want to give that up yet."

"The only advice I can provide is for you to follow your heart," he counseled.

Carollyn smiled at her grandfather, a small tear forming in her eyes. Gently they embraced each other. There was silence with the exception of rain lightly pattering on the porch, increasing to louder thumps on the roof, and then slow again to a light tapping.

The grandfather studied his beautiful granddaughter. "The rain is tears of angels welcoming new souls into heaven," he whispered.

The four sat at the kitchen table being serenaded by two birds. Charkey would say something, and his understudy would attempt to repeat it. Though it was hard to keep their attention on the food, the boys managed to complete their entire meal.

After dinner Carollyn and the captain sat on the porch, drinking cappuccinos, as the boys cleaned the kitchen. After the chore was done the boys quickly returned to the task of teaching the young bird how to be a good mimic.

In the distance they could see a cruise ship slowly floating by on the soft waves, carrying vacationers to exotic and romantic destinations.

"If I were a passenger on a cruise ship, do you know what I would want to take with me?" the captain asked.

"No, what?" Carollyn asked.

"A bottle of Alka Seltzer," the man laughed. "They give you so much food, I would be sure to get a stomachache."

Carollyn laughed. Then her face turned serious as she pulled an envelope from the pocket of her sundress. For a few minutes she fidgeted with it but didn't say a word. The old man looked at her and then returned his eyes back to the sea. The rain clouds had traveled to a new destination, leaving a clear sky. Slowly a few stars ignited signaling the others to all come alive.

"Is that the letter Nathaniel told me about?" the old man asked, as he stared toward the sea.

Carollyn looked stunned. "What letter?"

"The one in your hand. Nathaniel said that the reason you came here was to deliver a letter from his grandmother."

"When did he tell you that?" Carollyn was a bit embarrassed that she would entrust a secret to an eight-year-old.

"He told me that night you arrived, when I was making his bed," the man replied, a tinge of sadness in his voice.

"Why didn't you say something to me?" Carollyn asked.

"I was waiting for you to decide if you wanted to give it to me," the old man confessed.

"I don't know what is in it," Carollyn apologized. "It is possible that it is mean-spirited, though I have never known Momma to be that way." Carollyn paused as a tear developed in her eye. "About a week before she died, she asked me to mail it to you upon her death."

"Why did you decide to be the pony express?" the man asked, suddenly feeling a bit older than his age.

"I always wanted to know you. I thought that if you were a grumpy old man, I would just leave the envelope on the table for you to find." She sniffled. "Or, perhaps that I could transform you into someone that would love me. Honestly, I'm not really sure what I was thinking. After the first night here, I discovered that you are a wonderful, bright, and witty man that is loved by many and that has the capacity to return that love. I will always cherish this week."

"You are now a part of my boys' and my lives; words can't describe how that makes me feel. In this short time you have helped me gain an entirely new perspective on life. I don't want this letter to hurt you, if it is unpleasant." Carollyn could sense the apprehension her grandfather was feeling.

A tear formed in the old man's eye. "Whatever Melissa wrote I probably deserve. She certainly had the right to say anything. As one of her deathbed requests, I am obligated to listen."

Momentarily they sat in silence, listening to the noise of the night. The seagulls joyously sang a melody with the crickets on percussion. The peaceful splashing of the waves on the shore served as back up.

Carollyn placed the envelope on the table. "Would you like to be alone?"

The old man continued to stare at the sea. "If you don't mind," he said slowly, "would you read the letter to me?"

Carollyn leaned over and hugged him. "Sure." Quietly, she debated if she should edit any less than charitable comments. After pondering on this for a few seconds, she decided to read it as stated by her mother, regardless of the content.

The giggles of the boys teaching their new friend how to speak could be heard in the background.

Carollyn apprehensively opened the envelope. There was a brief hesitation before she started to read it.

Dear Daddy,

I know it has been a long time since we last communicated, but there has not been a day that I haven't thought about you. I wished that I would have written this letter forty years ago. I have asked my daughter, Carollyn, your granddaughter, to mail it to you postmortem. I know in my heart, in spite of the past, if you knew I was dying of cancer that you would be at my side.

"I would have," the man mumbled, looking at the cracks in the wood floor.

I am sorry for all the pain and suffering that I caused you and Momma. From the experience of my pregnancy and running away, I have learned never to run away from the problem. The right thing for me to do was to stay at home and fight it out with you. I know in the end, you would not have stood in the way of me keeping Carollyn. I also feel in the end you would not have prevented me from marrying Laurence.

"If we lived our lives in retrospect," the old man started, "we would make absolutely no mistakes. Unfortunately, we live our lives in real time. If you would have stayed," the old man drifted into a dialogue with his daughter, "I'm not sure what I would have done. Wisdom would dictate that I would have done the right thing. However, what is right for me now isn't necessarily what would have been right for me then." The man let out a slight chuckle. "Actually what was right for me in 1965 and that which is right for me today have drastically changed."

I know that getting pregnant was a huge disappointment to you, especially getting pregnant to an African-American. If the same would have happened to some of my girlfriends, their parents would have been horrified, as you. They would also worry about what the neighbors would say about them having a black baby. I know you had absolutely no concerns over the neighbors, you just didn't think races should mix. I do appreciate, no matter how petty it might be, that the neighbors' opinion didn't matter.

"You are wrong about that," the man mumbled. "Actually, my bigotry and chasing you away was the scandal of the town for several years. Some folks thought I was totally right, others thought I was just a mean old man. Your Uncle Gus, though I wouldn't admit at the time, hit it right on the head. He said that when we are all dead and in the ground, the only thing that remains is the soul. The soul has no color. Melissa, I was wrong, I am truly sorry." The old man sat stoically staring at the waves.

Carollyn stood up for a second, to switch the light on. Before sitting down, she massaged her grandfather's shoulders.

I feel fate brought Laurence and me together. Under most circumstances I would never have dated an African-American, partly because of your reaction, mainly because I shared some of your prejudices. One night I was doing my usual stroll on the beach. I was down by the old pier when three older men approached me. I believe they were college boys from out of town. They started flirting. When I chose not to respond, they decided to have their way with me anyway. The one boy ripped the strap on my blouse, and then shoved me to another. That boy tore the other strap before shoving me to the next. I was screaming and fighting, kicking and scratching. The third boy threw me on the ground, and ripped my pants open.

Horror covered the man's face, as it did Carollyn's.

The next thing I knew, Laurence appeared out of nowhere, pulling the boys off me. They immediately attacked him, grabbing and swinging. He had the adrenaline of ten men. His punch knocked one of the boys out; another had blood squirting from his nose. One of the boys swung a piece of driftwood at Laurence, landing several blows to his back before he was able to disarm him. It was all so bizarre; it was like a Batman show. Everything was in slow motion. I felt so helpless; all I could do was watch.

As I said, those hoodlums got their shot in on Laurence too, but he didn't quit until they retreated. The unconscious boy was carried by the others. After the fracas, he knelt down by me, to make sure I was okay.

A surge of rage filled the old man's heart. His face turned red as he clenched both fists. "I wish you would have told me," the old man said. "I would have found those boys and taken care of them."

I sat there crying for fifteen minutes, with Laurence holding me as though I was a baby. Honestly, he may have been more frightened than I. Once I regained some composure, he helped me tie the straps of my blouse so as not to expose myself.

Though the event occurred over forty years earlier, anger continued to pump through the old man's veins as though it was yesterday.

Laurence escorted me to the periphery of our house, until I could barely see the outline of you sitting on the porch. I said good-bye to him there. As usual, you and Charkey were sitting on the porch waiting for me. I remember kissing you on the cheek and saying good night. You protested, because I always sat down for our talks. That night I couldn't. If I told you what had happened, you would have found those boys and killed them.

I went into the house and said good night to Momma, who was sewing new cushions for the boat, and went to bed. The next week I ran into Laurence at school. He was respectful and shy; he really didn't want to talk. I went out of my way to be nice to him, because of what he had done. Over the next few months I got to know him better. One day I came to the realization that he wasn't black, he was just another person.

"That's right," the man exclaimed, "that's something it took me a while longer to learn."

Eventually we started to date. Then one thing led to another, and here I am. I have no regrets about falling in love with Laurence. He has treated me like his queen since the first time I met him. There has been nothing that I wanted that he wasn't willing to provide, no matter the sacrifice. We have a wonderful daughter that has blessed us with two beautiful grandsons. I hope one day you have the opportunity to meet them. They will enrich your life.

The man looked at Carollyn. "They already have."

When we left Daytona we didn't know where to go. Neither of us really liked Florida. After discussing it, we decided to go to Savannah. I guess we settled there because our family roots sprout from there. Maybe I was looking for a sense of belonging, or maybe just to try to make sense of the family tree. Laurence studied at the University of Savannah; in between diaper changes I finished my high school diploma. After graduation, we decided to move again. This time we landed in Chicago. Laurence became very successful in the banking industry. I went back to college eventually earning a master's degree in education. Until the time of my illness I taught art at a local high school. Working with kids has been a very rewarding experience.

"You always were a brilliant artist. I knew one day you would make use of it. That you became a teacher doesn't surprise me. As a teenager you always seemed to take to the young children. I am very proud of you."

It's strange; but you were right when you said that Laurence and I would have a difficult time fitting in because we were biracial. Of course I thought at the time it was just your racial hatred surfacing. Over the first few years we discovered that society did look at us funny. In Savannah and then in Chicago we tried to attend numerous churches. Unfortunately, we were snubbed in most, if not all. That really hurt me. I always thought God loved all people regardless of their skin color. Growing up, church was always something I looked forward to. It became something I loathed.

"You never missed a Sunday. I remember on the few Sundays that I would attempt to play hooky to go fishing, you would scold me. It seems like just yesterday you took your first communion. It was Easter Sunday. You wore a lovely pink dress with white ruffled lace around the neck, which your mother sewed. We were so proud of you."

The man paused as he watched a shadow of a couple jogging down the beach. "You always enjoyed singing in the choir. Thankfully, you received your voice from your mother." The man nodded his head towards Carollyn, signaling her to continue.

Unfortunately, the church wasn't the only place frowning on us. We had apartment complexes refuse to rent us a room. Laurence's African-American friends looked down on me; my white friends down on him. As time went on, the hatred, distrust, and ignorance of biracial couples slowly dissipated. Eventually we found a church that accepted us and friends that cherished us. I was able to handle the tough times because of you and Momma. Watching the two of you taught me how to love. Love endures all things.

"I thought about you in 1967 when the Supreme Court ruled that it was unlawful for states or local government to ban biracial marriages. I guess that is when I started to realize just how silly people's prejudices were. It is good that we as a society have grown to accept all diversity. It is a shame so much has been lost in the process. Hopefully a day will come when all men are judged by their hearts and not the color of their skin or the religion they practice." The old man chuckled and shook his head. "I think I may have plagiarized the Reverend King on that one."

At the encouragement of Laurence and some of our friends, I placed some of my paintings in a gallery on consignment. To my surprise, but no one else's, they sold. That I made money on something I loved was of no consequence. The very fact that something I created could be appreciated and treasured by others was so humbling yet so thrilling.

I still remember the first paint set you bought me. You were responsible for helping nurture my love of art. Thank you.

"It was you that provided me with the appreciation of art. You could capture anything on canvas exactly the way it appeared. Because of your paintings, I started studying the beauty of nature. You opened my eyes."

I hope you weren't too hard on Momma for sending Laurence and me money from time to time that first year we were in Savannah. We probably would not have been able to survive without it. Even without the money, there was no chance of me returning home after your ultimatum over the phone. I figured you found out when Momma cancelled the trip with Renda to Jacksonville. We had planned to rendezvous there so she could meet Carollyn. When I called to confirm the meeting, and to make sure you weren't coming, she cancelled the trip. Momma said that she could no longer deceive you; that it wasn't right to send money without you knowing. She asked us to come home, saying that she would smooth things over with you. I adamantly refused. That was the last time I spoke with her. She didn't know our address or phone number, so she could never get back in touch. I guess those first few years we lived in paranoia that one day you would show up at the door.

"I never knew Emma was sending money," the man whispered in despair, knowing that his wife would have to sneak behind his back to help their daughter. "I wish she felt comfortable enough to tell me. Obviously, that was my fault. Truthfully I probably would have been furiously self-righteous. I remember her and Renda planning a trip to Jacksonville. Emma was going to a wedding of one of Renda's friends. At the last minute she decided not to go."

"For the next several months, she was sad. I tried everything to cheer her up; nothing worked. One day she snapped out of it and we never discussed it again." A tear streamed down the old man's cheek.

The paranoia followed us to Chicago. I remember once when Carollyn was six or seven years old, we were taking one of our frequent trips to the Lincoln Park Zoo. I wanted to study the tigers for a painting I was working on. As we were passing the primates, I saw a man that resembled you. Immediately, I broke into a cold sweat. Carollyn and I rushed back to the bus stop. It was several months before we returned to the zoo. Even though I was petrified I did not tell anyone about this, not even Laurence. I guess I was worried that people would think I was silly.

The old man's jaw dropped. Carollyn paused for a few minutes, to give the man a chance to process the information, before continuing.

Over the years I kept in touch with my classmate Heidi. At one time her first husband supplied the restaurant with seafood. She kept me up to date with all the happenings in Daytona. In the early seventies she got a divorce and moved to Orlando. I continued to keep in touch with her, but her gossip was a bit delayed. She wrote to me in 1976, right after Momma died. She felt really bad that she had not known that Momma was sick. I was heartbroken. I must have cried for a month. If only I had known she was dying, I would have been on the first plane to Daytona. There is no way I could have not been there to say good-bye. I never would have allowed you the burden of facing it alone. I am so sorry. My not being there, also, made it impossible for me to have any type of reconciliation with you. I could not have looked you in the eyes after I failed you when you needed me most. It was as though I lost you too.

"I knew you would come, if you knew your mother was sick. Melissa, you didn't fail anyone by not being here, you didn't know. Remember I was the one that chased you away."

I still have the pearls Momma gave me for my sixteenth birthday. Those being the set she wore for your wedding made them special. Today I cherish them even more. I can still remember in detail your wedding picture. Daddy, you looked so handsome in your gray pinstripe tuxedo. The tails and walking stick made you appear to be royalty or perhaps like a movie star. You were a handsome man. Momma looked elegant in her long satin white gown, with a rose pattern and high neckline. Her long silky auburn hair tied in a bun was the perfect compliment to your blond hair. The two of you could have been on the cover of Life magazine you looked so complete.

Growing up I always admired the love you shared with each other. It may seem morbid, but I will wear the pearls at my funeral. After the funeral I am leaving them to Carollyn. I hope that she will treasure them as much as I have.

"That was a long time ago. Your mother was a beautiful bride. At times when I shut my eyes I can still see your mother and me standing in front of the altar at the First Methodist Church. To my right was your Uncle Gus. Always the kidder, he kept me loose by reminding me he had a car running in the back if I wanted to make an escape." The man paused. "I never wanted to escape. Standing to your momma's left was Lisa, in a pale yellow gown. There was never a prettier bride than my Emma. The only person missing from the ceremony was Denny."

The man coughed. "If your marriage was only half as good as mine, then you were blessed. There is not a day that goes by that I don't grieve over your mother. The preacher once told me that I should celebrate the time we had together. That has been difficult to do with her not here. Maybe if you had not left, you would have been able to help me through the memories."

I continue to correspond with Heidi. She has told me that you and Charkey are both doing well, which pleases me. I miss that old bird; but not nearly as much as I miss you and Momma. Heidi says that over the years of you have hired some African-Americans; even at one time had one as a manager. I'm glad you overcame the racial hurdle. Hopefully, you now know that it is the heart that makes a human being. I also hear that you are renovating the restaurant. C.C.'s was always your pride and joy; it's nice to know that it is receiving a face lift. I am also pleased that you have so many of my paintings hanging on your walls. It gives me a sense of immortality.

"We miss you too," the man sobbed. "I dreamt of one day of us managing the restaurant together and maybe even expanding it. Those dreams were lost a long time ago. Yes, my racial bigotry was the catalyst for the implosion of the fantasy."

The old man paused to wipe tears from his face. "You are right that it is the heart that makes the person. The black manager you speak of is Vanessa. That dear girl is like a daughter to me. I truly love her. Even so, there is no way she could ever replace you. In a way, your marriage to Laurence opened my eyes to an entirely new outlook on people."

"Unfortunately, my action surrounding the renaissance of thinking was a high price to pay."

There were so many times I wanted to come home to see you and Momma. Once, after Momma died, I almost took a plane to Orlando. Actually, I had purchased the ticket. I wanted to visit her grave. I just wanted to feel the dirt where she lay. At the last minute Laurence talked me out of it. He was afraid that I wouldn't be able to handle the stress. Or perhaps he was worried that I would visit you, and you would reject me. Sometimes we reject ourselves by not reaching out to the ones we love. I'm now sorry that I didn't make the trip.

"I visit your momma's grave every week, usually on Sundays after church. I know one day soon that I will be laid to rest beside her. We bought her a real nice pink marble tombstone. Above our names is our wedding picture. Inscribed under your mother's name is: forever the queen of my heart."

He paused briefly. "I still attend the Methodist Church, though I stopped teaching Sunday school years ago. After Emma's death I donated a pew to the church in honor of your mother."

On numerous occasions over the years I called Charkey's just to hear, "Thanks for calling Caribbean Charkey's, can I help you?" On more than one occasion I asked for you, but hung up before you came to the phone. It was always a treat when I could hear Charkey screeching in the background. The times you answered the phone, I tried to speak, but the words could not escape my mouth. In case you wondered, I did miss you. Even without talking to you, your voice brought me comfort.

"I missed you too."

Carollyn instilled some wisdom in me that is probably the force behind this letter. I apologized to her for all of my shortcomings as a parent. She placed her hand on mine and smiled. She said, "As adult children we have the responsibility to remember all the things our parents did right and avoid focusing on their minor shortcomings. Most parents do so much more good than they do wrong." If I would have heard those words of wisdom years ago, maybe we would not have missed out on a life of discovery.

The man reflected on the words. He remembered the days he had with his father. It didn't matter how crude his father was at times, or irritable. He didn't always agree with his daddy; in fact many times they disagreed, but he respected him and cherished their short time together. In the end his father did far more good than harm. Because of his father he was able to be the man he had become.

The peach-colored moon hung effortlessly suspended over the sea. The sound of fireworks exploding in the distance brought the boys hurtling out of the house. They raced to the beach to watch the spectacular display of colors igniting the night sky.

Daddy, you and Momma gave me life through my birth. You provided me so much more. As a child you taught me about art, through our building of sand castles. Then you bought me my first paint set. Remember the picture Momma took of me with that homemade smock and easel wearing the beret?

The man reflected for a second about the picture in an antique gold picture frame hanging in the guest bedroom.

Our long walks on the beach taught me about nature and gave me subjects to re-create. Our fishing trips taught me about the preciousness of life. I remember after catching a grouper one day, you made me keep it on my line dangling in the air instead of dropping it in the bucket You said, "watch the way this fish flutters in the air trying to prevent its destiny from being fulfilled. A fish with a small brain and very limited, if any, ability to reason, holds life so valuable that it doesn't want it to end. Grasp life with all the preciousness of this fish." Those were wise words, truer today, as I battle this dreaded disease, than ever before. You taught me how to live; your spiritual wisdom has provided me with the courage to die.

Carollyn had to stop reading for a moment to wipe the tears from her eyes.

I loved Momma with all my strength. Even still, I was always a daddy's girl. We had a special bond. Whenever Momma would scold me, you would make it right. You were my protector and confidant. I could share all my dreams and aspirations with you. Other than my decision to marry Laurence you always encouraged me to fulfill my destiny.

"You were Daddy's girl," the man agreed, "my special little girl."

Daddy, I hope that you will take the time to learn who your granddaughter is. I hope one day she will be welcomed into your home with her husband and children. There are so many things that you can share with them. I know that the two of you would fall in love with each other. I hope that me keeping her out of your life hasn't poisoned her mind against you. I have instructed Laurence that if you should write to her, that he should forward the correspondence without delay. He, though he admits to having reservations, has agreed to do so. Laurence is a good man. If you have an opportunity, take the time to make peace.

A flock of five pelicans flew in formation over the porch.

"I'm grateful to say that Carollyn, the children, and I are finishing a wonderful week of getting acquainted. There are so many of your qualities in her, and then again I would expect that as she is your daughter. The boys are both spitfires. They are both full of love and energy, a total pleasure to be around."

"The next visit, I hope, will include the entire family, including Laurence. I am grateful to have my family back." The man reflected on his phone conversation with Laurence. "I have spoken to Laurence. I asked him for his forgiveness. He said he has forgiven me. I hope one day we can sit down and break bread with each other. I don't know much about him; but we share our love for you, Carollyn, and the boys. With that we should be able to put our differences to the side."

As for the things you have done wrong, I forgive you. I regret that I was unable to do it sooner. If I had we would have had a joyous reunion; now we must wait until we meet in heaven. If you can find it in your heart to do so, forgive me. As for me, I chose only to take the good times with me to my resting place. In I Corinthians 13:13 we read, "And now abides faith, hope and love, these three; but the greatest of these is love." I have faith that one day soon I will be in the loving arms of my heavenly father. I have hope that one day that I will be reunited with my earthly father in heaven. Because Daddy, I love you. I always have and I always will.

Love,

Melissa

A meteorite crisscrossed the galaxy.

The old man looked towards the countless stars in the sky. "I love you," he whispered, "Melissa, I love you."

Chapter VII

Monday

The sun is rising over the lonely ridge, the moon is sinking through the depth of the quiet sea, a new day is here for the night is gone. The day has brought sunshine along with a little rain. I run through the day not knowing where to or why, birds hover singing over my head while serpents snap at my naked feet. I sit to watch the autumn leaves fall and swish away with the howling wind. I lay to rest awhile to ponder on the miracle of day and night. All is quiet now I don't know why, the moon is rising over the lonely ridge the sun is sinking through the depth of the quiet sea. The night is here for the day is gone.

The purple-gray haze encapsulated the early morning sky concealing the true intent of the sun. A pink mist hovered over the eerily calm sea. Silence governed the usually loud seagulls.

The phone rang at 6:15 AM, initially rousing suspicions of something being amiss. Carollyn answered the phone in somewhat of a panic. To her relief it was Jeremy Feldstein, calling to say that a pygmy whale had beached itself overnight. He and his boys were going to the site to witness the rescue attempt. They wanted to know if Jason and Nathaniel would like to join them. Without hesitation, Carollyn said yes and went to wake her young men.

The Feldsteins arrived to pick up the boys thirty minutes later; quickly they were on the way to the crowd gathering around the whale. The sky remained undecided as to what it was going to do. Cody was happy to see the boys again, and introduced his brothers, Jeremy IV, who was referred to as Jay, and Isaac as they drove to where the whale lay.

There was a crowd of just fewer than two hundred and fifty onlookers staring curiously at the nine-and-a-half-foot stranded mammal. Some of the witnesses reported seeing it late the previous night lazily floating in the surf. It had apparently beached itself on the shore around five in the morning.

A visiting businesswoman said she was jogging and saw it ride to shore on a large wave. There was a yellow crime scene tape preventing the intruding public from getting too close. County workers were busy pouring buckets of seawater on it to keep it from drying while waiting for rescuers from Sea World to arrive.

"Why is he on the beach?" Nathaniel was the first to speak.

"The tide brought him in," Jay instructed, "probably because he is sick and is too weak to resist the current."

"Can we push him back in?" Nathaniel continued the questions.

"It wouldn't do any good," Cody volunteered. "If he is sick, he would just die in the water and wash back to shore. His only hope is if the doctors from Sea World can find what's wrong with him and cure it."

"Do you think that will happen?" Jason asked.

"Doubtful," Jeremy said with a concerned voice. "Pygmy sperm whales generally are deep water mammals. We know very little about them. Without information it is difficult even to develop holistic medicine to assist in the healing process."

"This could even be their way of dying, leaving the herd and going ashore to die. It may be of noblest intent." Jeremy looked at the whale. "The chance for his survival even with the proper treatment is minimal. This is one species that seems to really loathe captivity."

"Are you suggesting that it would rather die than live in captivity?" Jason asked.

"History would seem to dictate that," Jeremy said sadly. He looked at the boy. "Wouldn't you?"

"What do you think is wrong with him?" Isaac asked.

"He probably has a viral infection or some type of bacteria that affects his tracking system. It is really difficult to say," Jeremy answered as he stared at the whale.

The haze above cleared enough to reveal forming storm clouds that were about to engulf any blue in the sky.

"Jeremy," a voice called from the other side of the yellow line.

"Mike, how are you," Jeremy greeted. "Are you in charge of this operation?"

"King for a day," he quipped sarcastically. "Who's your crew today?"

"I have my three sons and two young friends."

Mike looked at the kids surrounding Jeremy. "So, you kids want to help?"

They all rushed across the line to assume their orders. Mike instructed the older boys to assist in the bucket detail. Nathaniel was asked to sit by the whale and talk to it in a soothing voice, as he rubbed it with a wet towel.

"What's the estimated time of arrival for the crew from Sea World?" Jeremy asked.

"Hopefully within the hour," Mike said, looking at his wristwatch. "They are usually pretty responsive. I hope the storm doesn't slow them. According to the weather report there is a nasty front passing through Orlando."

"There is not much hope, is there?" Jeremy asked. The answer was already apparent.

"The chance of this poor guy surviving is about as good as me winning the lottery."

"How often do you play?"

"Never," Mike responded, as he stared at the ground and shook his head.

The miasma had vaporized, revealing the storm that was preparing to embark on its voyage of rage. The birds were fluttering and squawking as if warning each other of the pending fury. The nature of the weather did not deter the rescuers of their mission.

"Please, don't die," Nathaniel whispered to the whale. "I know that you are sad and lonely, but we are going to make you feel better. Soon you can go back and be with your mother." The innocent child looked at the whale's blunted snout and wondered if maybe it was on the beach because it ran into a ship. "Mr. Whale, did you run into a ship?" He knew the whale couldn't answer. "I'm so sorry you're not feeling well. Maybe when you are at the animal hospital at Sea World you will be able to play with Shamu."

The rain started to drizzle; still the volunteers continued the work. There was not a speck of blue in the sky. The waves began to hurl onto the shore. The buoys toppled recklessly in the waves trying to stay afloat. The clouds hastened to open up as a wild river gone astray poured from the heavens. Many of the onlookers ran shrieking for shelter; the ardent warriors continued undeterred with the task. The rain washed the saltwater the whale needed for survival off of it faster than it could be replenished.

Soon the rescuers from Sea World arrived. The veterinarian quickly assessed the whale's condition. One of the technicians drew a blood sample.

"Is he going to die?" Nathaniel asked the busy doctor.

At first the man ignored the question, fearing that an answer would be a prompt for more questions. Then, reflecting on an old horse doctor who took the time to quench his curiosity as a child, he reconsidered his rudeness. "I hope not," he said without looking up from the examination.

"What's wrong with him?"

The man thought for a second. "I wish I knew. We do not know a lot about pygmy sperm whales because they are basically deep water mammals. They are really difficult to study and understand their habits. Basically, the only time we see them is when they are stranded." The deep compassionate concern could not flee from his eyes.

"Is he going to die?" Nathaniel asked again, a tear forming in his eye.

The man looked at him, sympathetically. "We're going to do everything we can. If he survives it is in large part because of the rescue effort you put forth today."

The rain slowed to a drizzle.

"Let's go," the man yelled to his team. Quickly the crew moved in, gently rolling the nine-hundred-pound whale onto a giant tarp. "Son," he said to Nathaniel, "We need your help carrying him to the van." The workers, including the boy, all grabbed a piece of the tarp.

"On the count of three," the man commanded. "One ... two ... three." The crew slowly but deliberately carried the patient to the awaiting van. Several paramedics scrambled into the back so they could continue to hydrate the whale. As the ambulance sped away, Nathaniel waved good-bye, tears streaming from his eyes.

The exhilarated, drenched heroes returned to Jeremy's SUV for the return trip to the captain's house.

"Boys," Jeremy started, "you all did a wonderful job."

"I hope our effort wasn't wasted," Jason said solemnly.

"No effort is wasted if it is done for the right reason," Jeremy coached.

"What if the whale dies?" Jason asked, sadness reflected in his voice.

"There is a good chance he will die," Jeremy said, realistically. "Right now we do not know the outcome. If we would have done nothing the outcome would have been certain."

"It's like when your football team plays a superior team," Isaac said. "If you feel defeated, you will probably lose. If you have a positive attitude, you may beat the odds."

"And you may not," Jason countered.

"In your heart you will know you gave it everything you had. At that moment it doesn't matter what the score is; you on a personal level have won," Isaac advised.

Jason knew that Isaac was right. Though his outer appearance appeared solemn, his soul was rejoicing that the effort was made.

They decided to a stop at an IHOP for breakfast. Their conversation switched from the whale to little Charkey and then drifted to the wildlife refuge.

The sky had shed the rain clouds and was turning into a light blue. A faint outline of the moon continued to hover over her domain.

Soon the peril of the whale, while still in the back of their minds, was forgotten in conversation and conscious thought. The love and respect the Feldsteins held for all God's creatures was inspiring. Jason and Nathaniel gained the realization that they shared the earth with all creatures. The world was no longer a testament of man's superiority, but rather a sacred garden of a loving God's creative vision.

As they drove back to the house, the boys were more aware of the birds flying over the sea. It would be a mighty dreary world if people drove all other coinhabitants of the planet into extinction. A bulletin announced over the radio that the whale had arrived safely to Sea World. Chance of survival remained slim.

"I still don't understand why the whale might die," Nathaniel asked. "They got to the hospital."

Jeremy looked through the rearview mirror at Nathaniel and said, "Unfortunately, medical science doesn't always have the answers. Sometimes, it may be nature's way to keep the sea from becoming overpopulated."

There was silence. Over the radio they heard the disc jockey announce the next song: "From the *Lion King* and Elton John, 'The Circle of Life.'"

Maybe this song will explain it," Jeremy advised.

Everyone listened intently as the song started; Nathaniel sang softly along with the radio.

"The Buddhists believe that death is simply a continuation of life," Jeremy said as he looked into the rearview mirror at the boys.

"Yet it seems so final," Jason said as a frown formed on his face.

"Maybe it seems final due to the limitation of our minds," Jeremy suggested. "If we open our minds to the possibilities that await us we may embrace death as a new beginning, not an end." Jeremy tapped his brakes as a teenage driver swerved in front of his SUV. "Followers of the Tao believe you should not fear death or desire it, but put your energy into enjoying life."

Cody opened a book that was in the back seat. He looked at Jason and said, "The Chuang-Tzu states: 'The true men of old did not know what it was to love life or to hate death. They did not rejoice in birth, nor strive to put off dissolution.'"

"'Unconcerned they came and unconcerned they went. That was all. They did not forget whence it was they had sprung, neither did they seek to inquire their return thither. Cheerfully they accepted life, waiting patiently for their restoration (the end). This is what is called not to lead the heart astray from Tao, and not to supplement the natural by human means. Such a one may be called a true man. Such men are free in mind and calm in demeanor.'"

Jay entered into the conversation, "Jesus taught us that God knows all of the feathers on a sparrow and looks after all of his creatures." He paused for a second before continuing, "Therefore we must believe that God will take care of the whale and all of his creatures, including man."

Jason looked a bit bewildered as he considered the conversation.

Cody continued "in the sixth chapter of Matthew it states, 'Take therefore no thought for the morrow, for morrow shall take thought for things itself.'"

Jeremy eased the vehicle to a stop at a red light, and then turned towards Jason and said, "I believe what both spiritual teachings are instructing us to rejoice in today. Do not worry what tomorrow might bring,"

Once again silence fell over the group as they listened to the end of the song.

When the song ended, Nathaniel smiled as he said, "That is my favorite song and movie."

"From the moment we are born," Jeremy philosophized, "we are preparing for death; it is our certain end. The area in between are the memories and the enriching experiences that we share with future generations."

A small drizzle from a renegade storm cloud fell from the sky.

Jeremy continued his lecture. "Long after we exit our physical bodies our vibrations will live on through the laughter of family, through things we said, and deeds we have done. Whether the whale dies today or lives another ten years, it has impacted all of our lives; it will live on."

Jason stared at the rain hitting the pavement, bouncing in the air once before settling into a puddle. "Then what is the point of life?" he asked.

"Life is a gift," Jeremy said as he smiled. "Life is an opportunity to grow through experiences in this existence and all future lives."

Jason was puzzled somewhat by the conversation. He reflected to recent death of his grandmother. "Are you saying that we should not be sad when a family member or friend dies?" Jason asked.

"No," Jeremy said with passion, "I am not saying that at all. It is natural to be distressed over the loss of a loved one." He paused for a second as he turned onto the road heading towards the captain's house. "Anytime we have to say good-bye to someone that we love it should be difficult. However, I believe that it is good, also, to celebrate the life that was."

Again there was silence for a few minutes.

Jeremy continued to explain his viewpoints. "God has provided us with our body. Many spiritual teachers refer to it as a temple. During our time on earth it is our duty to take care of it with proper nutrition and exercise. It is natural that we become concerned when the body begins to fail or a disease attacks it. However, if we focus on the end, then we are failing to do what God wants us to do. We should live and experience all that we can in this lifetime."

"What happens to us after death?" Jason asked.

"Until we die, we truly don't know," Jeremy mused. "Some feel that we go to heaven, others feel that we are recycled to earth by reincarnation. Some think, which I would dispute, that we simply return to the earth."

The man paused for a few seconds and then continued, wondering if the conversation was becoming too deep. "Scientists report that we are all made of energy particles. If this is true we can never be destroyed, only redistributed. So, I believe that we live on. Since we will continue to inhabit the planet it is our responsibility to take care of it, not just for future generations but for ourselves. However, as opposed to worrying about what happens after death; I propose that we celebrate that time between birth and death."

"Life is a celebration," Isaac agreed.

"Embrace every second of each breath you take. Life is a wonderful adventure," Jeremy concluded.

The remainder of the drive home was made in silence.

In the afternoon the old man sat on the porch, enjoying a cold glass of lemonade. By the palm tree, Carollyn with the boys sat in the sand building the sand castle originally designed by her grandparents. Nathaniel carefully provided the instructions so the castle would turn out just right.

Carollyn's mind drifted back to her fifth birthday in Savannah. Her parents were laughing as she ran for more water for the mortar mix. They were talking about plans for the future. Her mother carefully instructed her how to make each tower. When the castle was finished, she took a stick to draw hieroglyphic drawings on the outside of the fortress.

Then she and her mother walked along the beach to collect shells to use for the windows and drawbridge of their fortress. It was an enchanting afternoon of discovery, filled with love and acceptance.

The family was poor, yet they could still embrace the pleasures of life. Poor may have been the wrong way to remember those years. They had very little money, but they were rich in happiness and love.

Suddenly, there was the flashback of the angry men. This time she focused on her father's face. For years she had wondered why he had allowed the men to bully him. Now the answer was clear; the fear on his face wasn't for his safety. Her father's concern was directed toward her and her mother. The reason her parents refused to discuss the incident was that they always felt it a minor inconvenience, not a major embarrassment. Her father showed great constraint in walking away from potential trouble. Silently, she prayed to God that the angry young men in Savannah had found happiness.

The warm transformation of thought was interrupted by the rough voice of the old man.

"Mighty fine castle," he boasted. "I see Nathaniel has the eye of a great architect."

"He should," Carollyn beamed. "He had one of the finest teachers of sand."

Carollyn stood and brushed the sand off her legs; then hugged her grandfather. "I love you," she whispered as she kissed his cheek.

"What is that all about?" the old man said as his face blushed.

"In this past week you have taught me more about life than I have learned in all the weeks of my life. You are an incredible man."

The old man was speechless.

"I love you too," both boys chimed in.

"I love the three of you more than words will ever express," the man said, his voice cracking with emotion.

A teenaged boy and girl were wading through the water nearby, navigating a fluorescent green box kite.

"The unique thing is, your love needs no words," Carollyn said, hugging him again. "Your love is shown by your actions."

The man was unsure as what to say. "Why don't we go eat dinner? As promised, I made my famous chicken tetrazzini."

The castle stood majestically under the palm tree. The old man and Carollyn started toward the house arm in arm as the two boys ran ahead. As they walked in, a group of college-aged kids jogged past the house, carefully dodging the castle.

The boys' plan to work on their water skills after dinner was altered by an early evening rain shower. The thunder roared and hissed as the lightning lit up the sky. The waves displayed their rage as they slammed to the shore.

To pass the time, the man pulled out a box filled with pictures for Carollyn to sift through as the boys tackled his coin collection. They all sat around the big dining room table that up to this point had not been used.

The captain wheezed a bit as he talked. "I barely use the dining room since Emma passed on. Just doesn't seem quite the same."

Carollyn looked at him with concern, realizing that there was nothing that she could say that had not already said about wearing oxygen during the day. "Eating in the kitchen is nice and is really quaint."

The boys started eagerly sorting through the old coins. Carollyn settled down with a cup of tea to look at pictures.

"What's this?" Nathaniel asked, holding up a bill.

The man looked at it carefully. "This is a five dollar bill from the state of Georgia printed in 1862," he started. "The man in the center is James Oglethorpe, the colonial founder of Georgia. There is a fort named after him in North Georgia."

Nathaniel lost interest, but Jason continued to pay attention to the lecture.

"Under Oglethorpe is the Georgia coat of arms. Of course, the Roman numeral five on both sides of the note indicates that is worth five dollars. On top at the left it tells that the note was engraved in Milledgeville, Georgia."

"Did every state print their money?" a curious Jason asked.

"Yes, as well as money that was backed by the Confederate government. This money was a result of U.S. coins being hoarded and obviously was in short supply. The paper money was backed by bonds, pledges, and/or redeemable for goods and services."

"So it was kind of like a barter system," Jason said.

"I guess so, at times." The old man reflected on the statement. "Anyway, it could be used for anything from land purchases, buying supplies, and paying taxes. Of course when the war ended, it became worthless."

"Other than a collector item," Jason piped in.

"Where did you get it?" Nathaniel asked while focused on other coins.

"It was passed down by Grandpappy. I'm not sure where he received it. It may have been part of his pay for fighting in the war." The man chuckled. "I'm not sure if he kept it for prosperity sake or because he thought the South would rise again."

"Probably because he hoped the South would rise again," Jason joked sarcastically.

The wind made sounds as if someone was knocking on the door. The light from the chandelier flickered, faded, and then returned to normal.

"According to my history teacher, 1862 was the year that the war started to intensify," Jason mentioned. "The Union started to get organized and started really making strategies to defeat the South."

"The battle of Antietam, Maryland, occurred on September seventeenth of that year," the old man began his lecture.

Jason listened intently, as did Carollyn as she was looking at pictures.

"General Lee was taking his troops into Maryland in attempts to push an offensive into the north as well as recruit new volunteers. The battle at Antietam had the most causalities of any other single battle in the Civil War." The man stopped for a second, staring at a nonrelated picture on the wall. "Over twenty-four thousand men were killed."

"Who won?" Jason asked.

"Historians have a tendency to disagree on that. Some say the South because they lost two thousand less men. Others will argue the North. Yet a third group will argue that it was a draw."

"What do you think?" Carollyn asked, not looking away from the photos.

"Beyond a doubt the North with a slight asterisk," the captain quipped. "Because there was no decisive victory, Great Britain delayed recognizing the southern states as a separate country, therefore making no decision as if to give them assistance. Secondly, by Lee's failure to push the war into the North, it provided Lincoln the time and political support to issue the Emancipation Proclamation in 1863."

"And the asterisk?" Carollyn pondered.

"If General George McClellan would have followed Lee into Virginia, as ordered by the commander and chief, the war would have ended two years earlier."

"Why didn't he follow Lee?" Jason asked.

"Good question; however, I don't have the answer. McClellan claimed that he did not have enough troops or supplies, and they needed more training." The man hesitated for a moment to collect his thoughts. "It is speculated by some that he was against Lincoln's policies, so was not willing to carry out the orders. In theory—if the war was prolonged, people would become weary and things would return to the way they were."

The man coughed. "There are some who will argue that McClellan resented taking orders from a 'civilian.' Therefore for ego sake he ignored the president's commands."

"What happened to him?" Jason asked.

"Eventually, Lincoln's patience became exhausted, and he was replaced." The man sipped some tea. "In 1864 he was the Democratic nominee for the presidency. The Democratic platform centered on a speedy end to the war. However, McClellan did not totally embrace the party's proclamation. He claimed that it was not his personal intent to bring an expedient close to the war. According to McClellan, he wanted to ensure victory. Several months prior to the election, the Union won a string of decisive battles which catapulted Lincoln back into the White House."

"What do you think would have happened if the general won?" Jason asked.

"I'm not sure. The course of the war was all but decided by election day. A McClellan victory may have prolonged it a few months, but as I said, the South's defeat was inevitable." The man took another sip of tea, "Or he could have negotiated a settlement with the South immediately upon taking office. Again historians can only speculate." The man sneezed.

"Bless you," Carollyn whispered as she gazed at him lovingly.

"McClellan seemed to have a habit of talking out of both sides of his mouth. I am not sure he even understood his viewpoints."

"Sounds as if he would fit in well with present day politicians," Jason said.

The man looked out the window to check the rain, "I think the change that would have occurred would be during reconstruction. He could have created such chaos that the country would never have recovered. It is a good thing that Lincoln won."

"I thought you didn't like Lincoln," a puzzled Jason replied.

"I never said that," the old man defended himself. "I was simply serving a different point of view. Mr. Lincoln was an excellent president. He was probably the best man to lead us through the travesty of the Civil War. I do not feel that his ideas for reconstruction were necessarily the best." The man thought for a second. "But that is a story for another time."

"Just as my old history teacher suggested," Jason started, "coins are a great way to study history."

"What is this one?" Nathaniel asked, holding a large copper coin the size of a half dollar.

"That's a large cent," the man stated. "Prior to the smaller penny we have today, all pennies were this size. They were minted from 1793 to 1857. When they first started to mint them horses were used to power the press that engraved them. The large cents were replaced by the Indian head penny, which was replaced by the Lincoln penny."

"Just think," Jason said to his younger brother. "President Lincoln may have held this very penny."

"Really?" Nathaniel asked, looking toward his great-grandfather for verification.

"Really," the old man nodded.

The wind continued to howl outside as rain smashed against the windows.

"Granddad," Carollyn broke in, holding an old black and white photo. "Who is this man in the photograph with Uncle Luther?" She paused for a few seconds. "I have seen him in several pictures."

The man took the picture and stared at it, putting his hand to his chin. "That is old Mickey Sampson," the man mused. "He and Luther were friends for years. They traveled together; at times they were in the restaurant business together. Most of the time they were inseparable."

"He was a bachelor too?" Carollyn asked, already sensing the answer.

"President Clinton said it best: 'Don't ask, don't tell,'" the old man mused.

"I see," Carollyn acknowledged awkwardly.

An attentive Nathaniel's curiosity perked up. He asked, "Don't tell what?"

Carollyn tapped Nathaniel's hand and said, "Never mind."

Nathanial gave her a perplexed look and then returned to the coins.

"There was a lot of that back in those days," the man continued. "It just wasn't something we would talk about. I guess it was tabloid, but it was Uncle Luther, so my family ignored it."

There was a deafening roar of thunder, and then a streak of lightning flashed passed the window. For a moment the lights flickered.

"It must have been terrible for Uncle Luther and Mickey having to keep their love a secret," the old man said. "I can't imagine if Emma and I had to hide our love affair."

"It is good that times are changing," Carollyn agreed.

"Mickey was a few years younger than Luther," the man volunteered, "so I got the privilege of knowing him. Grandma Ruth insisted that he come over every Sunday for dinner. As she said, we were the only family he had."

"That was very insightful of her," Carollyn said, admiring her great-grandmother's values.

"Uncle Mickey, as we called him," the captain continued with the fond recollection, "was a kind gentleman. He never had a bad word to say about anyone. Many of the poor folks in town had food to eat because he personally saw to it." The man sneezed. "The verse in the Bible that reads, 'I was hungry and you feed me, in jail you visited me,' described him completely. He would entertain Rufus and me for hours with stories. He and Luther had some wild adventures."

"Who is Uncle Mickey?" Nathaniel cut in.

"Never mind," his mother redirected, "Just a relative."

"But who was he?" Nathaniel pleaded.

Jason distracted him with some coins so his great-grandfather and mother could finish their conversation.

"Allegedly, once they went camping in the Everglades," the man started.

"Allegedly?" Carollyn clarified.

"Allegedly," the old man repeated. "One morning they stumbled across a bear den. There were two very young cubs sleeping by themselves. Uncle Mickey woke them so he could get a picture of Uncle Luther playing with them." The man stopped to clear his throat and snorted a laugh. "As Mickey is snapping the picture, momma bear returns."

"Oh no," Carollyn exclaims.

"The bear chases them into a lake. Thinking they were safe, they started laughing hysterically as the bear retreated." The man paused to take a sip of tea.

"I have a feeling this is not the end of the story," Carollyn said, a wide smile on her face in anticipation of the remainder of the tale.

"The two fools stumbled into an alligator nest." The old man had a difficult time concealing his laughter. Both boys stared at him, wondering what was so funny. "So they hightailed it out of the water with an angry gator on their heels. They shimmied up a tree for safety. On the way up Luther ran his shoulder into a bee hive."

Carollyn and the boys begin laughing hysterically.

"They jumped out of the tree and dashed back to the campsite, packed their tent, and fled the Everglades."

"That sounds a bit farfetched," Carollyn said, continuing to laugh.

Her grandfather looked at her seriously. "Young lady," he said, "this is your family history; you should be proud of it."

Carollyn tried to contain the laughter. "I'm sorry," she whimpered.

The man held a straight face for as long as he could, and then started to laugh.

"All of Mickey's stories were like that. He swore that they were all true." The man stopped for second. "Regardless, they were always entertaining."

"Where's the picture of the bears?" Nathaniel demanded.

The man laughed. "They supposedly dropped the camera when they jumped from the tree."

"He sounds as if he was a character," Carollyn remarked.

"He was; I loved him dearly," the man said. A sparkle appeared in his eye.

"How old were you when Uncle Mickey died?" Carollyn asked.

"About eleven, or maybe twelve," the man said. "One Sunday he didn't show up for Sunday dinner, so Daddy sent Rufus to his house to find him." The man paused. "Rufus found him sitting on the sofa with his pajamas on, stiff as a board."

"That must have been terrible for Rufus," Carollyn said sympathetically.

"It would have been a lot worse," the old man quipped, "if he didn't have his pajamas on."

Carollyn laughed. She pulled out another picture and studied it carefully.

"Granddaddy," she started as she handed the photograph to the old man, "Who are the other two people in this wedding picture of Grandpappy?"

The man glanced at the photo even though it was not necessary. "The maid of honor was Lucille, my grandmother's sister. About two weeks after the wedding, she mysteriously died. No one knows what she died of." The man showed no emotion in his voice.

"The best man is RJ Worthington of Atlanta, Georgia." The old man paused for a moment. "RJ served in the Battle of Chickamauga with Grandpappy. I believe," the man hesitated, "that he was the first man that Charkey pulled to safety. He was grazed on the side of his head with a bullet that knocked him out. Anyway, he and Grandpappy remained friends after the war, so he made the trip down for the wedding."

The man stared at the picture a little harder. "I guess we should write the history on the back of the pictures so future generations will know the family history."

"Maybe we can work on that later tonight," Carollyn suggested.

"Nonsense," the man continued, "this is your last night here. Let's enjoy it." There was another pause. "Anyway, the Worthington family and our family have kept in contact over the years. They still live in Atlanta. RJ's great-great-grandson is an attorney. He was just down for a visit several months ago. He stayed a few days. I took him fishing. We had a real good time."

"So much family history," Carollyn sighed, "that I never knew about."

The rain diminished to a drizzle. Before long it had totally subsided. The sun decided to make an encore appearance for the day. The waves continued to show their anger by heaving to the shore.

The boys assisted the captain in putting away the mementos after each taking a few additional souvenirs. Then they returned to the beach to attempt to master the waves with their boogie boards. The captain stood knee deep in water, shouting instructions and encouragement. The current was stronger than usual, knocking the old man off balance several times. Even with the strong tide he maintained his post, enjoying the kids' folly just as much as they.

As the moon slowly showed its head into the starless night, it was time to give up the quest of victory over the water. The boys returned to the living room to expand the vocabulary of their fowl.

The old man and Charkey sat on the porch to relish the sounds of the night.

Carollyn joined the old man on the porch for a cup of herb tea. When she had finished her tea Carollyn excused herself for a leisurely walk down the beach.

The cool breeze coming off the Atlantic was refreshing. The aroma of seaweed, saltwater, and sand blending into a sorbet of fragrance was now becoming a distinctive smell that Carollyn would not soon forget. The sun had continued on its nightly pilgrimage around the globe. One by one the stars commenced illuminating the sky. All the birds were bedded for the night. The only sound was the rhythmic swishing of the ocean onto the seashore, eroding the sand at one moment and then redistributing it at another.

The solitude was welcoming to Carollyn; the only company she needed was her thoughts. She walked silently, barefooted, on the periphery of the vast and marvelous Atlantic. A quote from Anne Frank drifted in to her consciousness: "How lovely to think that no one need wait a moment, we can start now, start slowly changing the world."

During the past week her grandfather had helped inspire a metamorphosis in her level of trust in human nature to change. There was a new insight into the pathology of mankind and the healing process. Indeed, after that dreadful day shared by her momma and grandfather in 1966, the old man had played a role in shaping and reshaping many people's lives.

Her caring grandfather had looked at Vanessa and maybe for the first time saw a human instead of a young black lady. She was a real person that had experienced a great loss and consequently had needs. Maybe he could see a bit of Melissa in her; after all, Melissa had lost her father also, in a different way. He rose to the occasion and made sure those needs were met. Through his love and faith she was able to rise above her meager beginnings.

Then there was Marissa, who from all accounts was a lost soul searching for a direction. Instead of dictating which way she should go, he empowered her to regain her confidence and find her own way. Just because her way was a bit different, he never once ridiculed her.

Tears came to her eyes when thinking about his love for Gus who, even though was beyond the state of recognition, realized that he was loved by the old man.

Remembering things her mother had said, it was evident that he had more of a positive influence on her life too. The letter from her mother bore testament that even though they were estranged, they remained bound by a powerful force. There was reluctance on the part of her father and husband for her to make this trip, especially with the boys. Indeed she had her own hesitations; however, she felt drawn by a strange energy to seek out her grandfather.

Even as a child she was curious about him; not so much her grandmother, but she wanted to know him. Maybe it was because of the painting of the man fishing. Though she was never told she knew instinctively that it was him. To her the picture exuded love and belonging. Carollyn was never sure whether the love came from her mother's enthusiasm for the beach and art or if it came from the man. Now she knew it was both. Carollyn relished in the fact that not only had her grandfather been blessed by having caring people around him, he blessed them in ways that he was too humble to recognize.

The tired man sat comfortably in the old tattered red-and-green-plaid chair with Charkey perched behind his left shoulder, watching the waves roll in and out. He had just finished tucking the exhausted boys in for the final time, at least for this trip. The two old friends were alone with their thoughts.

"Charkey," he said softly, "The Lord has answered our prayers. We have our family back. Even though I might not deserve it he has showered us with grace."

The captain yawned and stretched his arms high above his head. "Carollyn has two sisters now that will keep our memories alive long past the time that we are gone. The boys have a new set of cousins to build their memories with. If only Emma could see us now."

"That letter from Melissa relieved a lot of strain from my heart," he sighed. "It was her way of making peace. I'm glad she wrote. I only wish that peace could have been made forty years ago. I used to think that the heartaches in my life were punishment for my many sins. I was wrong; the trails were all opportunity to grow into a kinder, wiser man."

The old man chuckled to himself. "It would have been nice if I didn't need all the lickings to get it right."

The ocean was darkening as it fell deeper into the night. The mystifying whoo of an owl, boarding in a tree in the front yard, floated through the air. Occasionally a beacon of light would shine from a distant boat. Other than that all was still.

"Emma," Charkey shrieked, fluttering his wings, to interrupt the silence.

"Emma?" The old man sat straight in his chair and peered toward the beach. It was Emma walking barefoot through the sand being illuminated by the light of the blue moon. The long, wavy auburn hair of his Venus blew lightly in the wind. Unmistakably it was Emma.

"Emma," the man whispered. As soon as he mentioned her name, she disappeared.

"My Emma," he whispered again, "My Emma." Resigned, he leaned back in the chair.

Carollyn returned from her excursion, finding the old man and bird sitting silently on the porch.

"Nice walk?" her grandfather asked.

"The best," she smiled. "Hope you two old birds weren't waiting up for me."

The man remembered all the times he had waited on the porch for Melissa to return from outings with friends or dates. As soon as she made it to the porch, he lit a cigar. She would pull up a chair next to his, then prop her feet on top of his knees. They would sit and talk for twenty or thirty minutes. After a while Emma would join them with a glass of lemonade for Melissa and a mug of beer for him. The three would talk and listen to the gentle sounds of the ocean until time to go to bed.

Then the many lonely nights he spent there after she ran away, hoping in vain she would return. "Just keeping the sea company," he quipped. "She looked lonely."

Carollyn smiled. "The sea has been your friend for quite some time."

"'All of us have in our veins the exact same percentage of salt in our blood that exists in the ocean; therefore, we have salt in our blood, in our sweat, in our tears. We are tied to the ocean. And when we go back to the sea, whether it is to sail or to watch it, we are going back from whence we came.'"

Carollyn shook her head. "You are definitely the king of quotes! Who is this one from?"

The man grinned slightly. "President John Kennedy."

"You are one of the most educated men I have ever known," she beamed with pride.

The man chuckled. "I earned my PhD from the Book-of-the-Month Club."

"You know many great scholars were self-educated," she insisted.

"So, I've heard," the man said, looking directly at his granddaughter as he marveled at her beauty.

Carollyn bent down and kissed the man's forehead. "I'm a bit exhausted; if you don't mind I'm going to turn in."

"Sleep well," her grandfather said.

The enchanted lady paused for another moment, lovingly staring at the old man. "It is going to be sad leaving tomorrow."

The man coughed. "In the words of the immortal Dr. Seuss, 'Don't cry because it is over, smile because it was.' Now before I get mushy, get off to bed. We can say our good-byes in the morning."

"Don't stay out here long, you'll catch a chill," she coaxed in a motherly tone.

"We will be going to bed soon," the old man said with a smile. "Just want to listen to the crickets finish their symphony."

"They seem like they are working on a masterpiece," Carollyn whispered, as she lovingly looked at her grandfather.

The old man smiled.

"Remember your oxygen," she pleaded.

"Ah ..." the man grunted, waving his hand backward, urging her to the door.

Carollyn stood in the door for a long minute continuing her stare of admiration toward her grandfather. Casually she returned to his side.

The exhausted lady sat on the edge of a chair. "Granddaddy, I truly admire the life you have led."

The man looked a bit bewildered. "I haven't done anything special."

"Excuse me for disagreeing," Carollyn started. "You haven't done anything that wasn't special. You have tremendously influenced the lives of many people. Renda was able to know her father because you kept his memory and legacy alive. It is something you didn't have to do, but you did it anyway."

"Denny would have done the same if things were reversed," the man protested.

"Of course, but it wasn't done out of obligation. It was done out of love. Through your help Vanessa and Marissa were able to complete their education. Thousands of people that visit the restaurant return because of your inviting nature. Those two ghost hunters drove out of their way not for the food but for the effect you had on them."

"They said they returned because of great seafood," the man quipped, having difficulty with the compliments.

"I'm sure they enjoyed the food. However, it was the time you took to listen to their intriguing tales that motivated them to return. The innate ability you possess to allow your thinking to evolve is inspiring. Most people will hold onto preconceived notions for a lifetime. When you discover that your ideas are outdated or wrong you allow them to change."

"Emma taught me that," the man boasted. "The book of Genesis said that woman was created from a rib of a man. God created her to be a helpmate. She was a helpmate in nudging me to the correct conclusion. I guess she loved me into being a better man." The man paused for a second. "When love didn't work she used that rib God gave her to knock me over the head."

Carollyn smiled. There was a moment of silence as they both stared at the endless sea. Tears of appreciation formed in Carollyn's eyes.

"The influence you had on Jason and Nathaniel this week is incredible. They have an entirely new outlook on life. In a week's time you taught them the wisdom of acceptance and love. Through your eyes they now understand the importance of looking for good in all people."

"I'm not sure I did all that," the man protested. "I'm not quite saint material."

"To me you are," Carollyn whispered. She stood from the chair and kissed him on the forehead. "I love you, Granddad," she said with a smile.

He returned, "I love you," a tear streaming down his cheek.

Carollyn reached her bed and within seconds was fast asleep, forgetting her nightly phone call to her husband. Blissful dreams occupied her slumber.

The old man and Charkey fell asleep on the porch with a full moon and a chorus of stars watching over their slumber.

The moon and stars quietly disappeared from the sky. The sea was tranquil. Without warning the red sun suddenly poked its head up over the horizon; within seconds the perfectly round ball rose into the sky. The rays of a newly born day eagerly danced on the turquoise sea.

The waves splashed playfully on the soft sand. In the distance dolphins rose and fell in and out of the horizon, as a bald eagle majestically soared over. A slightly discolored orange crab hobbled unhurriedly back to the sea. A pygmy sperm whale floated inconspicuously on his side, revealing its yellow stomach in the surf, and then slowly submerged to its home in the depth of the sea. The only sounds were those of the seagulls shouting early morning wake-up calls.

Along the eternal white sandy beach a young woman in a familiar blue sundress with white polka-dots walked deliberately toward the house. Stepping off the porch, the captain, who had regained his right eye and lost the limp, walked slowly toward her. A rejuvenated Charkey burst into flight, frantically circling the two lost lovers.

The couple embraced, exchanging a prolonged passionate kiss. The man lovingly garnished her long slender neck with a navy blue scarf, accented with red and green.

They turned to the beach and started a fresh journey, hand and hand, down a golden path. Soon the beach was empty; only the footprints remained.

Epilogue

The creative is the place where no one else has ever been. You have to leave the city of your comfort and go into the wilderness of your intuition. What you'll discover will be wonderful. What you'll discover will be yourself.

—Alan Alda

The sun's rays bounced off the asphalt runway, beaming back into the early morning purple haze, creating a dazzling light show. The Boeing 727 lowered her nose toward the runway. As the plane taxied to the terminal, the voice of the captain boomed over the intercom.

"On behalf of our crew we would like to welcome you to Orlando, Florida. The temperature is a humid eighty-four degrees; but seems like a hundred and twelve. The forecast for the next three days is plenty of heat with a slight chance of precipitation in the late afternoon. We hope you enjoy your stay in the land of Mickey."

Jason quietly fidgeted with the antique money clip his great-grandfather had given him seven years earlier. He ran his fingers over the engraved sterling silver wolf as he stared at its face. "My father gave this to me prior to me leaving for the war," the old man had told him. "He said the wolf was a sign of wisdom and strength." The wolf had originally belonged to his great-great-grandfather who had carried the clip to World War I; now it was his. Hopefully, it would provide him with all the wisdom he needed.

As the other passengers crowded the aisle to disembark; the twenty-one-year-old man stared in quiet contemplation out the window. A lot had changed in seven years. The summer he met his great-grandfather changed his life. A boy that had looked at all things as either black or white had grown into a man that could see the gray in between. He realized that life was a great wondrous adventure that would take many turns. Life was the opportunity that God provided each man to expand the dimensions of his soul and mind. It was man's responsibility to grow and learn.

His great-grandfather's life was an inspiration on how to fulfill the Creator's plan. He was constantly evolving as a person; quietly changing into the person God intended him to be.

Jason's mind reflected back to the conversation with his great-grandfather on their fishing trip. "In the beginning of life we are given a large blank canvas with an assortment of paints. Through our life we are the artist of our destiny. Sometimes we can change the sandspur into a beautiful flower. Sometimes, the paint has dried and the sandspur must remain as it is. Ultimately, when our time is up, we have to put down the brush and the painting is finished."

Jason smiled. "I have some new scenes to paint," he said to himself.

Two years earlier he thought his future looked bleak, after being cut from his second attempt of playing collegiate baseball. The inability to hit a curve ball cursed him. He was a fine high school player, but the skills needed at the next level were far superior to his. It was frustrating because he spent hours at the batting cage attempting to master the curve and the slider, but it seemed as if practice made it worse. The dream of being a major leaguer was over. Failure was new to him, and he despised it.

Jason glanced at the emptying aisle and then returned his attention to the window. The ground crew was experiencing some trouble in opening the cargo door. It seemed as if some luggage had jammed the door. Three overweight men with their shirttails hanging out continuously tugged on the door with no luck. Finally, a graying man with long skinny arms reached through the narrow gap and dislodged the item that was causing the chaos. The men all enjoyed a laugh as they started to unload.

Jason's eyes glanced down to the space between the seat and window. Stuck in the crack was a lady's mauve-colored wallet. Quickly, he shoved his hand into the crack and retrieved it. He looked around the emptying plane to locate the owner. There was no one there.

He attempted to get a flight attendant's attention; but she rudely attempted to rush him off the plane so they could get ready for the next flight. Not sure that he was doing the right thing, Jason stuffed the wallet into his carry-on bag. He was afraid if he turned it in the flight crew would not make an effort to find the owner. It was his reasoning that he could take on the responsibility of locating the owner. Jason was sure that was what his great-grandfather would have done. He stood, reached into the overhead storage compartment, grabbed his other bag, and slowly exited the plane.

The weary young man shuffled through the terminal toward the exit. A book on display in front of the bookstore caught his attention. He stopped to admire Vanessa's third book, *How to Maintain Change*, for a few minutes. His great-grandfather would have been proud of her; he was proud of her.

Vanessa and David eagerly greeted him as he ambled out of the terminal. He embraced Vanessa tightly, then turned and shook David's hand.

"How was the flight?" Vanessa asked.

"Fine," Jason said, displaying a slight smile. He shook his head and continued, "It is really surreal coming here alone. I've never flown by myself before; I've always had Nathaniel or Mom or Dad with me." He paused for a second. "The entire flight I kept reflecting back on Grandpa and things he said. It's funny, I only knew him that one week, yet it seems like a lifetime."

David laughed and said, "He had that effect on a lot of people." David put a firm hand on his shoulder. "Besides, you have been coming here every summer for the past seven years; I would expect the captain to wear off on you." There was a brief pause. "I am convinced that his spirit still takes up residence at Charkey's."

Vanessa laughed and then nodded in agreement. "Sometimes when I am there, I sense someone looking over my shoulder. It is either Daddy or Charkey." Vanessa's scientific mind challenged what she had just blurted out. She smiled and shook her head.

"Maybe both," Jason offered. His mind drifted to the weeks ahead when he would be spending nights alone in the old house. He wondered if his great-grandfather would be there watching over him. To some that may have been a frightening thought, but to Jason it was comforting.

A young mother tugging her toddler by the arm cut in front of Jason, almost knocking his bag out of his hand. She gave him an angry scowl as if it were his fault as she continued to rush through the airport.

"I saw your book in the bookstore in the terminal," Jason mentioned. "Congratulations!"

Vanessa smiled shyly and said, "Thank you."

"Of course, I've already read it," Jason continued. "I think it could be your best."

Again, Vanessa smiled whispering, "Thank you."

"Most self-help books are great at instructing a person to change," David began his commentary. "But few discuss how to maintain that change."

Jason smiled, but said nothing.

"The book does a great job on motivating the reader to continue to grow and avoid the pitfalls of going backwards," David continued the endorsement.

"My favorite chapter was on gratitude," Jason said, partially because he wanted to validate that he really read the book.

Vanessa smiled and asked, "What stood out to you in that chapter?"

"The focus it placed on having continuous thankfulness for all of our blessings. Even if things do not seem to be going the way we would like them." Jason glanced at a bookstore as they walked by and noticed Vanessa's book in a prominent place. "I particularly liked the suggestions of doing a thirty-day calendar listing a different gratitude each day."

Vanessa smiled, pleased that Jason found the book useful. "Other than family," she began her question, "what was your top gratitude?"

The young man did not hesitate in the answer, "Trees. I wrote in my journal that tree limbs stretch toward heaven, reminding us that God is the creator of all. That their leaves serve as filters to ensure that we breathe clean air."

"That is poetic," David chimed in.

The trio walked in silence to baggage claim. Jason watched as people rushed from and toward the terminal. He could not help but wonder where they were headed to.

Idle chitchat followed them to the car. Soon they were on I-4 driving toward Daytona.

"You know, you guys didn't have to pick me up," Jason offered. "I could have rented a car or taken a shuttle."

"Twenty-one-year olds are not allowed to rent cars," David reminded him. "And we would never allow you to ride the shuttle. Besides, this is a new beginning for you. How could we not be here for you?"

Vanessa chimed in. "You are our nephew."

"As promised, I have my old car waiting for you at the house. You can use it as long as you need," David reminded him.

"Thank you," Jason said, almost apologetically.

As the blinding sun nonchalantly continued its emergence from the sea the car continued in silence, except for the sound of the radio, towards Daytona.

"This is KMIM 98.7 Daytona Beach, more music less talk. This one going out to Jason Bowers from Marissa: 'Hero' by Mariah Carey."

Jason was a bit embarrassed by the announcement. Vanessa turned to look at him in the back seat and smiled. The young man noticed David glancing at him through the rearview mirror. Casually he returned their smiles.

Jason's looked at scenery. Green trees lined the flat road providing the highway with definition and purpose. Birds soared through the air, occasionally taking a rest on one of the tree limbs. Cows lazily strolled around their field. Purple flowered weeds sprouted from the side of the road. The sun had began a game of hide and seek behind newly formed clouds.

Jason noticed an orange butterfly gently fluttering on the side of the interstate. A small tear formed in his eyes. The tear perplexed him, as he quickly wiped it with his forearm so it would not be noticed. He wasn't sure if the tear was generated from the memory of his grandmother's painting and her loss; or was it a tear of joy for all those who have loved him. Perhaps it was a symbol of what the future may hold.

As the song continued, he pondered all these thoughts. Memories of the week he spent with his great-grandfather seven years earlier came to his mind. Thoughts of him frequently entered his mind. The man epitomized love, understanding and wisdom. Grandpa is the real hero, Jason thought to himself.

As the song ended Jason felt a warm felling inside himself. The dedication was a nice gesture by Marissa. He was looking forward to seeing her. Even though during the previous four summers he worked at Charkey's, this was different. Jason was coming home to stay.

Over the next three months he would need to learn everything he needed to know about running a business. Marissa had been a good caretaker, but now it was time for her to move on. She had other aspirations, though she wasn't certain as to what they were, and it was time for her to follow them. It was a tremendous undertaking for such a young man.

His great-grandfather's will left the restaurant in a trust that dictated a percentage of the profits go into an account for future operating expenses and the rest to be divided between his adopted family and his natural heirs. Vanessa, as executor of the trust, showed great faith in appointing Jason as the new manager of Charkey's.

Jason wasn't sure it was a coincidence that Marissa's decision was made shortly after he graduated with a business degree or if Vanessa and Marissa planned it that way. Regardless, he had big plans for the restaurant.

It was his dream to open new locations and eventually franchise it. His undergraduate thesis was a detailed report on Ray Kroc's franchising plan. If he could duplicate the plan, on a small scale, his great-grandfather's legacy would live forever.

"Are you going to take a few days to settle in before you start?" Vanessa asked, though she knew the answer.

"There will be time for that later," Jason offered. "I have a lot to learn over the next few months." He paused. "The lesson will start this afternoon."

Vanessa smiled, thinking of his desire to do a good job.

"Why don't you rest today and start tomorrow," David advised. "There should be a good surf this afternoon."

"Granddaddy once said tomorrow was for people who didn't want to succeed."

"He also preached that a productive person needed to find a balance between work and play," Vanessa reminded.

"That is why we're closed on Sundays." Jason paused. "On Sunday I will play."

Vanessa laughed. "You remind me so much of Daddy. It will be great to have you close by."

"I only hope I can live up to his reputation."

Vanessa smiled. "I think you already have."

Again silence filled the car. David suggested that they stop for breakfast; however, Jason insisted on going to the house. It was unclear as to if he felt he was imposing on their day or if he was just eager to get started on his. Whatever the reason, they complied with the request and drove him to his new home. After a few minutes of idle conversation they left to drive back to Orlando.

As soon as they were out of the driveway, Jason slipped out the back door and jogged to the waiting ocean. He stared at the slow moving aqua waves for a few minutes, then carefully selected five shells from the sand and stuffed them in his jeans pocket. Once again he gazed at the lonely sea and then retreated to the house.

Jason picked up the car keys and headed out the door. Work was beckoning, but first there was business to attend to.

Jason drove the fire engine red Honda Accord slowly through the back streets, carefully taking in the scenery. Large brick houses neighbored with smaller weathered ones. Kids raced each other on bicycles, weaving in and out traffic, having no fear of danger. Mothers were pushing their babies in strollers. He turned right on a familiar narrow winding lane, using an old trailer court as a landmark. Slowly he steered the car down the road for several miles until he found the meadow he was searching for. Veering toward the left he entered through the old steel gate onto a dusty gravel road. After a few feet he pulled to the side, and turned the key off.

He strolled through the overgrown lawn, his sandaled feet feeling the dampness of the grass. After stepping over several mud puddles Jason arrived at his first stop. Reaching into his pocket he pulled out a red and white shell, reverently placing it on the marker. The young man took a step back and stared at the reminder that a man had once lived.

On top of the white tombstone was a faded cross. The epitaph read: "A mere man yet a hero."

Dennis O'Reilly's name was carved into the stone. Jason noticed that time had not been kind to the memorial. Covering the front and side was green mold. There were numerous chips and nicks over the surface of the stone. At the base of the stone was a pot of faded artificial flowers.

"Denny," Jason mused, "My great-grandfather was so proud of you. You were a man among men. Though I never had the opportunity to know you, your legend will always be in my heart." He bowed his head in silent prayer, asking for God's blessing on his soul.

Jason then turned and strolled a few hundred feet to the site where Gustavo Harrison was laid to rest just two years earlier. Quietly, he placed a pure white shell on his headstone. Then he read the epitaph out loud: "A generous man and a good friend to all."

"Uncle Gus," Jason said with a smile on his face, "Grandpa said you had a passion for life. You were a good friend. I hope you are in the sea in the sky with him and Denny fighting a large marlin."

The young boy looked at weeds growing around the plot. He then focused on the iron rods that surrounded the cemetery. Wild unruly vegetation slowly twirled their way around the fence post, encapsulating the stately beauty that was meant to be. Slowly, he shook his head in dismay as to the condition of the garden. He vowed to make a difference. Jason then said a prayer for the soul of the departed friend of his great-grandfather.

Jason's final stop was to where his great-grandparents were reunited. The rose marble headstone stood in grandeur among the other stones. It was not nearly as humble as the man was in life. The headstone slowly curved at the top, with a cross mounted in the center.

The epitaph was simple: "Pure love that was meant to be." The names were inscribed in bold old English script. He read the family name out loud: Eberhart. Underneath to the left was his great-grandfather's name: Vladimir "Buddy." In between his name and Emma Jane's was a carved likeness of Charkey.

Carefully he placed a gray shell above his great-grandmother's name. "Grandma, though we never met, I know you well. I pay honor to the heritage you provide me." Silently, he said a prayer of thanks to God for the life his great-grandmother had. Then he placed a multicolored shell above the name of Charkey. "What can I say," he began. "You were one silly bird, but one heck of a historian. I miss your cackling." Then he stood back for a few minutes, looking at the gravesite and reflecting on the brief period of time he had known his great-grandfather. Slowly, he once again approached the monument. A tear formed in Jason's eye as he placed the last shell, a boat shell, on the marker.

Jason sat on a bench next to the gravesite, as his great-grandfather had done for years. Quietly, taking in the family plot where many of his ancestors were laid to rest. There was Grandpappy and Grandma Ruth bonded together for eternity next to Uncle Luther. A few feet from Luther's marker was one for Michael "Mickey" Sampson. The epitaph read: "A man of wild yarns ... or was he?"

"At least you can be beside each other now," Jason whispered.

Beside his great-great-grandfather and grandmother were the remains of six-year-old Allison and the bones of Uncle Rufus.

Turning to his great-great-great-grandfather's grave, he winced as he did every time he looked at it. "Grandpappy," he said out loud, "I hope you are not too offended that this black boy is in charge of continuing the family tree." He laughed softly to himself. "Maybe you and Sergeant Charkey are in heaven playing a game of gin." He noticed a few wild violets poking up around the tombstone. Somehow, he felt that Grandpappy was in the sky looking down with understanding and acceptance.

"Grandpa," he said softly. "I'm here to stay. I graduated from the University of Illinois last month with a degree in business administration and finance." He paused to watch one squirrel chase another up a nearby tree. "I graduated summa cum laude, which made Mom and Dad really proud." He paused. "Grandpa Laurence says that I inherited my business mind from him. I hope that I received part of it from you, also."

"Mom is doing well. She left private practice last year and is working as a researcher. With so many people in our family having cancer, she feels that her energy should be spent trying to find more effective treatments. The company she is working for is affiliated with a hospital in Arizona that specializes in an integrated approach to medicine."

"The money obviously isn't as good, but she went into medicine to help people, not to get rich. Since she decided to make the switch she seems much more relaxed. I think her real passion is research."

"Dad is doing well; he is still working as the administrator at the hospital. He has been real supportive of Mom's career move. He had been encouraging her to do that for years."

"You would be extremely proud of Nathaniel. He is really blossoming into a fine baseball player. His coach switched him from third base to second base. Last season he led the conference in fielding percentage and batting average. The picture of you in your Red Sox uniform is still taped to the mirror on his dresser. Nathaniel said that you are his inspiration. If he keeps it up, he will make it to the major leagues. I wish some of your baseball talent would have rubbed off on me." He laughed. "I just couldn't convince the other team not to pitch curve balls to me. Oh, by the way, Nathaniel's team is called the Buffalos. I thought you would get a kick out of that."

A stray black and white cat carefully meandered through the overgrown grass as if looking for prey.

"Little Charkey is doing well. Once I get settled in, he will be returning to Daytona." Jason watched as a couple of orange butterflies with black spots hovered over the modest marker of his great-great-grandfather.

"I'll be taking over as manager at Charkey's in a few months. I guess you know that Marissa is leaving." Tears welled in his eyes. "I know I'll do a good job. I want to make you proud."

The young man hesitated for a few seconds. "Grandpa, I'm scared, really scared. I've read all the business principles. On paper I can demonstrate the perfect business plan. But in real life, I haven't done any of this. What if I fail?"

The usually confident boy hung his head toward the ground. The bright rays of the sun were suddenly occluded by a dark cloud. He reflected back on a discussion he had with his great-grandfather as they sat on the porch years before. "Jason," he had coughed, "sometimes the future looks cloudy because of unforeseen circumstances. There will always be 'what ifs' and other obstacles. You will never know if you can accomplish something unless you try. The very act of not attempting to reach your goals is an act of failure." The old man looked out at the stars for a few seconds. "Franklin Delano Roosevelt made it quite clear, 'You have nothing to fear but fear itself.'" The captain had pointed toward the North Star. "In all things reach for the stars and you will be okay."

Jason peered at the tombstone. "Thank you Grandpa," he whispered. He stood for a few minutes staring at his great-grandfather's name. "Lord be with the souls of my great-grandparents. I pray that they are happily reunited with my grandmother and their dear friends. May eternal happiness and peace be theirs. Amen."

Jason sat on the hood of the car for a few minutes, staring at the old burial grounds. It saddened him to think that most of the souls buried there were long forgotten. He was appalled by the disarray of everything. The lawn maintenance people obviously were overpaid and mostly under supervised. The only plots that showed any sign of regular visitors were those of his grandparents. "How soon people forget," he said, looking toward the heavens.

He shut his eyes lightly, imaging a garden full of roses and other flowers. A rust-colored red brick walkway weaved around the tombstones. In the middle a large flowing water fountain to attract birds to serenade the residents of the peaceful haven. Opening his eyes, he smiled, and whispered, "Why not?" When it was time, he slid behind the wheel of the car for the drive home.

As Jason pulled out of the cemetery an early Florida afternoon thunderstorm blinded him, temporarily forcing him to the side of the road. As he was waiting for the weather to clear, he pulled the medallion his mother gave him before he left out of his pocket. Carefully he studied the inscription: *The future belongs to those who believe in the beauty of their dreams—Eleanor Roosevelt.* "Yes," he whispered, "yes."

As quickly as it struck, the storm retreated. The only remnants of the squall were a few scattered clouds in an otherwise blue sky. The rearview mirror reflected a transcendent rainbow arching over the old cemetery, ending at the captain's grave.

Jason carefully unpacked his clothes, folded those needing folding and hanging those that needed hanging. Going through his carry on bag, he discovered the lady's wallet that he had found on the plane. He opened it up in search of identification. After searching through a large amount of money and several credit cards, he discovered a driver's license belonging to a Tamara Lasserus of Sanford, Florida.

Jason picked up the phone and called information in hopes of retrieving the number. Silently, he wondered why he didn't just turn it into the flight attendants, other than being fearful that they would not make the effort. The only listing in Sanford was for T. Lasserus; Jason decided to take a chance on the number. After four rings, the phone was answered.

"Hello," a sweet, sensuous voice floated through the receiver.

Jason's mind reflected to the picture on the license of an attractive young lady, probably in her early twenties. In the picture she had shoulder-length, frizzy auburn—closer to red hair. Mounted on her face were thin black-rimmed glasses that provided her with a studious mystique. "I'm looking for Tamara," he started politely.

"May I ask who is calling?" the voice on the other end asked, trying to recognize the caller.

"My name is Jason," the boy stuttered, wishing he would have turned the wallet in. "I found something that belongs to her."

"My wallet?" a shrill reply came over the phone. "I lost that over a month ago."

Suddenly relieved, Jason continued. "I found it on the plane this morning. I was afraid that the airline may not make an earnest effort to find you, so I decided to take it upon myself. It was between the seat and the window; somehow it got wedged down there."

"Oh my," she blushed. "I called the airline and they said they searched the plane thoroughly and found nothing."

"There are several credit cards in there, and a fair amount of money. I rummaged through it trying to find your driver's license."

"I am so glad you found it," Tamara sighed.

"If you would like I can mail it to you." He hesitated for a few seconds. "Or if you don't mind the drive, I'm starting a new job as manager at Charkey's in Daytona tonight."

"I love Charkey's," she interrupted.

"Good," he blurted out. "Why don't you come over tonight; dinner will be on the house, and you can get your wallet." He paused for a second. "It is okay if you bring your boyfriend or husband or a friend," Jason stuttered, trying not to sound pushy.

"I don't have a boyfriend or a husband," was a quick reply. "However, I'll see if one of my girlfriends can come with me."

"Great," Jason responded.

"However, since you found my wallet, I'm not sure that it is right for me to expect you to buy dinner," Tamara said.

Jason smiled. "It's a tradition started by my great-grandfather. I insist that dinner is on the house."

"Thank you," Tamara whispered. "I'll plan on being at Charkey's around eight."

"I look forward to meeting you," Jason said.

After the phones were hung up, the young man glanced at the driver's license, this time staring at her birth date. "She just turned twenty-one; maybe I have found my first new friend in Daytona," he whispered.

Jason quickly showered, put on a new pair of tan pants and a nice button down shirt, and started toward the restaurant. As he slowly walked towards Charkey's, he watched the waves from the sea glide effortlessly into the shore just as they had they had for eons. Seagulls fluttered about the beach looking for scraps. The more industrious pelicans gracefully dove into the water in search of prey.

"Welcome," Marissa greeted Jason as he stepped onto the porch. She hugged him. "It is good to have you home," she said in the middle of the hug.

Jason smiled broadly. "It is nice to be back." He gave her a tight embrace.

Marissa took a step back to look at him. "I must say you are certainly dressed managerially." She smiled as she shook her head. "Daddy would be proud of you." There was a momentary pause. "I'm certain he is looking down from heaven, smiling ear to ear."

A seagull swooped between them, in search of a french fry, momentarily startling them.

They both laughed.

"I want to make him proud," Jason whispered, staring at floor, then back at Marissa. "This is all happening so quickly. At times it is a little scary."

Marissa gave him a knowing smile. "When your grandfather first told me that I was going to manage Charkey's I was terrified."

"How did you handle it?" Jason quizzed, looking for answers.

Marissa smiled. "I just did it."

"How did you just do it?" Jason asked.

Marissa smiled again. "I just did it," she chirped. "You will too! Let's get started." She turned and walked into the restaurant before he could continue the conversation. Jason, glanced toward the sea for a few seconds, shook his head, and then dutifully followed Marissa into the restaurant.

Though he held summer jobs at the restaurant while in college, Marissa started the training process as if he had never been in the business. Jason's duty for the first night was to greet guests and escort them to their table.

Numerous old faces came in that night to welcome his return to Daytona. Renda was the first to greet him, followed by the Feldsteins, and then many others. Everyone was happy that Jason had returned.

At 7:00 PM, Jason noticed that a couple that had occupied a corner table by the picture window were leaving. He casually walked over to Trudy, who was bussing the table.

"We're going to hold this table," Jason said.

"Hold it?" Trudy quizzed. "When did we start taking reservations on a Monday night?"

Jason smiled. "It's a one-time thing," he said with a laugh.

"You're the boss," she said, chuckling to herself while carry a tray of dirty dishes toward the kitchen.

Jason looked out the window at the ocean. The sun was setting on the other coast, but he could still see a faint reflection beaming on the water. Orange rays danced lazily across the waveless sea. Soon a full moon would be taking its post over the Atlantic.

Jason returned to the hostess station. Three girls waited patiently to be seated. Jason picked up three menus, and then gave the guests a slight smile. "Three?" he asked knowingly, holding up three fingers.

"No, there are just two of us," said one of the girls, pointing toward her companion and back to herself.

Jason's heart skipped to his throat as he looked at the girl that had previously been eclipsed by the others. She was tall and slender. Not skinny, but slender. Her slightly curly red hair draped her shoulders. Jason peered through her black rectangular framed glasses into her deep green eyes. Blue specks around the outer rim of her iris made her eyes sparkle.

Marissa walked up behind Jason, took two of the menus out of his hand, and escorted the two girls to a table.

Tamara smiled. "Are you Jason?"

Jason was dumbstruck.

"I'm sorry, I'm about an hour early," she whispered.

Jason attempted to regain his composure. "That's okay," he stuttered. "I'm sorry," he said, "I'm being rude." He extended his hand. "I am Jason." He paused for a second. "I didn't expect you to be so beautiful," he blurted. "I mean, your license doesn't do you justice." Jason covered his face with a hand. "I don't know what I mean," he muttered.

Tamara let out a nervous giggle. "Thank you," she said. She blushed slightly. Though she was attracted to Jason, she did her best to conceal it.

An older couple walked through the door and stood behind Tamara.

Marissa, came from behind and retrieved the third menu. "If you follow me," she said to Tamara, "I'll show you to your table." Looking at Jason, she smiled. "Jason has arranged for you to have a nice corner table with a view of the Atlantic."

Tamara looked at Jason. "Thank you," she said as she followed Marissa.

"I will be over in a little bit to check on you," Jason offered. He did not take his eyes off of her until she was seated.

For the next fifteen minutes Jason busied himself seating guests and helping to bus tables. Every few seconds he glanced toward Tamara.

"Break time," Marissa said, tapping Jason on the shoulder from behind.

Startled, he turned toward her. "You have to quit sneaking up on me like that," he gasped.

"That's fine," she said with glee, "break time."

"That is okay," Jason said, "I'll take my break later."

Marissa stared at him, one hand on her hip, the other on his right shoulder. "I am still the boss," she scolded. "Actually, you don't need to take a break. You are going to take the rest of the night off."

"But ..."the young man started to protest.

Marissa gave him a love tap on his cheek. "I said you are off. Your princess awaits you."

"Excuse me?" Jason asked trying to sound shocked.

"Your princess awaits you," Marissa repeated. "She said that you are hot and she wants to get to know you." Marissa paused, and gave him another love tap on the cheek. "Now go," she whispered.

"Tamara said that?" Jason asked.

"Her vibrations spoke to me," Marissa reassured him. "Now go."

Jason stared toward Tamara, then back to Marissa, then back to Tamara. Butterflies fluttered around in his stomach.

"Stop stalling." Marissa coaxed. "I am never wrong about vibrations." She glanced in the direction of the young lady. Tamara was gazing at the lonely sea "Why do you think she came alone?"

Jason considered the question.

Marissa did not give him an opportunity to answer. "She came alone so she could check out the possibilities."

A lightbulb flashed in Jason's head. Perhaps she was right. "Thank you," he mumbled as he moved toward the office to retrieve Tamara's wallet.

Trudy placed Tamara's dinner on the placemat in front of her. "Is there anything else I can get you?" she asked. An obvious routine question, but articulated in the most sincere tone. It gave each patron the feeling that they were Trudy's personal guest.

"No thank you," Tamara smiled. "Everything looks delicious."

"Would you like a bit of company?" Jason asked, stepping to the side of the table.

Tamara smiled as the waitress retreated. "I was hoping you would join me." She motioned for young man to sit down.

Jason sat down across from her, nervously placing the wallet on the seat next to his. Realizing what he had done he picked it up again. "I believe this is what you came for," he said shyly, handing her the wallet.

"Thank you," she whispered. "I also came to meet the noble knight that retrieved the wallet for me."

Jason smiled, bashfully lowering his head.

They sat in silence for a few minutes as Tamara daintily ate her food. They both stared at the waves gently drifting toward shore. For a brief moment two seagulls amused them as they fought over morsels of food on the beach.

"How is everything?" Jason stuttered.

Tamara smiled. "It's fine. It is always good here."

"Do you come here often?"

"Every time I come to the beach," she replied. "I try to get to Daytona at least once a month. I find the ocean is revitalizing. So refreshing. This might seem silly but it is as though it calls out my name."

Jason smiled broadly. "'All of us have in our veins the exact same percentage of salt in our blood that exists in the ocean, and, therefore, we have salt in our blood, in our sweat, in our tears. We are tied to the ocean. And when we go back to the sea; whether it is to sail or to watch it, we are going back from whence we came.'"

"Did you just make that up?" Tamara asked with an expression of amazement on her face.

"I wish I could take credit for it," Jason said, obviously becoming more relaxed. "It's a quote my great-grandfather taught me." There was a brief pause. "I believe he was quoting President Kennedy." Jason paused for a second. "You would have liked him. He was an extraordinary man … along with being the master of quotes."

A wide smile covered the girls's face, revealing light freckles on her nose. "It sounds like his great-grandson is somewhat of an extraordinary man himself."

For the next hour the two engaged in idle talk, which drifted into deeper conversation. They discussed all their hopes and dreams. As Jason had, Tamara received a degree in business administration. She was preparing to take night classes in preparation for an MBA.

After an hour of talking, Marissa appeared at their table with a bottle of wine and two glasses. "I thought that you kids would like a little wine," she said in a matronly tone.

"Thank you," they both said simultaneously.

Looking towards the staircase, Marissa continued, "Tamara, you should have Jason take you to the moonlight deck for the wine. Italian wine always tastes better outdoors. It has something to do with the fresh air oxygenating with the grapes," she said, having no idea what she was talking about. "Besides," she continued, "he will amaze you with his knowledge of the heavens. On clear nights he can point out five or six planets."

Jason stared at Marissa, trying not to laugh at her slight exaggeration.

"That's sounds delightful," Tamara responded before Jason had a chance to reply.

Jason smiled at the matchmaker and then turned his attention to Tamara. "I'm not sure we will be able to spot that many planets, but let's see what we can do."

Jason and Tamara walked to the staircase as closely as possible without touching each other.

Trudy joined Marissa as she watched them go upstairs. "So they are going to do a little star watching?" Trudy mused.

Marissa giggled. "I think the only stars they are going to see will be in each other's eyes."

Trudy shook her head and smiled. "Then, I guess they won't be seeing stars."

Puzzled, Marissa looked at her. "What do you mean?"

"How do you expect them to see stars when their eyes are going to be closed?" she joked. Trudy pranced over to the stairway and put the chain across the entryway to prevent other guests from imposing on the stargazing.

Tamara walked to the railing. Leaning on it she gasped. "I have never been up here," she sighed. "It is so beautiful."

Jason smiled. "Yes, it is quite a view." Slowly, he poured the wine into the glasses. He walked over to Tamara and handed her a glass.

Tamara took a small sip of the wine. "Thank you," she whispered. Then she placed the glass on the railing. "I wonder how long it has to sit here before it begins to oxygenate?" she asked, smiling pleasantly.

They both laughed.

An evening mist was beginning to sweep off the sea. Through experience Jason knew that it would not take long for the entire view of the stars and the sea to be occluded. He pointed toward a bright star, slightly to the right of the moon. "That is Mars," he whispered. Then he quickly scanned the heavens in search of Saturn.

Tamara ignored the astronomy lesson. Staring directly into his face, she admired the strong jawbone running to a square chin that was accented with a dimple. His deep sensitive hazel eyes calmed her heart. Though he was a tall, muscular man, he spoke in a soft soothing voice.

Jason started to point in the direction of Saturn before he noticed that Tamara was not paying attention. Slowly he turned toward her. He placed his left hand on her right shoulder. Carefully he ran his other hand through her hair, starting at the top of the head, stopping when he reached the back of her neck.

To Tamara, Jason's hands were an anomaly: so strong, yet his touch was so gentle. She placed her right hand on Jason's waist. Tenderly, she placed the other hand on his chest. Tilting her head slightly, she gazed into his eyes.

Their eyes locked in silence for what seemed an eternity as they searched each others eyes as if they were revealing the mysteries of their souls. Finally, Jason's head bent slightly as their lips touched lightly. After the first kiss, Jason's head retreated a few inches. Tamara's head followed his; this time the kiss had more passion, Tamara retreated.

As Tamara stared at Jason she could feel her lips quiver. Her legs felt as though they were going to collapse. Jason marveled at the sweetness of her lips.

Jason's left arm slipped from her shoulder to her back as he pulled her into him. Tamara's arm circled to his back before climbing to his shoulder blades. Again, their lips touched. In an instance passion resonated through their bodies as their mouths collided.

When they had finished, they turned their attention to the now almost totally invisible sea. The full moon barely emitted its light through the haze. All the stars had gone into hiding. The only sounds were those of the raucous sea slamming to the shore.

Tamara picked up her glass of wine. "What should we drink to?" she asked.

Jason lifted his glass to hers. "Possibilities," he said, smiling.

A meteorite shot through the haze on its journey to earth. For a few seconds the couple stopped to watch as it illuminated the sky.

Jason heard the rough, salty voice of his great-grandfather, as if he was standing next to him, say, "Welcome home."

Tamara turned back to Jason. "To possibilities," she said raising the wine glass to her lips.

The End

LaVergne, TN USA
01 October 2009
159521LV00003B/8/P